The Official MongoDB G

Resilience, scalability, security and performance

Rachelle Palmer

Jeffrey Allen

Parker Faucher

Alison Huh

Lander Kerbey

Maya Raman

Lauren Tran

‹packt›

The Official MongoDB Guide

Portfolio Director: Sunith Shetty
Relationship Lead: Sathya Mohan
Project Managers: Sathya Mohan & Aniket Shetty
Content Engineer: Saba Umme Salma
Technical Editor: Aniket Shetty
Copy Editor: Safis Editing
Indexer: Rekha Nair
Production Designer: Deepak Chavan

First published: September 2025

Production reference: 1080126

Published by Packt Publishing Ltd.
Grosvenor House
11 St Paul's Square
Birmingham
B3 1RB, UK.

ISBN 978-1-83702-197-0
www.packtpub.com

Contributors

About the authors

Rachelle Palmer is the Product Leader for Developer Database Experience and Developer Education at MongoDB, overseeing the driver client libraries, documentation, framework integrations, and MongoDB University. She has built sample applications for MongoDB in Java, PHP, Rust, Python, Node.js, and Ruby. Rachelle joined MongoDB in 2013 and was previously the director of the technical services engineering team, creating and managing the team that provided support and CloudOps to MongoDB Atlas.

Jeffrey Allen is a Technical Writer at MongoDB, based in the New York City area. He focuses on server documentation and works closely with Product and Engineering teams to develop examples that reflect real-world use cases, especially pertaining to data modeling and the MongoDB query language. Before joining MongoDB, Jeff worked as a full-stack web developer. Jeff also enjoys playing guitar and piano, and produces electronic music in his spare time.

Parker Faucher is a self-taught Software Engineer with over six years of experience in technical education. He has authored more than 100 educational videos for MongoDB, establishing himself as a knowledgeable resource in database technologies. Currently, Parker focuses on Artificial Intelligence and Search technologies, exploring innovative solutions in these rapidly evolving fields. When not advancing his technical expertise, Parker enjoys spending quality time with his family and maintains an avid interest in collecting comic books.

Alison Huh is a New York City-based Technical Writer on MongoDB's server documentation team. In addition to the core database, she focuses on documenting MongoDB user tools such as Compass, Mongosync, and IDE extensions. Outside of MongoDB, Alison is currently pursuing her M.A. in Instructional Technology and Media at Teachers College, Columbia University, exploring the intersections of design, digital media, and learning. In her free time, Alison loves going on runs, crafting small trinkets, and experiencing live music.

Lander Kerbey is a Technical Writer at MongoDB, specializing in Atlas Stream Processing. Prior to MongoDB, he worked at InterSystems, documenting various parts of the HealthShare suite, along with their various data analytics tools. His 11 years of experience as an educator informs his approach to documentation, as he strives to create "Aha!" moments for users.

Maya Raman is a Technical Writer and sometimes-software engineer at MongoDB. She is passionate about the intersections between the environment, art and literature, technology, and people. She is based in New York City and likes to spend her time hanging out in Prospect Park, even in winter.

Lauren Tran is a Technical Writer at MongoDB with a background in Communications and Computer Science. She is on the Server Documentation team and mainly specializes in Information Architecture, Time Series data, and Search. Lauren is passionate about creating accessible and inclusive documentation that caters to diverse audiences. She is based in Chicago following four years in New York City and in her free time, enjoys reading on the beach at Lake Michigan and listening to Taylor Swift music.

About the reviewers

Sarah Evans is a Curriculum Engineer at MongoDB, where she specializes in making complex technical concepts accessible for all learners. With over ten years of experience in software engineering, education, and developing curriculum for technical bootcamps, she's all about making learning MongoDB less intimidating and more exciting. When she's not helping developers level up their database skills, Sarah can be found having spontaneous dance parties with her family, exploring the great outdoors with her dog, or tending to her garden.

Manuel Fontan is a Senior Technologist on the Curriculum team at MongoDB. Previously he was a Senior Technical Services Engineer in the Core team at MongoDB. In between Manuel worked as a database reliability engineer at Slack for a little over 2 years and then for Cognite until he re-joined MongoDB. With over 15 years of experience in software development and distributed systems, he is naturally curious and holds a Telecommunications Engineering MSc from Vigo University (Spain) and a Free and Open Source Software MSc from Rey Juan Carlos University (Spain).

Table of Contents

Chapter 3: Developer Tools   63

Chapter 4: Data Modeling and Index Optimization   85

Chapter 6: Database Operations   151

Chapter 8: MongoDB Atlas   219

Chapter 9: Atlas Search 279

Preface

In today's fast-moving technology landscape, data sits at the core of how we build smarter applications and deliver world-class experiences to our users. As systems become more interactive and personalized, you need a database that is not only flexible and performant but also deeply aligned with how modern software is built. MongoDB was created to support that vision; from its expressive document model to its intuitive query language, MongoDB delivers developer-first features that streamline the way teams work with data.

Whether you're a developer, architect, data engineer, or someone supporting modern data applications, this book is your guide to working with MongoDB. It will help you write expressive queries, design efficient data models, secure your deployments, and use advanced features such as aggregation, full-text search, and Atlas automation. Each chapter delivers knowledge and teachings rooted in best practices and real-world use cases.

The content in this book is modular, allowing you to focus on the areas most relevant to your role or project. Newcomers may benefit from reading chapters sequentially to build foundational knowledge, while more experienced readers can jump into topics such as modeling strategies, Atlas automation, or security architecture. The goal throughout is to help you apply MongoDB confidently and effectively to modern application demands.

How this book will help you

This book provides the knowledge and tools to confidently build and scale MongoDB-powered applications. From querying and modeling to aggregation and deployment, each chapter offers practical techniques, clear examples, and useful insights.

You'll also learn how to monitor performance, implement security best practices, and use the MongoDB Atlas platform for cloud deployments, search features, and simplified operations.

Who this book is for

This book is intended for developers, database professionals, architects, and platform teams who want to understand and use MongoDB effectively. Whether you're working on web apps, APIs, mobile services, or backend systems, the concepts here will help you structure data, improve performance, and deliver value to your users. Prior experience with MongoDB isn't required, but familiarity with databases and programming will be helpful.

What this book covers

Chapter 1, Introduction to MongoDB, introduces key concepts, the document model, and use cases.

Chapter 2, MongoDB Architecture, explains core system design principles and how they support scalability and resilience.

Chapter 3, Developer Tools, explores productivity features, IDE integrations, and AI-enhanced development workflows.

Chapter 4, Data Modeling and Index Optimization, covers schema strategies and indexing techniques to support efficient access patterns.

Chapter 5, Queries, shows how to filter, project, and sort data using MongoDB's expressive query language.

Chapter 6, Database Operations, discusses data operations, deployment practices, and foundational security configurations.

Chapter 7, Security, delves deeper into authentication, authorization, encryption, and compliance strategies.

Chapter 8, MongoDB Atlas, guides you through deploying and managing MongoDB in the cloud, including automation and scaling features.

Chapter 9, Atlas Search, explores platform-native capabilities such as Atlas Search, triggers, and serverless services.

To get the most out of this book

You will require the following software:

Software covered in the book	Operating system requirements
MongoDB version 4.4 or newer	Windows, macOS, or Linux
MongoDB Atlas Shell	Windows, macOS, or Linux
MongoDB Shell	Windows, macOS, or Linux

After reading this book, we encourage you to check out some of the other resources available at `https://www.mongodb.com/developer` and `https://learn.mongodb.com/`.

Download the example code files

The code bundle for the book is hosted on GitHub at `https://github.com/PacktPublishing/The-Official-MongoDB-Guide`. We also have other code bundles from our rich catalog of books and videos available at `https://github.com/PacktPublishing`. Check them out!

Download the color images

We also provide a PDF file that has color images of the screenshots/diagrams used in this book. You can download it here: `https://packt.link/gbp/9781837021970`.

Conventions used

There are a number of text conventions used throughout this book.

`CodeInText`: Indicates code words in text, database table names, folder names, filenames, file extensions, pathnames, dummy URLs, user input, and X/Twitter handles. For example: "To disable mirrored reads, you can set the `mirrorReads` parameter to `0.0`."

A block of code is set as follows:

```
db.adminCommand( {
    setParameter: 1,
    mirrorReads: { samplingRate: 0.0 }
} )
```

When we wish to draw your attention to a particular part of a code block, the relevant lines or items are set in bold:

```
db.settings.updateOne(
    { _id: "balancer" },
    { $set: {
        activeWindow: {start: "<start-time>", stop: "<end-time>"}
    }},
    { upsert: true }
)
```

Bold: Indicates a new term, an important word, or words that you see on the screen. For instance, words in menus or dialog boxes appear in the text like this. For example: "Select **System info** from the **Administration** panel."

Warnings or important notes appear like this.

Tips and tricks appear like this.

Get in touch

Feedback from our readers is always welcome.

General feedback: If you have questions about any aspect of this book or have any general feedback, please email us at customercare@packt.com and mention the book's title in the subject of your message.

Errata: Although we have taken every care to ensure the accuracy of our content, mistakes do happen. If you have found a mistake in this book, we would be grateful if you could report this to us. Please visit http://www.packt.com/submit-errata, click **Submit Errata**, and fill in the form.

Piracy: If you come across any illegal copies of our works in any form on the internet, we would be grateful if you would provide us with the location address or website name. Please contact us at copyright@packt.com with a link to the material.

If you are interested in becoming an author: If there is a topic that you have expertise in and you are interested in either writing or contributing to a book, please visit http://authors.packt.com/.

Share your thoughts

Once you've read *The Official MongoDB Guide*, we'd love to hear your thoughts! Scan the QR code below to go straight to the Amazon review page for this book and share your feedback.

https://packt.link/r/183702197X

Your review is important to us and the tech community and will help us make sure we're delivering excellent quality content.

Free Benefits with Your Book

This book comes with free benefits to support your learning. Activate them now for instant access (see the "*How to Unlock*" section for instructions).

Here's a quick overview of what you can instantly unlock with your purchase:

PDF and ePub Copies	Next-Gen Web-Based Reader

Free PDF and ePub versions

Next-Gen Reader

Access a DRM-free PDF copy of this book to read anywhere, on any device.

Use a DRM-free ePub version with your favorite e-reader.

Multi-device progress sync: Pick up where you left off, on any device.

Highlighting and notetaking: Capture ideas and turn reading into lasting knowledge.

Bookmarking: Save and revisit key sections whenever you need them.

Dark mode: Reduce eye strain by switching to dark or sepia themes.

How to Unlock

UNLOCK NOW

Scan the QR code (or go to packtpub.com/unlock). Search for this book by name, confirm the edition, and then follow the steps on the page.

Note: Keep your invoice handy. Purchases made directly from Packt don't require one.

1

Introduction to MongoDB

MongoDB is the world's most popular NoSQL document database. Rather than using traditional relational tables, it stores data in a flexible, JSON-like format. Developers value it for its ease of scaling, strong security features, and reliable performance. With tools such as AI-enhanced search, sharding, and encryption, MongoDB offers a comprehensive platform for handling diverse data needs.

MongoDB 8.0 is the fastest and highest-performing version of MongoDB yet, performing around 32% faster than the previous version of MongoDB (Source: https://www.mongodb.com/company/blog/mongodb-8-0-improving-performance-avoiding-regressions). In addition to performance gains, MongoDB 8.0 delivers various improvements in aggregation, security, sharding, replication, and more, such as the following:

- Sharding enhancements distribute data across shards up to 50 times faster and at up to 50% lower starting cost, lowering the infrastructure cost of getting started by up to $5,000 (USD) per year
- Improved support for a wide range of search and AI applications at higher scale and lower cost, using quantized vectors (compressed representations of full-fidelity vectors) that require up to 96% less memory and are faster to retrieve while preserving accuracy
- Expanded support for MongoDB's Queryable Encryption, a groundbreaking innovation developed by the MongoDB Cryptography Research Group, to also support range queries

This book provides a comprehensive overview of what MongoDB, particularly version 8.0, can offer for your development needs. While we strive to be comprehensive and current, MongoDB is constantly adding new features. For the most detailed and up-to-date information, check out the MongoDB documentation at https://mongodb.com/docs.

In this chapter, we're going to cover the following topics:

- Why MongoDB?
- Who uses MongoDB?
- MongoDB architecture
- What's new in MongoDB 8.0?

Why MongoDB?

MongoDB is the preferred developer data platform for several reasons:

- **Flexibility**: MongoDB lets you work with data without locking you into rigid schemas. This makes it easier to adapt your application as your data changes, or when handling formats that benefit from a flexible data store, such as unstructured or semi-structured content.
- **Scalability and performance**: MongoDB is highly scalable and performant, allowing it to support both large-scale applications and smaller individual projects.
- **Security**: MongoDB offers various security methods from user authentication and authorization to data and network encryption, including 8.0 support for OIDC authentication and authorization, and range queries in Queryable Encryption.
- **Query language**: MongoDB offers a powerful query language that you can use to access your data, simplifying common operations such as findOne and updateOne. It also offers indexing capabilities for increased query efficiency.
- **Developer-friendly data format**: MongoDB stores data in a document format that resembles the structure of objects in many widely used programming languages, which helps simplify data handling and speeds up the development process.
- **Quick start**: MongoDB's simplicity and user-friendly setup make it easy to start using.

Plainly, MongoDB is simple to use. You can interact with your deployment in various ways, such as through programming language drivers, methods in the MongoDB Shell, and database commands. MongoDB provides a simple and streamlined interface for creating, updating, and interacting with data. For example, consider a Python developer attempting to insert a document by using the Python driver:

```python
from pymongo import MongoClient
# Connect to MongoDB
client = MongoClient('mongodb://localhost:27017/')
db = client['mydatabase'] # Specify the database name
collection = db['mycollection'] # Specify the collection name
```

```
# Create a document to be inserted
document = {
    'name': 'Chinazom',
    'email': 'chinazom@example.com'
}
# Insert the document into the collection
result = collection.insert_one(document)
# Check if the insertion was successful
if result.acknowledged:
    print('Document inserted successfully.')
    print('Inserted document ID:', result.inserted_id)
else:
    print('Failed to insert document.')
```

Easy! You don't need to create an ID for the document, because MongoDB automatically creates one for you. In this case, all the developer needs to define are the document's name, age, and email details.

Now, suppose the developer wants to retrieve this document by using a query. You can query for equality (for example, searching for documents in which the name is Chinazom). You can also query for inequality. In the following example, we are constructing a query to look for documents whose age is less than or equal to 25.

```
from pymongo import MongoClient
# Connect to MongoDB
client = MongoClient('mongodb://localhost:27017/')
db = client['mydatabase'] # Specify the database name
collection = db['mycollection'] # Specify the collection name
# Retrieve documents based on specific conditions
query = {
  'age': {'$lte': 25}, # Retrieve documents where age is less than or
equal to 25
}
documents = collection.find(query)
# Iterate over the retrieved documents
for document in documents:
    print(document)
```

This example shows how you can use a MongoDB query operator such as `$lte` to filter a query. MongoDB returns a document that is represented as a Python dictionary, where each field is a key-value pair in the dictionary. See the following example:

```
{
    '_id': ObjectId('60f5c4c4543b5a2c7c4c73a2'),
    'name': 'Chinazom',
    'age': 24,
    'email': 'chinazom@example.com'
}
```

As you can see, the `_id` field has been inserted by MongoDB and is represented as an `ObjectId` data type. The `_id` field is a unique and fast-to-generate identifier for each document. It is used as a document's primary identifier.

MongoDB has a suite of drivers in various programming languages that act as a translation layer between the client and server. By using these drivers, you can interact with the data with your native programming language. You can also interact with your data by using the MongoDB Shell, database commands, and other tools offered by MongoDB.

The mission of MongoDB is to be a powerful database for developers, and its features are developed with programming language communities and framework integrations in mind. This will become more apparent in subsequent chapters, where you'll learn about CRUD operations, sharding, replication, MongoDB Atlas, and more, all through the lens of a developer.

Who uses MongoDB?

MongoDB is used by many different industries, and its use cases span all kinds of situations and types of data. Users range from small businesses and start-ups, and even student projects, to some of the largest banks, automakers, and government agencies in the world.

MongoDB offers three different environments for you to create a database and store your data, each of which supports different developer needs:

- **MongoDB Atlas:** Atlas is MongoDB's cloud database service. It simplifies deploying and managing your databases, removing the user's responsibility to maintain hardware and keep up with software patches. You can provision your database through the Atlas UI and easily scale as necessary. When you use Atlas, you have access to additional features such as embedded full-text search via Atlas Search, vector-based search through Atlas Vector Search, and Atlas Stream Processing, which allows you to process streams of complex data. Atlas is used by those who want to focus on developing data models instead of spending resources provisioning and managing their database.

- **MongoDB Enterprise Advanced (EA)**: MongoDB EA is the commercial edition of MongoDB. It includes additional capabilities such as an in-memory storage engine for high throughput and low latency, advanced security features such as Kerberos access controls, and encryption for data at rest. EA is ideal for organizations that require self-managed deployments on-premises, in private clouds, or in hybrid environments. The EA subscription, through which you get MongoDB EA, includes 24/7/365 support and tools such as MongoDB Ops Manager to help simplify deployment.

- **MongoDB Community**: MongoDB Community is the free-to-use version of MongoDB. It includes support for basic operations such as queries, indexing, and aggregation. Because it is free and source-available, MongoDB Community is often used by small businesses and start-ups looking for a developer data platform with a low barrier to entry.

Please refer to the following resources for more information:

- `https://www.mongodb.com/try`
- `https://www.mongodb.com/docs/atlas/production-notes/`
- `https://www.mongodb.com/docs/manual/administration/production-notes/`
- `https://www.mongodb.com/blog/post/mongodb-8-0-raising-the-bar`

MongoDB architecture

This section offers a summary of some of the aspects of a typical MongoDB deployment. Read on to learn more about cluster architecture, sharded clusters, and collections.

Clusters

The typical MongoDB configuration is a replica set, also referred to as a cluster: a group of mongod instances that maintain the same dataset. mongod is the primary MongoDB daemon. By default, a replica set is a three-node configuration. Each node contains a complete copy of your database, allowing for redundancy and high availability: if one node goes down, you can still access the other two.

Nodes are generally categorized as primary or secondary nodes. The primary node receives all write operations from the client. Write operations are recorded on the oplog, which is a collection that keeps a record of all operations performed on the primary node. The secondary nodes then replicate this log and perform the operations on their datasets to ensure that they match the data on the primary node. Read operations are performed on the primary node by default. However, users can specify that operations should be performed on different nodes, such as the nearest node or explicitly secondary nodes.

If a primary node becomes unresponsive or unavailable, a healthy secondary node is promoted to primary. The replica set holds an election to choose which of the secondaries becomes the new primary. Various factors affect elections, such as responsiveness, node priority, and freshness of the data.

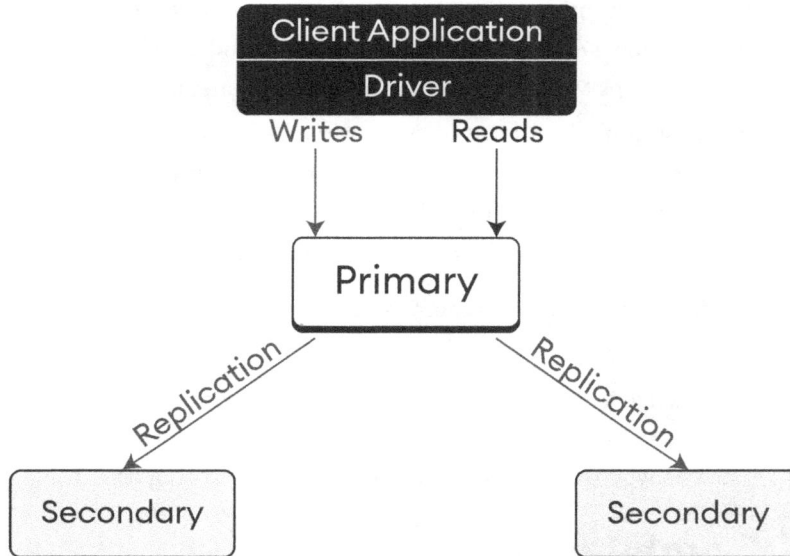

Figure 1.1: Replicated cluster architecture

Sharded clusters

Sharded clusters are useful when you want to further divide your data into replicated partitions while maintaining efficiency. Sharding is most useful when your application requires large datasets and high-throughput operations. Each sharded cluster consists of shards, or replica sets, over which data is distributed at the collection level. They also include mongos instances, which act as an interface between the client and server, routing a query to the appropriate shard or shards, as well as merging resultant data. The final aspect of a sharded cluster is a config server, which is a replica set that stores replication and configuration metadata for the cluster.

Starting in MongoDB 8.0, you can now unshard collections, as well as move unsharded collections between shards on sharded clusters. This offers you more flexibility in how you want to optimize your cluster's performance.

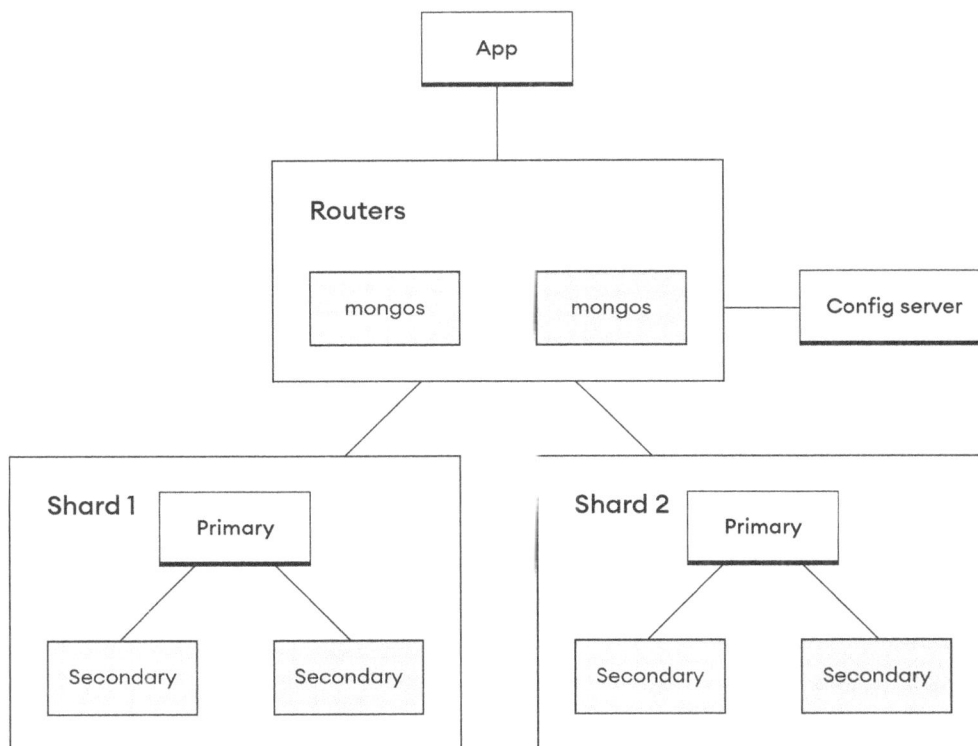

Figure 1.2: Sharded cluster architecture

To learn more about replication and sharding and their enhancements in MongoDB 8.0, check out *Chapter 2, MongoDB Architecture.* Also see the MongoDB documentation for the most up-to-date information.

Collections

A collection is a grouping of MongoDB documents. It is the equivalent of a table in a relational database. In MongoDB, collections do not enforce a schema for the data that is inserted into them.

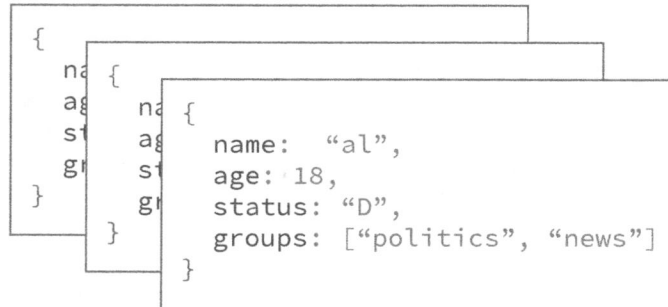

```
{
  name: "al",
  age:  18,
  status: "D",
  groups: ["politics", "news"]
}
```

Collection

Figure 1.3: Documents in a collection

Collections are assigned a **UUID**, or **universally unique identifier**. The UUID is especially useful in a sharded cluster when identifying which chunks of data belong to a specific collection.

When executing a query, MongoDB must scan every document in a collection to return query results. However, you can create indexes on specific fields at the collection level to more efficiently traverse through the data. For example, if you have a collection full of employee data and you often need to look up employee information based on the employee ID, you can create a collection-level index on the ID field to improve query performance.

Indexes store a small portion of the collection's data in a B-tree data structure, which allows searches in logarithmic time ($O(logn)$). The index stores the value of a specific field or set of fields ordered by the value of the field, allowing for easier traversal through the data.

What's new in MongoDB?

MongoDB 8.0 is the highest-performing version of MongoDB yet, with a focus on the following four areas:

- Performance optimization
- Encryption improvements
- Cost reduction and scaling improvements
- Increased resilience

Performance

MongoDB improves querying and transforming data, with up to 36% better throughput, 56% faster bulk writes, 200% faster complex aggregations of time-series data, and 20% faster concurrent writes during data replication. Overall, MongoDB 8.0 performs around 32% faster than the previous version of MongoDB. This means that you can perform operations faster with lower resource usage and costs.

Encryption

With a combination of authentication and authorization protections and encryption at rest, in transit, and in use, MongoDB protects data throughout its life cycle. Queryable Encryption, which offers robust encryption for in-use data, allows more flexibility in how you interact with your data, while ensuring that it is encrypted the whole time.

Cost and scaling

With sharding and replication improvements in MongoDB, horizontally scaling your application, or increasing the number of resources it uses, is faster and easier at a lower cost. MongoDB 8.0 distributes data across shards up to 50 times faster and at 50% lower cost than the previous version.

Resilience

To promote resilience of your application even under high-stress workloads, MongoDB includes improvements such as default maximum times for queries, upgrades to TCMalloc, and improvements to query settings.

Summary

With its flexibility and performance, MongoDB handles the low-level details so that you can focus on your application development. It's straightforward to set up and provides an efficient, developer-friendly environment.

The rest of this book details how MongoDB can support your needs and the different tools and features it offers. From MongoDB Atlas to Queryable Encryption to the MongoDB Shell, there are countless tools that enable you to use MongoDB to your advantage.

In addition to providing a robust, scalable infrastructure for your production deployments and managing high-performance tasks, MongoDB is also an excellent choice for learning and creating proofs of concept.

We will also cover how new features in MongoDB 8.0 will enable you to create faster and more resilient applications. In the next chapter, you will learn about how replication and sharding can aid you in building a reliable, available, and efficient database for your application's needs.

Happy developing!

Get This Book's PDF Version and Exclusive Extras

UNLOCK NOW

Scan the QR code (or go to packtpub.com/unlock). Search for this book by name, confirm the edition, and then follow the steps on the page.

Note: Keep your invoice handy. Purchases made directly from Packt don't require an invoice.

2

MongoDB Architecture

MongoDB is designed to support the evolving needs of modern applications through a developer-centric data platform based on a set of core architectural principles. In this chapter, we'll explore the architectural framework that powers MongoDB, with a particular focus on two foundational concepts: replication and sharding.

Replication plays a vital role in MongoDB's distributed design by enhancing both availability and fault tolerance. By maintaining several copies of your data across multiple servers, MongoDB ensures that your application can continue functioning even if one server fails.

Sharding is a horizontal scaling strategy for spreading data across several machines, called shards. Each shard stores a portion of the total dataset on a separate database server instance. As applications grow in popularity, and the volume of data they produce increases, scaling across machines becomes essential to ensure sufficient read and write throughput. When used in conjunction with replication, sharding can help create a robust and scalable MongoDB deployment.

This chapter covers the following topics:

- How to increase reliability and availability
- Best practices for replication and sharding
- New features in MongoDB 8.0

Replication

A replica set in MongoDB is a group of mongod processes that maintain the same set of data. It provides redundancy and high availability and is the basis for all production deployments. By having several copies of your data across database servers, replication ensures a degree of fault tolerance, protecting against the loss of a single database server.

Maintaining copies of data in different data centers can increase data locality and availability for distributed applications. In some cases, replication can provide increased read capacity as clients are able to send read operations to different servers.

A replica set includes one **primary node,** which handles all write operations and logs all dataset changes in its **operations log (oplog)**. The **secondary nodes** replicate the primary's oplog and implement the operations on their own datasets. This ensures that they mirror the primary's dataset. In the event that the primary becomes inaccessible, a qualified secondary will initiate an election to become the new primary.

By storing data across multiple servers, replication increases the reliability of the system. Furthermore, support for rolling upgrades lets you upgrade the software or hardware of individual servers without interruption, ensuring the continuous availability of the database. Replication significantly improves the performance of read-heavy applications, distributing the read load across multiple servers to ensure fast data retrieval.

Replica set elections

MongoDB employs a protocol built on top of the Raft consensus algorithm to execute replica set elections, ensuring data consistency across distributed systems. This protocol includes a voting mechanism used by replica sets to select which member will assume the primary role.

Replica sets can trigger an election in response to a variety of events, such as the following:

- Adding a new node to the replica set
- Initiating a replica set
- Performing replica set maintenance using a method such as `rs.stepDown()` or `rs.reconfig()`

Second members losing connectivity to the primary for more than the configured timeout (10 seconds by default for self-managed hosts or 5 seconds in MongoDB Atlas) may initiate an election to select a new primary, provided a majority of voting nodes agree the current primary is unreachable.

You should design your application's connection-handling logic to account for automatic failovers and the ensuing elections. MongoDB drivers can identify the loss of the primary and automatically retry specific read or write operations, offering an additional layer of built-in resilience to elections.

When a primary becomes unavailable, the secondary nodes vote for a new primary. The node most likely to be elected is determined by multiple factors, such as its configured priority and most recent write timestamp. This strategy minimizes the chance of rollback when a previous primary rejoins the set. After an election, nodes enter a freeze period that prevents them from initiating another election. This is designed to prevent continuous, rapid elections, which can destabilize the system.

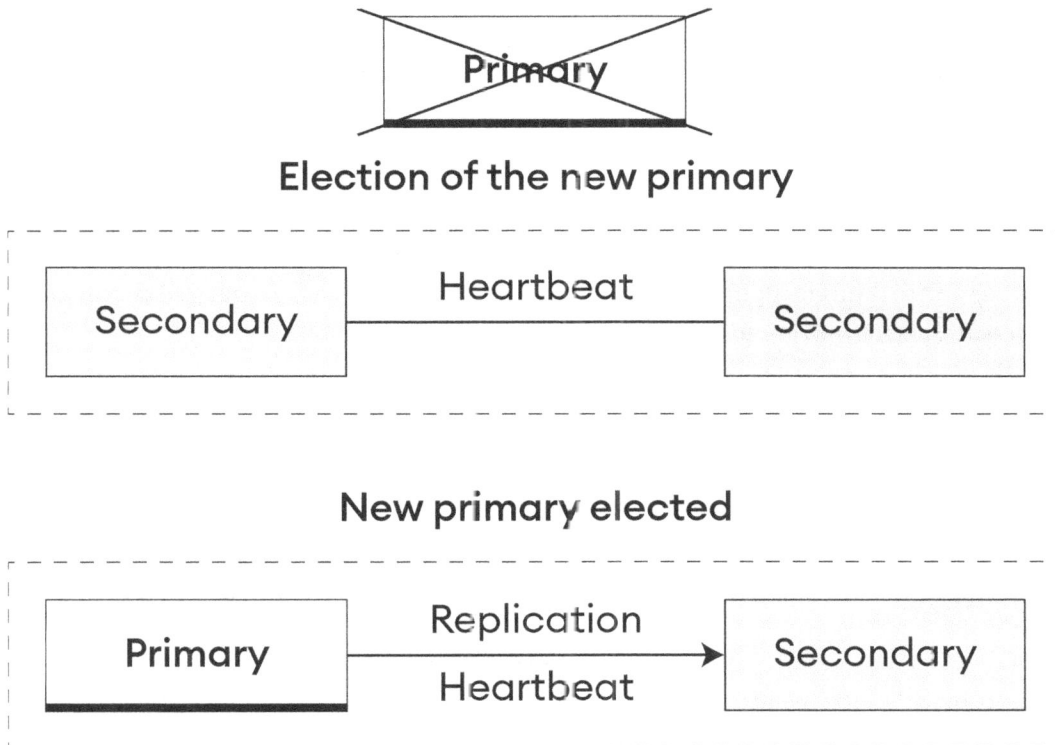

Primary

Election of the new primary

| Secondary | — Heartbeat — | Secondary |

New primary elected

| Primary | Replication ⟶ Heartbeat | Secondary |

Figure 2.1: Election of a new primary

Replica sets are unable to execute write operations until the election has successfully concluded. However, replica sets can still handle read operations if they're configured to target secondary nodes.

Under normal circumstances, with default replica set configuration settings, the average time taken for a cluster to elect a new primary should not exceed 12 seconds. This duration encompasses the time needed to declare the primary as inaccessible and to initiate and finalize an election. This timeframe can be adjusted by altering the `settings.electionTimeoutMillis` replication configuration option.

Replication election protocol

Currently, MongoDB replica sets only support protocol version 1 (pv1). pv1 reduces replica set failover time, accelerates the detection of multiple simultaneous primaries, and guarantees the preservation of confirmed {w: "majority"} writes.

With pv1, you can set the settings.catchUpTimeoutMillis replica set configuration option to prioritize between faster failovers and preservation of standalone writes. Infinite or larger values for settings.catchUpTimeoutMillis may reduce the amount of data that the other members would need to roll back after an election, but may increase the failover time.

In the case that two nodes in a replica set *transiently* believe that they are the primary, one of them will be able to complete writes with the {w: "majority"} write concern. This can occur when the node that can complete the write operations acts as the current primary, and the other node has not yet recognized its demotion, typically due to a network partition. In this case, clients that connect to the former primary might read stale data despite having requested primary read preference, and new writes to the former primary will eventually roll back.

Additionally, pv1 makes a "best-effort" attempt to have the secondary with the highest priority available call an election. This can lead to back-to-back elections as eligible members with higher priority can call for an election. However, pv1 limits priority elections to occur only if the higher-priority node is within 10 seconds of the current primary, and it causes arbiters to vote no in elections if they detect a healthy primary of equal or greater priority to the candidate.

Heartbeats

Replica set members send heartbeats (pings) to each other every two seconds. If a heartbeat does not return within 10 seconds, the other members mark the delinquent member as inaccessible.

Member priority

Once a stable primary is established, the election algorithm enables the highest-priority secondary to initiate an election. Member priority affects both the timing and outcome of elections, where secondaries with higher priority are likely to initiate an election sooner and win. Lower-priority members may briefly serve as a primary, despite higher-priority members being available. The process of elections continues until the highest-priority member becomes the primary. Members with a priority value of 0 can't become a primary and don't seek election.

Since a replica set can accommodate a maximum of 50 members, with only 7 of them being voting members, the inclusion of non-voting members enables the set to exceed the limit of 7. Non-voting members, characterized by having zero votes, must possess a priority of 0.

To learn more about voting and non-voting members, refer to the following documentation: https://www.mongodb.com/docs/manual/core/replica-set-elections/.

Mirrored reads

Mirrored reads in MongoDB reduce the impact of primary elections after an outage or planned maintenance. After a failover in a replica set, the secondary that takes over as the new primary updates its cache as new queries come in. Mirrored reads pre-warm the caches of electable secondary replica set members by having the primary mirror a sample of supported operations it receives to a subset of electable secondaries. Mirrored reads support the following operations:

- count
- distinct
- find
- findAndModify (specifically, when the filter is sent as a mirrored read)
- update (specifically, when the filter is sent as a mirrored read)

Mirrored reads use a default sampling rate of 0.01. You can configure the size of the subset of electable secondary replica set members that receive mirrored reads by setting the mirrorReads parameter. If you set a sampling rate between 0.0 and 1.0, the primary forwards a random sample of the supported reads at the specified sample rate to electable secondaries. If you set a sampling rate of 1.0, the primary forwards all supported reads to electable secondaries.

To disable mirrored reads, you can set the mirrorReads parameter to 0.0:

```
db.adminCommand({
    setParameter: 1,
    mirrorReads: { samplingRate: 0.0 }
})
```

Loss of a data center

With a distributed replica set, the loss of a data center may affect the ability of the remaining members in other data centers to elect a primary. If possible, distribute the replica set members across data centers to maximize the likelihood that even with a loss of a data center, one of the remaining replica set members can become the new primary.

Network partition

A network partition can split a primary into a partition with a minority of nodes. When the primary detects that it can only see a minority of voting nodes in the replica set, the primary steps down and becomes a secondary. If this happens, a member in the partition that can communicate with a majority of the voting nodes can hold an election to become the new primary.

Replica set oplog

The oplog is a unique capped collection that maintains a continuous log of all operations that alter the data housed in MongoDB databases. It can expand beyond its set size limit to prevent the deletion of the majority commit point.

Write operations in MongoDB are executed on the primary and subsequently logged in the primary's oplog. The secondary members asynchronously replicate and apply these operations. Every member of the replica set holds a copy of the oplog, located in the `local.oplog.rs` collection, enabling them to keep up with the current state of the database.

To support replication, all members of the replica set exchange heartbeats with each other. Any secondary member can import oplog entries from any other member. Each operation within the oplog is idempotent, meaning that, whether applied once or multiple times to the target dataset, oplog operations yield the same outcome.

Oplog buffers

Starting in MongoDB 8.0, secondaries write and apply oplog entries for each batch of data in parallel. For each batch of oplog entries, MongoDB uses two buffers:

- The `write` buffer receives new oplog entries from the primary, adds the entries to the local oplog, and sends them to the `apply` buffer
- The `apply` buffer receives new oplog entries from the `write` buffer and uses these entries to update the local database

The oplog window

Oplog entries carry timestamps. The **oplog window** refers to the time interval between the most recent and earliest timestamps in the oplog. If a secondary node loses connectivity with the primary, it can resynchronize using replication only if the connection is reestablished within the duration of the oplog window. MongoDB allows you to define both a minimum duration (in hours) and a specific size for retaining an oplog entry.

If the oplog has filled up to its maximum configured capacity, and the oplog entry has exceeded the specified retention period based on the host system's clock, the system will discard the oplog. Additionally, without a specified minimum oplog retention period, MongoDB begins truncation of the oplog from the oldest entries, ensuring the oplog doesn't exceed the configured maximum size.

Oplog size

When you start a replica set member for the first time, MongoDB creates an oplog of a default size if you do not specify the oplog size with the `oplogSizeMB` option.

Refer to the following table for the default oplog size on different operating systems:

Operating System	Storage Engine	Default Oplog Size
Unix	WiredTiger	5% of free disk space
Unix	In-memory	5% of physical memory
Windows	WiredTiger	5% of free disk space
Windows	In-memory	5% of physical memory
64-bit macOS	WiredTiger	192 MB of free disk space
64-bit macOS	In-memory	192 MB of physical memory

Table 2.1: Default oplog size on different operating systems

The default oplog size has the following constraints:

- The minimum oplog size is 990 MB. If 5% of free disk space or physical memory, depending on your storage engine, is less than 990 MB, the default oplog size is set to 990 MB.
- The maximum default oplog size is 50 GB. If 5% of free disk space or physical memory, depending on your storage engine, is greater than 50 GB, the default oplog size is set to 50 GB.

In most cases, the default oplog size is sufficient. For example, if an oplog is 5% of free disk space and fills up in 24 hours of operations, then secondaries can stop copying entries from the oplog for up to 24 hours without becoming too stale to continue replicating. However, most replica sets have much lower operation volumes, and their oplogs can hold much higher numbers of operations.

If you can predict your replica set's workload to resemble one of the following patterns, you might want to create an oplog that is larger than the default size. Alternatively, if your application predominantly performs reads with a minimal amount of write operations, a smaller oplog may be sufficient. To change the oplog size after you start a replica set member, use the `replSetResizeOplog` administrative command.

Consider setting a larger oplog size in the following workload scenarios:

- **Bulk update operations**: The oplog must translate bulk updates into individual operations in order to maintain idempotency. This can use a large amount of oplog space without a corresponding increase in data size or disk use.

- **Deletions equal the same amount of data as inserts**: If you delete roughly the same amount of data as you insert, the size of the operation log can become large without a significant increase in disk use.

- **Large number of in-place updates**: If a significant portion of the workload is made up of updates that don't increase the size of documents, the database records a large number of operations that don't change the quantity of data on disk.

Replica set deployment architecture

In production environments, a common approach is to deploy MongoDB as a **three-member replica set**, which offers both redundancy and high availability. While it's best to avoid overly complex configurations, the architecture should ultimately align with your application's requirements.

Here are some general best practices to follow:

- **Use an odd number of voting nodes** to avoid split-brain scenarios during a network partition. This ensures a majority can still form and continue accepting writes.

- If your replica set includes an even number of voting members, aim to add another data-bearing node. If that's not feasible, you can introduce an **arbiter**, which participates in elections but doesn't store data.

- For specialized tasks such as backups or analytical queries, consider adding **hidden or delayed nodes**. These members won't serve client reads but are valuable for offloading certain workloads.

- To protect against data center outages, make sure at least one replica set member is hosted in a **separate data center**, improving resilience in the face of regional failures.

Strategies for deploying replica sets

A replica set can have up to 50 members, but only 7 voting members. When you deploy your replica set, ensure that there is an odd number of voting members. If you have an even number of voting members, deploy another data-bearing voting member or, if constraints prohibit another data-bearing voting member, deploy an arbiter.

Replica set arbiter

An **arbiter** takes part in primary elections, but it doesn't store a copy of the data and cannot become a primary. As a result, you may run an arbiter on an application server or other shared resource. With no copy of the data, you can place an arbiter in environments that you would not place other members of the replica set, depending on your security policies.

> Avoid deploying multiple arbiters in your replica set. While arbiters *do* contribute to the number of nodes in a replica set used to calculate a majority in relation to the {w: "majority"} write concern, the presence of multiple arbiters makes it less likely that a majority of *data-bearing nodes* will be available after a node failure. As a result, the presence of multiple arbiters prevents the reliable use of the majority write concern and, consequently, cannot ensure that writes will persist after the failure of a primary node.

Hidden replica set members

Hidden members cannot assume the primary role and remain unseen by client applications. Despite being invisible, hidden members retain the ability to participate and vote in elections. Hidden nodes can be used as dedicated replica set members to perform backup operations or to run some reporting queries. To set up a hidden node and prevent a member from being promoted to a primary, you can set its priority to 0, and also configure the hidden parameter to true, as shown in the following example:

```
cfg = rs.conf()
cfg.members[n].hidden = true
cfg.members[n].priority = 0
rs.reconfig(cfg)
```

You can also configure **delayed members**, which are hidden members that replicate and apply operations from the source oplog with a deliberate delay, representing a previous state of the set. Delayed members act as a continuous backup or a live historical record of the dataset that can provide a safety net against human error. They can facilitate recovery from failed application updates and operator errors, such as accidental deletion of databases and collections.

For example, if the current time is 08:01, and a member has a delay set to one hour, the most recent operation on the delayed member will be no later than 07:01:

```
cfg = rs.conf()
cfg.members[n].hidden = true
cfg.members[n].priority = 0
cfg.member[n].secondaryDelaySecs = 3600
rs.reconfig(cfg)
```

Fault tolerance

Fault tolerance refers to a replica set's ability to continue operating in the event that several members become unavailable. You can calculate the fault tolerance of a set as the difference between the number of members in the set and the majority of voting members needed to elect a primary. If a replica set is unable to elect a new primary, it cannot accept write operations.

Consideration of fault tolerance can help ensure high availability, data integrity, and flexibility for your MongoDB deployment. For example, if you have an application that requires continuous uptime and can't afford interruptions, fault tolerance ensures that the database remains accessible to your application and users.

Fault tolerance is affected by replica set size, but the relationship is not direct. Although adding a member to the replica set does not always increase the fault tolerance, the addition of replica set members can provide support for dedicated functions such as backups or reporting.

Refer to the following table to calculate the fault tolerance for a replica set:

Number of Members	Majority Required to Elect a New Primary	Fault Tolerance
3	2	1
4	3	1
5	3	2
6	4	2

Table 2.2: Calculated fault tolerance for a replica set

Adding capacity ahead of demand

Existing members in a replica set must have spare capacity to support the addition of a new member. You should always add new members before the current demand saturates the capacity of the replica set.

Geographic distribution

While replica sets provide basic protection against single-instance failure, replica sets whose members are all located in a single data center are susceptible to data center failures. To protect your data in case of a data center failure, distribute replica set members across geographically distinct data centers to add redundancy and provide fault tolerance if one data center becomes unavailable.

If possible, use an odd number of data centers, and choose a distribution of members that maximizes the likelihood that even with a loss of a data center, the remaining replica set members can form a majority or, at a minimum, provide a copy of your data.

By distributing replica set members across two data centers instead of one, the following apply:

- If one of the data centers goes down, the data is still available for reads
- If the data center with a minority of the members goes down, the replica set can still serve write operations as well as read operations
- If the data center with the majority of members goes down, the replica set becomes read-only

When possible, distribute members across at least three data centers. If the cost of the third data center is prohibitive, you can evenly distribute the data-bearing members across the two data centers and store the remaining member in the cloud, if permitted.

Read-heavy applications

Replica sets are designed for high availability and redundancy. Secondary members typically operate under similar loads to the primary; however, you should avoid directing reads to secondaries.

If you have a read-heavy application and need to replicate data to another cluster for reading, consider using other tools, such as **Mongosync**. **Mongosync** is a tool that replicates data and writes from one cluster to another until the sync finalizes. You can use mongosync to perform one-time data migrations between MongoDB clusters with minimal downtime.

> To learn more about mongosync, refer to the following documentation: `https://www.mongodb.com/docs/mongosync/current/`.

Alternatively, you can use the `secondary` or `secondaryPreferred` read preference mode. Though the data that you read on a secondary might be stale compared to the primary, these read preferences can be helpful in the following scenarios:

- If you have a replica set with members that are distributed across different geographical locations, you can use `secondaryPreferred` to direct reads to the nearest secondary node. This can reduce latency for users who are geographically closer to a secondary node than to the primary node.

- If you have an application for analytics or reporting, reading from secondary nodes can help prevent these operations from affecting the performance of the primary node. This can be especially helpful when the analytics workload is read-intensive and doesn't require the most up-to-date data.

Example deployment architectures

The following section includes sample deployment architectures that leverage some of the strategies for deploying replica sets listed in the previous section. Each example outlines the roles of each member, strategies used in the architecture, and possible use cases for the specific deployment type.

Primary with two secondary members

Consider the following example, where a three-member replica set uses the **Primary-Secondary-Secondary (PSS)** architecture:

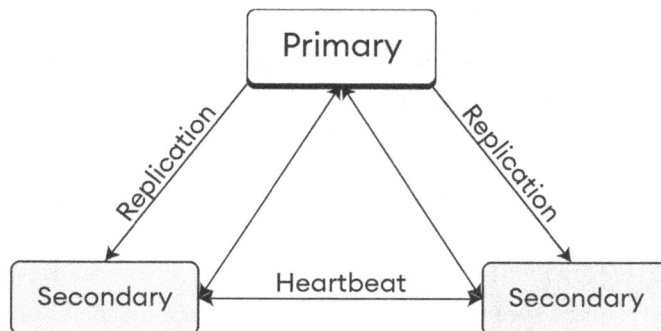

Figure 2.2: A replica set with one primary and two secondaries

This example represents the standard replica set deployment for a production system. With two secondaries, this deployment provides two complete copies of the dataset at all times and will have a majority if the primary goes down. When a secondary detects that the primary is unavailable, it can initiate an election. The two secondaries each vote for one of the secondaries to be the primary (typically the one with the highest priority or the most up-to-date oplog) and continue normal operation. When the old primary comes back online, it rejoins the replica set as a secondary member.

Primary with a secondary member and an arbiter

Consider the following example, where a three-member replica set uses the **Primary-Secondary-Arbiter (PSA)** architecture:

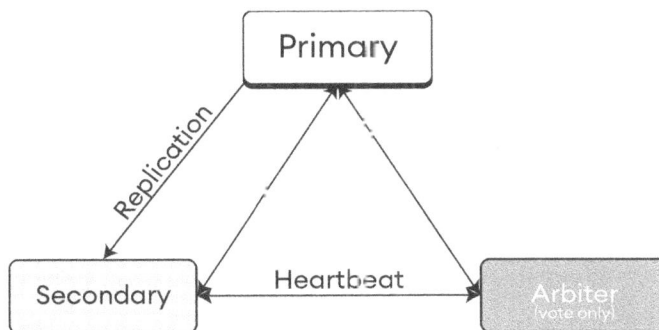

Figure 2.3: A replica set with a primary, secondary, and arbiter

This example represents an alternative to the standard PSS deployment architecture. This deployment may be used in cases where circumstances, such as cost, prohibit you from adding a third data-bearing member. Since the arbiter doesn't hold a copy of the data, these deployments provide only one complete copy of the data. If the primary becomes unavailable, the secondary and arbiter will elect the secondary to become the new primary.

Though the use of an arbiter requires fewer resources, consider the following performance impacts before you decide to deploy this configuration:

- This configuration can equate to more limited redundancy and fault tolerance since arbiters don't hold a copy of the data
- The default write concern, {w: "majority"}, can cause performance issues for PSA deployments if a secondary becomes unavailable or lags
- If you use a global default read concern of "majority" and the write concern is a numeric value less than the size of the majority (2 in this example), your queries may return stale data

Three-member replica set distributed across two data centers

Consider the following example, where a three-member replica set distributes its members across two data centers:

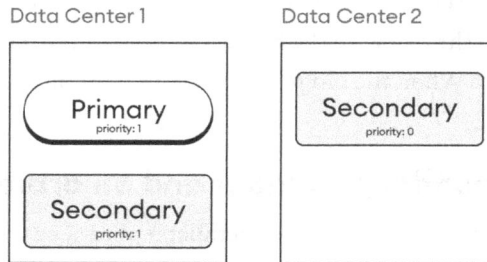

Figure 2.4: A three-member replica set distributed across two data centers

This example takes advantage of geographically distributed replica set members. Although we typically recommend using an odd number of data centers, this configuration of two data centers makes the most sense for a three-member replica set to ensure that there is at least one, if not a majority, copy of the data available to read from in case a data center is lost due to a power outage, network interruption, or natural disaster.

For example, if **Data Center 1** goes down, the replica set becomes read-only since the majority of members have gone down, but a copy of the data is still preserved in **Data Center 2**. Because the secondary member in **Data Center 2** has been configured with a priority of 0, it cannot become the primary. This is to avoid having a single node that accepts writes as a new primary, which could cause data inconsistency when **Data Center 1** comes back online. If **Data Center 2** goes down, the replica set remains writable as the members in **Data Center 1** make up the majority with a running primary.

Five-member replica set distributed across three data centers

Consider the following example, where a five-member replica set distributes its members across three data centers:

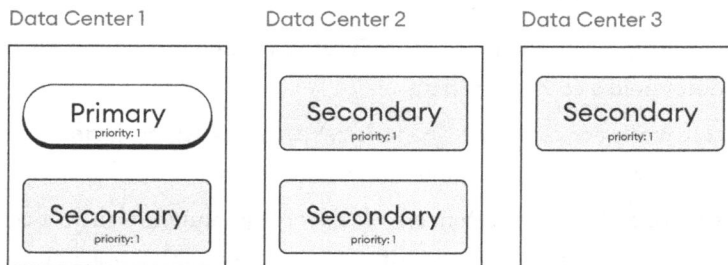

Figure 2.5: A five-member replica set distributed across three data centers

Similar to the previous example, this configuration makes use of geographically distributed replica set members. However, with more members, we can distribute the nodes across an odd number of data centers, which increases the likelihood that even with a loss of a single data center, the remaining replica set members can form a majority.

In this example, if any single data center goes down, the replica set remains writable as the remaining members make up a majority and can hold an election, if needed.

Alternatively, you may want to configure your deployment so members in one data center can be elected as the primary before members in other data centers. The following figure shows how you can set priority values, so the members in **Data Center 1** have a higher priority than those in **Data Center 2** and, subsequently, **Data Center 3**:

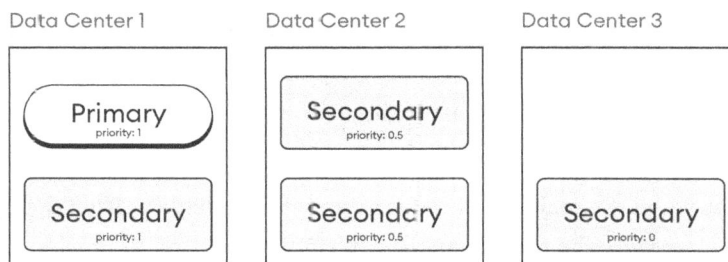

Figure 2.6: A five-member replica set distributed across three data centers with modified priority values

Write concern

A **write concern** controls how MongoDB acknowledges write operations within a replica set. It defines the level of assurance the system must provide before confirming that a write was successful. Essentially, it determines how many nodes must record the write before it's considered complete.

A write concern is configured using the following options:

```
{ w: <value>, j: <boolean>, wtimeout: <number> }
```

Each field in this structure plays a specific role in controlling the durability and behavior of write operations:

- **w**: Specifies the required number of replica set members that must acknowledge the write. You can set the w field to the following values:

  - **0**: No acknowledgment. This provides the least durability but the highest performance.

- **1**: Acknowledgment from the primary node.
- **majority**: Acknowledgment from the majority of the replica set members (default).
- **<number>**: Acknowledgment from a specific number of replica set members.

- **j**: Requests acknowledgment that the write operation has been written to the on-disk journal. If set to true, the write operation waits for a journal acknowledgment.

- **wtimeout**: Sets a time limit, in milliseconds, for the write concern. If the specified level of acknowledgment is not reached within this time, the write operation returns an error. This error does not mean the write won't complete or be rolled back; it prevents the write from blocking indefinitely.

By default, MongoDB uses the { w: "majority" } write concern. The majority is calculated as half of the voting members plus one (rounded down). However, if the number of data-bearing voting nodes is less than this majority, such as in deployments that include arbiters, the default write concern effectively falls back to { w: 1 }.

Starting in MongoDB 8.0, write operations that use the "majority" write concern return an acknowledgment when the majority of replica set members have written the oplog entry for the change. This improves the performance of "majority" writes. In previous releases, these operations would wait and return an acknowledgment after the majority of replica set members applied the change.

You can also set a global default write concern on both replica sets and sharded clusters. This default applies to all operations that don't explicitly define their own write concern. To configure the default read or write concern globally, use the following command:

```
db.adminCommand({
    setDefaultRWConcern: 1,
    defaultReadConcern: {<read concern>},
    defaultWriteConcern: {<write concern>},
    writeConcern: {<write concern>},
    comment: <any>
})
```

A write concern can influence both the performance and the durability of your data. Take the following examples:

- A lower write concern, such as { w: 0 }, can enhance performance by reducing the latency of the write operation. However, it risks data durability.

- A higher write concern, such as { w: "majority" }, ensures that the data is durable by waiting for acknowledgments from the majority of nodes. However, this can introduce some latency in the write operation.

Read preference

In MongoDB, read preference controls how clients choose which replica set members to use for read operations. By default, all reads are sent to the primary member in a replica set. However, you can configure the read preference to route queries to secondary members instead, which can help distribute load, enhance performance, and increase availability, especially in read-heavy applications.

MongoDB supports five read preference modes:

- **primary**: All read operations read from the current replica set primary (default)
- **primaryPreferred**: Reads are directed to the primary member if available; otherwise, they are routed to secondary members
- **secondary**: All operations read from the secondary members of the replica set
- **secondaryPreferred**: Reads are directed to the available secondary members, if any; otherwise, they are routed to the primary member
- **nearest**: Read operations are directed to the member with the lowest network latency, irrespective of the member's status

Changing the read preference can influence both the performance and availability of your data. For example, if you use secondary or secondaryPreferred read preference, the following apply:

- Distributing read operations to secondaries can enhance performance by reducing the load on the primary
- If the primary is unavailable, read operations can still be served by secondary members if the read preference mode allows it

In addition to the read preference modes, you can also specify the following options:

- **Tag sets**: Tag sets allow custom read preferences to be associated with custom tags for replica set members. Clients can then target read operations to members with specific tags. Consider the following when creating tags:
    - While they always apply with the secondary read preference, tag sets with primaryPreferred and secondaryPreferred read preferences only apply if your application selects a secondary for a read operation

- When setting tag lists with the nearest read preference, MongoDB selects the matching member with the lowest network latency

- You cannot set this option with the primary read preference

- **Max staleness**: Staleness refers to the lag in replication from the primary to the secondary. This option allows you to specify how stale a secondary can be before the client stops using it for read operations. You can set the max staleness value with the maxStalenessSeconds option. Consider the following when setting the max staleness value:

  - This option is meant to be used for applications that can read from secondaries and are trying to avoid reading from secondaries that have fallen too behind in replicating the primary's writes

  - You cannot set this option with the primary read preference

If the read preference includes both a maxStalenessSeconds value and a tag set list, the client filters by staleness first and then by the specified tags.

> To learn how to configure tag sets and the max staleness value, refer to the following documentation:
>
> - https://www.mongodb.com/docs/manual/core/read-preference-tags/
> - https://www.mongodb.com/docs/manual/core/read-preference-staleness/

Read concern

A read concern determines the consistency and isolation properties of the data read from replica sets and sharded clusters. By adjusting the read concern, you can control the visibility of data in read operations to ensure the desired level of consistency and isolation for your deployment.

Refer to the following table for information on supported read concern levels:

Read Concern Level	Description	Availability
`local`	Returns the most recent data available to the MongoDB instance at the start of the query. The `local` read concern doesn't guarantee that the data has been written to a majority of the replica set members. Default for reads against the primary and secondaries.	Available for use with or without causally consistent sessions and transactions.
`available`	Returns data that is currently available in the distributed system at the time of the query. This level provides the least amount of latency but does not guarantee consistency.	Not available for use with causally consistent sessions and transactions.
`majority`	Returns data that has been acknowledged by a majority of replica set members. This level ensures that documents returned by the read operation are durable, even in the event of failure. For operations in multi-document transactions, the majority read concern provides its guarantees only if the transaction commits with the majority write concern.	Available for use with or without causally consistent sessions and transactions.

`linearizable`	Returns data that reflects all successful majority-acknowledged writes that completed prior to the start of the read operation. This level provides the highest level of consistency. `linearizable` read concern guarantees only apply if read operations specify a query filter that identifies a single document. Furthermore, the following criteria must be met for the `linearizable` read concern to read from a consistent snapshot: • The query uses an immutable field as the query's search key • No concurrent updates mutate the search key of the query • The search key has a unique index that the query uses • Always set `maxTimeMS` with the `linearizable` read concern in case a majority of data-bearing nodes become unavailable	Not available for use with causally consistent sessions and transactions. You can specify this read concern for read operations on the primary only.
`snapshot`	Returns majority-committed data from a specific point in time across all replica set members. This level provides its guarantees only if the transaction commits with the `majority` write concern. If a transaction is part of a causally consistent session, upon transaction commit, the transaction operations are guaranteed to have read from a snapshot of majority-committed data that provides causal consistency with the operation immediately before the start of the transaction. If a transaction is not part of a causally consistent session, upon transaction commit, the transaction operations are guaranteed to have read from a snapshot of majority-committed data.	Available for all read operations inside multi-document transactions with the read concern set at the transaction level. Also available for the following methods outside of multi-document transactions: • `find` • `aggregate` • `distinct` (on unsharded collections)

Table 2.3: MongoDB read concern levels and their availability

To learn about causal consistency and transactions in MongoDB, refer to the following documentation:

- https://www.mongodb.com/docs/manual/core/causal-consistency-read-write-concerns/
- https://www.mongodb.com/docs/manual/core/transactions/

Read concern can influence both the consistency and isolation of your data. Take the following examples:

- If you set a higher level of read concern, such as majority or linearizable, you can ensure that the data returned is consistent across replica set members
- If you use the snapshot read concern, you can isolate a transaction from concurrent writes, ensuring a consistent view of the data throughout the transaction

Compaction

You can leverage compaction to release unneeded disk space, taken up by data and collection indexes, to the operating system. To do this, run the compact command on one of your deployment's secondary nodes. The command has the following syntax:

```
db.runCommand({
    compact: <string>,
    dryRun: <boolean>,
    force: <boolean>,
    freeSpaceTargetMB: <int>,
    comment: <any>
})
```

You can specify the following compact options:

- **compact**: The name of the collection you want to run compaction on.
- **dryRun**: If set to true, returns an estimate of how much space, in bytes, compaction can reclaim from the targeted collection. If dryRun is enabled, the compact command doesn't perform any kind of compaction and only returns the estimated value.
- **force**: (Optional) If enabled, forces compact to run on the primary member of your replica set.

- **freeSpaceTargetMB**: (Optional) Specifies the minimum amount of storage space, in megabytes, that must be recoverable for compaction to proceed. If there isn't enough storage space, compaction does not run.

- **comment**: (Optional) A comment to attach to the compact command. This comment appears alongside records of the compact command in log outputs.

To run compaction on a cluster that enforces authentication, you must authenticate as a user with the compact privilege action on the target collection. Before you run the compaction, consider the following:

- The primary does not replicate the compaction command to the secondary nodes
- A secondary node can replicate data while compaction is running
- Reads and writes are permitted while compaction is running
- Compaction is not supported on Atlas M0 and Flex clusters

Additionally, note that running compaction can lead to synchronization overhead due to the fact that it regularly checkpoints the database. On high-traffic databases, this can potentially delay or prevent operational tasks such as taking backups. To avoid unexpected disruptions, disable compaction before taking a backup.

Background compaction

In addition to the standalone compact command, starting in MongoDB 8.0, you can enable background compaction with the autoCompact command. If there is enough free storage space available, background compaction periodically iterates through all available files and continuously runs compaction without requiring you to manually run the compact command continuously. While the compact command targets only one collection at a time for compaction, the autoCompact command runs compaction on all collections on the node. The autoCompact command has the same requirements and performance considerations as the compact command.

The command has the following syntax:

```
db.runCommand({
    autoCompact: <boolean>,
    freeSpaceTargetMB: <int>,
    runOnce: <boolean>
})
```

You can specify the following options with the autoCompact command:

- **autoCompact**: Specifies whether to enable background compaction.
- **freeSpaceTargetMB**: (Optional) Specifies the minimum amount of storage space, in megabytes, that must be recoverable for compaction to proceed. If there isn't enough storage space, compaction does not run.
- **runOnce**: (Optional) If enabled, background compaction runs only once through every collection on the node. If a collection fails to compact when runOnce is set to false, MongoDB temporarily skips that collection and continues compacting the remaining collections.

TCMalloc performance optimization

Starting in MongoDB 8.0, MongoDB uses an upgraded version of TCMalloc that uses per-CPU caches, which locally store memory for a specific CPU core and drastically reduce memory fragmentation when compared to the previously used per-thread caches. As a result, the new TCMalloc helps reduce memory fragmentation and makes your database more resilient to high-stress workloads. This reduced fragmentation can improve the read performance of your replica set, especially secondaries that serve read queries.

Platform support

All operating systems that support MongoDB 8.0 also support the updated TCMalloc, *except* for the following:

- RHEL 8/Oracle 8 on the PPC64LE and s390x architectures
- RHEL 9/CentOS 9 / Oracle 9 on the PPC64LE architecture
- All Windows operating systems

Enabling Transparent Huge Pages (THP)

If you're running a self-managed MongoDB deployment on a Linux system, ensure that you enable **Transparent Huge Pages** (**THP**). Prior to MongoDB 8.0, we recommended disabling THP due to its negative performance impacts on database workloads with the old version of TCMalloc. However, the new version of TCMalloc relies heavily on THP.

This is because the new version of TCMalloc features a hugepage-aware allocator, which more aggressively releases hugepages to the operating system to reduce the total TCMalloc pageheap size. In other words, this can lead to more efficient memory usage, faster memory allocation, and lower overall memory consumption by MongoDB.

> For detailed instructions on how to enable THP for your Linux system, refer to the official documentation: https://www.mongodb.com/docs/manual/administration/tcmalloc-performance/#enable-transparent-hugepages--thp-.

Enabling per-CPU caches

To verify whether TCMalloc is running with per-CPU caches, run the following command:

```
db.runCommand({ serverStatus: 1 }).tcmalloc
```

In the output of the serverStatus command, ensure the following:

- tcmalloc.usingPerCPUCaches is true
- tcmalloc.tcmalloc.cpu_free is a value greater than 0

If you find that per-CPU caches aren't enabled for your deployment, make sure that you have disabled glibc rseq and are using Linux kernel version 4.18 or later. The new TCMalloc requires rseq to implement per-CPU caches, and if another application, such as the glibc library, registers a rseq structure before TCMalloc, TCMalloc can't use rseq.

Replication methods

In addition to built-in replication features, the MongoDB Shell (mongosh) provides a set of shell helper methods designed to facilitate interaction with a replica set. These helper methods serve as crucial tools for managing a replicated MongoDB deployment. Let's examine some of the important methods needed for managing replication in MongoDB:

- rs.add(): Adds a member to a replica set
- rs.addArb(): Adds an arbiter to a replica set
- rs.conf(): Shows the replica set configuration document
- rs.initiate(): Initializes a new replica set
- rs.printReplicationInfo(): Summary of the replica set's status as seen from the primary
- rs.status(): Provides a document detailing the current status of the replica set
- rs.reconfig(): Reconfigures an existing replica set, overwriting the existing replica set configuration
- rs.stepDown(): Triggers a transition where the primary becomes a secondary and the eligible secondaries hold an election

For a detailed list of replication methods, visit the following resource: https://www.mongodb.com/docs/manual/reference/method/js-replication/.

Replication commands

In addition to the preceding replication methods, you can also use replication commands for specific operations. For instance, replSetResizeOplog changes the size of the variable oplog in a replica set. The command takes the following fields:

- **replSetResizeOplog**: Set to 1.
- **size**: Specifies the maximum size of the oplog in megabytes. The minimum size that can be set is 990 MB, and the maximum is 1 PB. Explicitly cast the size as a double in mongosh using Double().
- **minRetentionHours**: Represents the minimum number of hours to retain an oplog entry, where decimal values indicate fractions of an hour (e.g., 1.5 means 1 hour and 30 minutes). The value must be equal to or greater than 0. A value of 0 means that mongod should truncate the oplog starting with the oldest entries to maintain the configured maximum oplog size.

You can use the following syntax with the relevant fields configured as shown below:

```
db.adminCommand({
    replSetResizeOplog: <int>,
    size: <double>,
    minRetentionHours: <double>
})
```

To learn more about replication commands, visit the following resource: https://www.mongodb.com/docs/manual/reference/command/nav-replication/.

Replication versus sharding

Replication and sharding are often confused with each other, but they serve fundamentally different roles. Replication involves creating multiple copies of the same data across different servers. Its primary goal is to provide fault tolerance, high availability, and redundancy, ensuring your application remains operational even if a node goes down. On the other hand, sharding is a horizontal scaling method that breaks a large dataset into smaller, more manageable pieces, called shards, and distributes those shards across multiple server instances. Each shard holds only a subset of the overall data, which improves performance and allows the system to handle more data than a single server could manage.

However, replication and sharding work together in that each shard must implement replication to maintain data integrity and availability. Each shard in a sharded cluster should be configured as a replica set to protect against data loss and system outages. If a shard's primary server fails and no replicated copy exists, any data stored exclusively on that shard becomes temporarily inaccessible. By replicating each shard's data across multiple nodes, MongoDB ensures that the cluster can continue operating even if individual servers go offline.

This architecture also supports rolling upgrades, which are updates that can be applied one node at a time without downtime, enabling smooth system maintenance with zero interruption to service.

The next section will take an in-depth look at sharding and its components.

Sharding

MongoDB supports horizontal scaling through sharding, which involves the distribution of data across multiple servers, divided into smaller pieces known as shards. Sharding plays an essential role in managing and organizing large-scale data.

Moreover, sharding allows for the creation of distributed databases to support geographically distributed applications, enabling policies that enforce data residency within specific regions.

Why do you need sharding?

Imagine your application's data is growing rapidly and starting to push the limits of your database. As data volume increases, you may encounter a range of issues, the most immediate being degraded performance. Queries that once returned results quickly may now take noticeably longer, slowing down your application and frustrating users with laggy or delayed responses.

Storage is another critical concern. Every system has practical limits on how much data it can store and manage efficiently. If your data growth outpaces your infrastructure's capacity, you risk hitting system limits or even encountering outages. To handle this kind of growth, there are two main strategies:

- **Vertical scaling** involves enhancing the resources of a single server by, for example, adding more RAM, upgrading to a faster CPU, or increasing disk space. While this can buy you time, there's a ceiling to how far you can scale one machine. Eventually, hardware constraints become a bottleneck.
- **Horizontal scaling** distributes the load across multiple machines. Rather than relying on one powerful server, the system splits the data and workload among several nodes. This approach can offer better scalability and often proves more cost-effective than high-end hardware upgrades. However, it also introduces added complexity in terms of system architecture, data distribution, and ongoing maintenance.

Key elements of a sharded cluster

A MongoDB sharded cluster consists of the following key elements:

- **Shard**: A replica set that stores a portion of the data in the cluster. The cluster can have anywhere from 1 to n shards, with each shard containing a distinct subset of the overall data. MongoDB Atlas offers different storage capacities for shards based on the cluster tier.

- **mongos**: A query router for client applications that efficiently manages both read and write operations. It directs client requests to the appropriate shards and consolidates the results from multiple shards into a coherent client response. Clients establish connections with mongos instances, rather than directly with individual shards. It is recommended to run multiple instances of mongos in production deployments to ensure high availability.

- **Config servers**: A replica set that serves as the primary repository for sharding metadata and configuration settings. This metadata encompasses the state and structure of the sharded data, including essential information such as the list of sharded collections and routing details. It plays a crucial role in enabling efficient data management and query routing within the cluster. Config servers can take the form of either a dedicated config server or a config shard:

  - A **dedicated config server** is a standalone config server without shard server functionality

  - Introduced in MongoDB 8.0, a **config shard** is a config server that also provides shard server functionality, meaning it can store application data in addition to the usual sharded cluster metadata

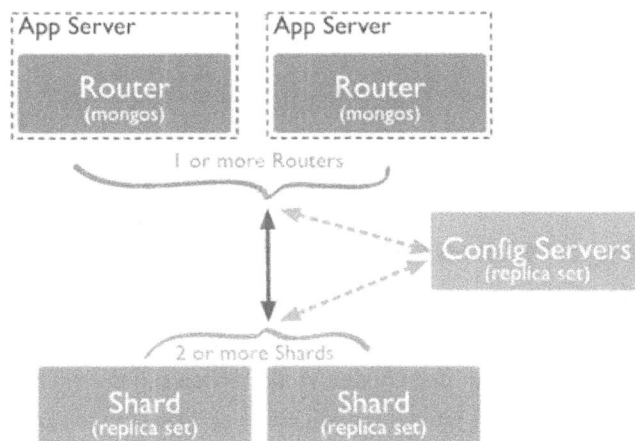

Figure 2.7: Components of a typical sharded cluster

In MongoDB, data sharding occurs at the collection level, meaning that the data of a collection is distributed across multiple shards within the cluster. It's important to note that each database in a sharded cluster has its own primary shard, which is responsible for storing all the unsharded collections within that database.

Also note that primary shards in sharded clusters are different from primary nodes in replica sets; they serve different purposes and are not related to each other.

When creating a new database, the primary shard is selected by the `mongos` process. It chooses the shard in the cluster that contains the least amount of data. The `totalSize` field returned by the `listDatabases` command is used as one of the factors in the selection criteria.

You can move the primary shard after its initial assignment by using the `movePrimary` command. The `movePrimary` command initially alters the primary shard in the cluster's metadata, then migrates all unsharded collections to the designated shard.

Config shards

Starting in MongoDB 8.0, you can configure a config server to be a config shard that stores your application data in addition to the usual sharded cluster metadata. Every sharded cluster must have a config server, but it can take the form of either a config shard or a dedicated config server. You cannot use the same config shard for multiple sharded clusters.

When choosing whether to use a config shard or a dedicated config server, consider the following:

- Use a **config shard** if your cluster has three or fewer shards
- Use a **dedicated config server** in the following instances:

  - You plan to use more than three shards
  - You plan to use time-series collections or queryable encryption
  - You plan to use queryable backups
  - Your application has demanding availability and resiliency requirements

Converting a replica set to a sharded cluster with a config shard

While you can't directly convert a replica set into a config shard, you can convert your replica set into a sharded cluster with a dedicated config server. Once you complete the initial conversion of your replica set into a sharded cluster, you can then run the `transitionFromDedicatedConfigServer` command to configure your dedicated config server to run as a config shard:

```
db.adminCommand({
    transitionFromDedicatedConfigServer: 1
})
```

After you run the `transitionFromDedicatedConfigServer` command, you can verify that your config server is running as a config shard by using the `listShards` command against the admin database, while you're connected to a mongos instance:

```
db.adminCommand({
    listShards: 1
})[ "shards" ].find( element => element._id === "config")
```

If your cluster uses a config shard, the output of the `listShards` command should resemble the following document, containing an `_id` value of `"config"`:

```
{
    _id: "config",
    host: "configRepl/localhost:27018",
    state: 1,
    topologyTime: Timestamp({ t: 1732218571, i: 13 }),
    replSetConfigVersion: Long('-1')
}
```

For detailed procedures on how to convert a replica set into a sharded cluster with a config shard, refer to the following tutorial: `https://www.mongodb.com/docs/manual/tutorial/convert-replica-set-to-embedded-config-server/`.

Transitioning from a config shard to a dedicated config server

If your sharded cluster uses a config shard, but you later find that a dedicated config server may be better suited for your application's workload, you can run the `transitionFromDedicatedConfigServer` command against the admin database of a mongos instance to convert your config shard into a dedicated config server:

```
db.adminCommand({
    transitionToDedicatedConfigServer: 1
})
```

When you convert a config shard to a dedicated config server, MongoDB moves all application data from the config shard to the other shards in the cluster.

This ability to transition between the config shard and dedicated config server provides increased flexibility for you to configure your application with respect to changing workload requirements and data volume.

Advantages of sharding

With an understanding of its key components, we can better understand the benefits that sharding can provide when managing and optimizing your MongoDB deployment. With the ability to distribute data across shards (as opposed to a standalone replica set, where each node contains the same data), sharding provides several advantages, such as the following:

- **Enhanced read and write speed**: Spreading your dataset across multiple shards allows for parallel processing. Each additional shard increases your total throughput, and a well-distributed dataset improves query performance. Multiple shards can process queries simultaneously, speeding up response times.

- **Expanded storage capacity**: Increasing the number of shards enhances your total storage. If one shard holds 4 TB of data, each additional shard adds another 4 TB. This allows for nearly limitless storage capacity, enabling scalability as your data needs increase.

- **Data locality**: Zone sharding allows you to distribute databases across different geographical locations, making it ideal for distributed applications. Policies can confine data within specific regions, with each region holding one or more shards, improving efficiency and adaptability in data management. In zone sharding, different ranges of shard key values can be associated with each zone, enabling faster and more precise data access based on geographical relevance.

- **Increased availability**: If one or more shards become unavailable, the sharded cluster can continue to perform partial reads and writes on the remaining available shards. This differs from replica sets in that the failure of a primary in a replica set can temporarily affect write availability for the entire set until a new primary is elected. Since sharded clusters distribute data across multiple shards, the other shards can still serve requests for the subset of data that they hold.

Data distribution

Correct data distribution in a sharded MongoDB cluster is vital to prevent bottlenecks and ensure efficient resource use.

Some key components for sharded data distribution include the following:

- **Shard key:** A field that MongoDB uses to distribute documents among members of a sharded cluster.
- **Zones:** A grouping of documents based on ranges of shard key values for a sharded collection.
- **Chunk:** A contiguous range of shard key values within a shard.
- **Range:** A contiguous range of shard key values within a chunk. A range can be a portion of a chunk or the whole chunk.
- **Balancer:** An internal MongoDB process that monitors the amount of data on each shard and migrates data between shards to attempt to achieve even distribution across shards.

The following sections provide more in-depth information on these key components.

Shard key

MongoDB performs sharding at the collection level, allowing you to choose which collections to shard. **Shard keys** determine the distribution of the collection's documents among the cluster's shards. They can take the form of either a single-indexed field or multiple fields covered by a compound index. You will learn more about indexes in *Chapter 4, Data Modeling and Index Optimization*.

Choosing the right shard key is one of the most critical decisions when sharding. A poorly chosen shard key can lead to inefficient data distribution, unbalanced load distribution across shards, and diminished query performance. These issues can overload some shards while underutilizing others, reducing system efficiency. In extreme cases, a single shard, known as a **hot shard,** could become a bottleneck that significantly impacts cluster performance. To avoid these performance impacts, choose the right shard key to optimize the performance of your sharded cluster.

To address problems stemming from a suboptimal shard key, MongoDB allows you to change your shard key either by **resharding a collection** or **refining a shard key**.

Resharding a collection

Data distribution fixes are most effective when you reshard a collection. If you want to improve data distribution and your cluster meets the following criteria, you should reshard the collection:

- Your application can tolerate a period of two seconds where the affected collection blocks writes due to an increase in latency

- The storage space available on each shard the collection will be distributed across is at least twice the size of the collection that you want to reshard and its total index size, divided by the number of shards:

  ```
  storage_req = ((collection_storage_size + index_size) * 2)/shard_
  count
  ```

- Ensure that the I/O capacity of your database is below 50%
- Ensure that your CPU load is below 80%

> The database does not enforce these requirements. Failure to allocate enough resources can result in the following:
>
> - The database running out of space and shutting down
> - Decreased performance
> - The operation taking longer than expected: In this case, consider deploying one member of each replica set in a site suitable for being a disaster recovery location

If your cluster doesn't meet the criteria to reshard, consider refining the shard key instead.

You can use the reshardCollection command to change your shard key or redistribute your data across your cluster. Prior to MongoDB 8.0, you had to specify a new shard key when running the reshardCollection command; otherwise, the command wouldn't have any effect. However, starting in MongoDB 8.0, you can specify the forceRedistribution option to reshard a collection on the same shard key.

Resharding a collection on the same shard key can be helpful in the scenario where you just added a shard to your cluster and need to redistribute your data onto the new shard. Previously, to redistribute data without changing the shard key, MongoDB would run a range migration, which was a much slower process than the current version of resharding.

Refining a shard key

Refining a collection's shard key allows for a more fine-grained distribution of data and can address situations where the existing key has led to jumbo chunks due to insufficient cardinality. To refine a collection's shard key, use the refineCollectionShardKey command. This command adds a single or multiple suffix fields to the existing key to create a new shard key.

For example, you may have an existing orders collection in a test database with the { customer_id: 1 } shard key. You can use the refineCollectionShardKey command to change the shard key to the new shard key, { customer_id: 1, order_id: 1 }:

```
db.adminCommand({
    refineCollectionShardKey: "test.orders",
    key: { customer_id: 1, order_id: 1}
})
```

Chunks

MongoDB organizes sharded data into distinct sections called chunks. Each chunk is characterized by an inclusive lower boundary (minKey) and an exclusive upper boundary (maxKey), which are defined by the shard key. These chunks contain an uninterrupted sequence of shard key values within a specific shard and are split only when moved across shards.

Jumbo and indivisible chunks

In MongoDB, when a chunk grows beyond the configured maximum size but cannot be automatically split, it is labeled as **jumbo**. This jumbo status signals that the chunk may cause balancing issues, as it can't be easily divided and moved.

The preferred way to clear the jumbo flag is to manually split the chunk. If the chunk can be successfully split into smaller parts, MongoDB will remove the jumbo designation. You can perform this operation using either the sh.splitAt() or sh.splitFind() method, which allows you to specify where the split should occur.

Sometimes, MongoDB cannot split a jumbo chunk any further. This often happens when the chunk contains documents that all share the same shard key value, making it indivisible. In these situations, you have a couple of options: you can modify the shard key and perform a resharding of the collection to create more granular chunks, or you can manually clear the jumbo flag to acknowledge the chunk's size without splitting.

To manually clear the flag, initiate clearJumboFlag in the admin database, provide the namespace of the sharded collection, and provide one of the following:

- The boundaries (bounds) of the jumbo chunk:

  ```
  db.adminCommand({
      clearJumboFlag: "sample.customers",
      bounds: [{ "x": 5}, {"x": 6}]
  })
  ```

- A `find` document with a shard key and value that falls within the jumbo chunk:

```
db.adminCommand({
    clearJumboFlag: "sample.customers",
    find: { "x": 5}
})
```

In the case where the collection employs a hashed shard key, avoid using the `find` field with the `clearJumboFlag` command. For collections with hashed shard keys, it's more appropriate to specify the `bounds` field.

Ranges

Ranges in MongoDB are closely related to chunks in that a range can either be a portion of the chunk or the whole chunk itself. MongoDB migrates data ranges automatically when there is an even distribution of sharded collection data across shards.

The default size for a range in MongoDB 8.0 is 128 MB. Though this default range size works sufficiently for most deployments, you may consider modifying this value due to hardware or workload requirements. For example, if you notice that automatic migrations use more I/O than your hardware can handle, you might want to reduce the range size to allow for more rapid and frequent migrations. You can specify a range size value between 1 and 1,024 megabytes, inclusive.

Pre-split ranges

In most cases, a sharded MongoDB cluster automatically creates, splits, and distributes data ranges across shards to balance the load. However, there are situations where MongoDB may not generate enough ranges quickly enough to keep up with your application's throughput demands.

If you're preparing to load a large volume of data into a new sharded cluster, **pre-splitting** the ranges can help ensure an even distribution of data from the start. This proactive step prevents any single shard from becoming a bottleneck during heavy data ingestion.

> You should only pre-split ranges for a collection that is currently empty. Attempting to manually split ranges for a collection that already contains data can result in irregular range boundaries and sizes. It can also cause the balancing behavior to function inefficiently or not at all.

To manually split empty ranges, use the `moveRange` command to distribute the empty ranges across the shards in your cluster. For a detailed example of how to manually move ranges, see `https://www.mongodb.com/docs/manual/tutorial/create-chunks-in-sharded-cluster/#std-label-create-ranges-in-a-sharded-cluster`.

Zones

You can create zones of sharded data based on a cluster's shard key. Each shard in a cluster can be in one or more zones. In a balanced cluster, MongoDB directs reads and writes for a zone only to shards that are inside that zone. You should consider applying zones in your deployment if you need to do the following:

- Isolate a specific subset of data on a specific set of shards
- Ensure that the most relevant data lives on shards that are geographically located closest to the application servers
- Route data to shards based on the hardware or its performance

Each zone covers one or more ranges of shard key values for a collection, and each range that a zone covers is inclusive of its lower boundary and exclusive of its upper boundary. When you define zones and zone ranges before you shard an empty or non-existent collection, the shard collection operation creates chunks for the defined zone ranges as well as any additional chunks that would cover the entire range of shard key values. It then performs an initial chunk distribution based on the zone ranges, which allows for faster setup of zoned sharding.

Balancer

Data in sharded clusters is distributed based on data size. To ensure a balanced distribution of data, a background process called the **balancer** keeps track of the data volume on each shard for every sharded collection. Once the amount of data for a sharded collection on a particular shard reaches a specific migration limit, the balancer attempts to redistribute data across shards, aiming for an equal data distribution per shard while honoring previously defined zones. By default, this balancing process is always enabled and runs on the primary of the **Config Server Replica Set (CSRS)**.

The balancing process for sharded clusters is completely invisible to the user and the application layer, although minor performance effects might be observed during execution. The balancer tries to mitigate this impact by attempting to limit a shard to participate in only one migration at a time. The balancer performs range migrations one after the other. With a sharded cluster consisting of n shards, MongoDB can perform up to n/2 (rounded down) concurrent migrations as long as they aren't performed on the same shard.

Another way that the balancer attempts to minimize performance impacts is by starting a balance round only when the data discrepancy between the most heavily loaded shard and the least loaded shard for a sharded collection hits the migration threshold.

A collection is considered balanced when the data variation between shards for that specific collection is less than three times the established range size for the collection. For example, if the range size is set at the default of 128 MB, a migration will be triggered if the data size difference between any two shards for a certain collection is at least 384 MB.

Balancing window

You can also set a specific timeframe for the balancer's operation to prevent it from interfering with production traffic. This is called the **balancing window**. You may want to schedule a balancing window in situations where your dataset grows slowly and a migration can impact performance. If you specify a different balancing window, it must be sufficient to complete the migration of all data inserted during the day.

To specify a balancing window timeframe, perform the following steps:

1. Connect to any mongos instances in the cluster by using mongosh.

2. Switch to the config database:

   ```
   use config
   ```

3. Run the sh.startBalancer() command to ensure that the balancer is not stopped.

4. Set the activeWindow field by using the updateOne() command:

   ```
   db.settings.updateOne(
       { _id: "balancer" },
       { $set: {
           activeWindow: {start: "<start-time>", stop: "<end-time>"}
       }},
       { upsert: true }
   )
   ```

5. Replace <start-time> and <end-time> with time values using two-digit hour and minute values (i.e., HH:MM) that specify the beginning and end boundaries of the balancing window:

   - For HH values, use hour values ranging from 00 to 23
   - For MM values, use minute values ranging from 00 to 59

For self-managed sharded clusters, MongoDB evaluates the start and stop times relative to the time zone of the primary member in the CSRS. For Atlas clusters, MongoDB evaluates the start and stop times relative to the UTC time zone.

> For more detailed information on managing the balancer, refer to the following documentation: https://www.mongodb.com/docs/manual/tutorial/manage-sharded-cluster-balancer/#std-label-sharding-schedule-balancing-window.

Sharding strategies

MongoDB supports two sharding strategies for distributing data across sharded clusters: **ranged sharding** and **hashed sharding**.

Ranged sharding

Ranged sharding involves dividing data into continuous sequences based on shard key values. Documents with similar shard key values are likely to be in the same shard or chunk. This allows for efficient queries where reads target documents within a contiguous range. Range-based sharding is the default method unless options for hashed sharding or zones are configured.

Ranged sharding is most efficient when the shard key has a combination of these characteristics:

- **High cardinality**: High cardinality allows MongoDB to create more chunks, giving the balancer greater flexibility to evenly distribute data and workload among shards. Whenever possible, choose a shard key with high cardinality. A low-cardinality key limits the number of chunks that can be created, which in turn restricts the effectiveness of horizontal scaling and can lead to performance bottlenecks.

- **Low frequency**: Frequency refers to how often each shard key value appears in the dataset. Ideally, shard key values should be evenly distributed. If a large portion of documents share just a few common values, it can lead to oversized chunks concentrated around those values. These imbalanced chunks can overload specific shards and become performance bottlenecks. If these chunks can't be split further because all the documents share the same shard key value, they become jumbo chunks, which prevent efficient rebalancing and reduce the overall scalability of the cluster.

- **Non-monotonically changing values**: Whenever possible, choose a shard key with values that change unpredictably to encourage more even distribution of inserts across the cluster. Using a shard key based on a value that consistently increases or decreases can lead to poor data distribution. If you use a monotonically changing shard key, new inserts will likely target a single chunk, often the one containing the highest range of values. This chunk becomes a hotspot for writes, leading to an uneven load across the cluster.

To help mitigate the risk of hotspots, MongoDB ensures that the MinKey and MaxKey chunks are not placed on the same shard. However, that alone isn't enough to solve write skew caused by monotonically changing values.

You can perform ranged sharding on both populated and empty collections. If you shard a populated collection, only one chunk is created initially. The balancer then migrates ranges from that chunk, if necessary, according to the configured range size.

If you shard an empty collection, MongoDB's behavior depends on whether you specify zones and zone ranges. If you don't specify zones for the empty collection, the sharding operation creates a single empty chunk to cover the entire range of the shard key values, and the balancer then migrates the initial chunk across the shards as appropriate. If you specify zones and zone ranges, the sharding operation creates empty chunks for the defined zone ranges as well as any additional chunks to cover the entire range of the shard key values. It then performs an initial chunk distribution based on the specified zone ranges. This initial creation and distribution of chunks allows for the faster setup of zoned sharding.

Hashed sharding

Hashed sharding involves computing a hash of the shard key field's value. MongoDB automatically computes the hashes when resolving queries that use hashed indexes, so your application does *not* need to compute hashes. Each chunk is then assigned a range based on the hashed shard key values. Although a range of shard keys may appear to be close in terms of their values, their hashed values are unlikely to fall within the same chunk.

Hashed sharding is best for shard keys with fields that change monotonically, such as ObjectId values or timestamps. Hashed sharding provides a more even data distribution across sharded clusters at the cost of reducing targeted operations, which are those that mongos routes to a single shard using the shard key and cluster metadata.

You can perform hashed sharding on both populated and empty collections. If you shard a populated collection with a hashed shard key, the operation creates an initial chunk to cover all shard key values.

If you shard an empty collection with a hashed shard key, MongoDB's behavior depends on whether you specify zones and zone ranges. Starting in MongoDB 7.2, if you don't specify zones for the empty collection, the sharding operation creates one chunk per shard by default and migrates the data across the cluster. Previously, the operation created two chunks by default. You can specify a different number of initial chunks with the numInitialChunks option to start an initial chunk distribution, which allows for faster setup of sharding.

If you specify zones and zone ranges, the sharding operation creates empty chunks for the defined zone ranges as well as any additional chunks to cover the entire range of the shard key values. It then performs an initial chunk distribution based on the specified zone ranges.

You can also create compound indexes with a solitary hashed field. To create a compound hashed index, specify "hashed" as the value of any single index key during index creation. A compound hashed index calculates the hash value for a single field in the compound index. This value, along with other fields in the index, becomes your shard key.

The following example creates a compound hashed index on the name field in ascending order, sets _id as the hashed field, and shards the planets collection:

```
db.planets.createIndex({ "name": 1, "_id": "hashed" })
sh.shardCollection("sample_guides.planets", {"name": 1, "_id": "hashed" })
```

Features such as zone sharding are supported by compound hashed sharding, where the prefix non-hashed field or fields define zone ranges, while the hashed field ensures a more equitable distribution of the sharded data. Additionally, compound hashed sharding can support shard keys with a hashed prefix, which helps address data distribution issues tied to fields that increase monotonically.

Hashed versus ranged sharding scenarios

The following table outlines several example scenarios of sharded data, recommends the best sharding strategy, and explains the reasoning for why the chosen strategy is better than the alternative:

Scenario	Best Sharding Strategy	Reasoning for Sharding Strategy
Social Media Platform: You manage a database for a social media platform that handles a large volume of user posts. Each post, stored in an app.posts collection, is associated with a unique post_id, which is a sequentially generated identifier. The platform experiences a high write load due to the continuous creation of posts. Common queries to the database include retrieving the most recent posts, fetching posts from specific users, and performing analytics on post data.	Hashed	**Hashed sharding would be better suited for this scenario because** post_id is a monotonically increasing value. Hashed sharding uses an automatically computed hash of the post_id value to determine shard placement. This ensures that posts are distributed evenly across all shards, regardless of their sequential nature. This uniform distribution helps prevent any single shard from becoming a bottleneck due to a concentration of writes or reads. If we were to use ranged sharding, with post_id being a monotonically increasing value, the chunk with the upper bound of key values would receive the majority of incoming writes. This would restrict insert operations to the single shard containing this chunk.

Scenario	Best Sharding Strategy	Reasoning for Sharding Strategy
Rideshare Application: You manage the database for a global rideshare app that manages a large volume of ride data, stored in an `application.rides` collection. Each ride is associated with a unique `ride_id`, which is a composite shard key consisting of a `city_code` value(representing different cities where the service operates) and a unique `_id` value for each ride. The app experiences a mix of read and write operations, with frequent queries targeting specific `city_code` values to retrieve all rides or analyze ride patterns and demand in a given city.	Ranged	**Since the app frequently queries for rides with specific** `city_code` values, ranged sharding would be better since it targets specific ranges of the shard key. Additionally, the high cardinality of the `city_code` field ensures that data is well distributed across shards. Each shard can handle rides for different cities, balancing the load and preventing any single shard from becoming a bottleneck. Hashed sharding wouldn't be as effective here because it would distribute rides randomly across shards. As a result, this could result in increased latency and resource usage when targeting specific `city_code` values because multiple shards would need to be queried.

Scenario	Best Sharding Strategy	Reasoning for Sharding Strategy
Streaming Platform: You manage the database for a content streaming platform that manages a large catalog of media content, including movies, TV shows, and music. Each media item is associated with a unique media_id, which is a composite key consisting of a genre and a unique _id value for each piece of content. Common queries on this database include retrieving all media items for a specific genre, as users like to filter for specific media categories, and analyzing popularity trends within genres.	Ranged	**Ranged sharding would be better for this scenario because of the non-monotonic nature of the** genre field. This ensures that data can be distributed across shards based on the genre, rather than in a sequential pattern, and it can allow for related data to be stored in the same shard. This way, queries against the genre field likely only need to access one shard. Similar to the previous rideshare scenario, hashed sharding would unnecessarily distribute each content item randomly across shards. This could lead to increased latency and resource usage when looking for specific genre values since the query would have to target multiple shards.

Table 2.4: Recommended Sharding Strategies Based on Application Scenarios

Production configurations

In a production cluster, ensure that data is redundant and that your systems are highly available. Consider the following for a production sharded cluster deployment:

- Deploy config servers as a three-member replica set
- Deploy at least two shards as three-member replica sets
- Deploy one or more mongos routers

> When possible, consider deploying one member of each replica set in a site suitable for being a disaster recovery location.

Having multiple mongos instances can support high availability and scalability. If a proxy or load balancer is between the application and the mongos routers, you must configure it for client affinity.

Client affinity allows every connection from a single client to reach the same mongos instance. For shard-level high availability, do one of the following:

- Add mongos instances on the same hardware where other mongos instances are already running
- Embed mongos routers at the application level

If you increase the number of mongos routers, performance can degrade. Your deployment should not have more than 30 mongos routers.

The following diagram shows a common sharded cluster architecture used in production:

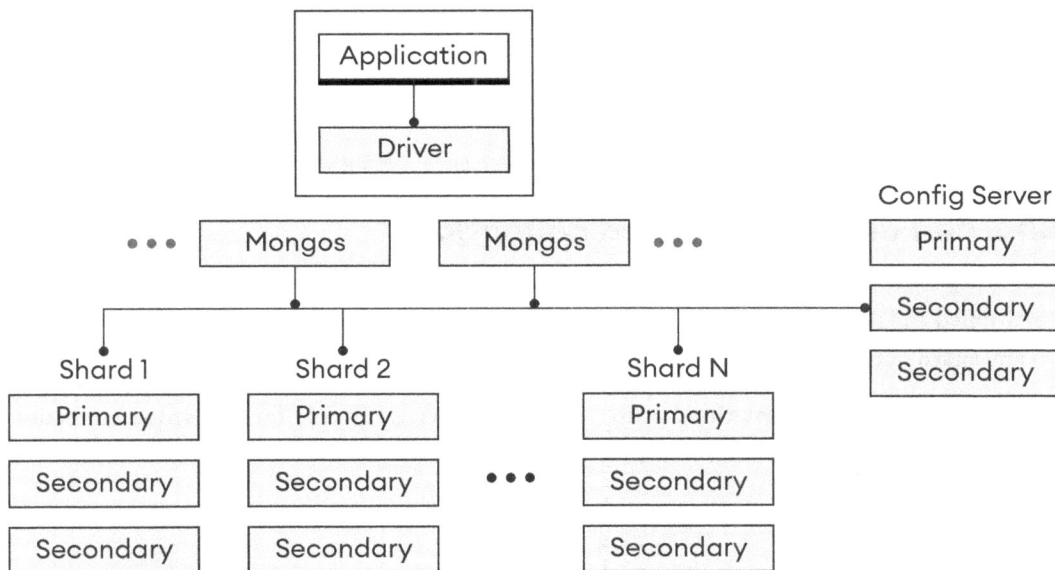

Figure 2.8: Example production sharded cluster architecture

Development configuration

For testing and development, you can deploy a sharded cluster with a minimum number of components. These non-production clusters will typically have the following components:

- One mongos instance
- A single shard replica set
- A replica set config server

The following diagram shows a sharded cluster architecture used for development only:

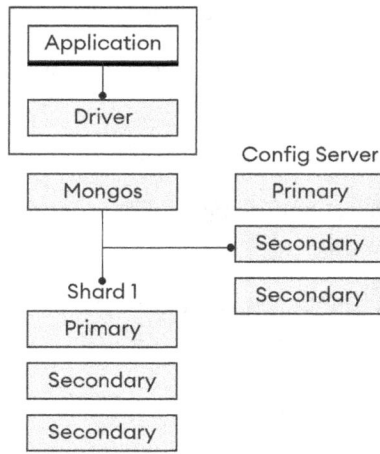

Figure 2.9: Example sharded cluster architecture for testing and development

Sharded and non-sharded collections

A database can have a mixture of sharded and unsharded collections. Sharded collections are partitioned and distributed across the shards in the cluster. Unsharded collections can be located on any shard but cannot span across shards.

The following figure shows the distribution of data across shards for a sharded collection (**Collection1**) and an unsharded collection (**Collection2**):

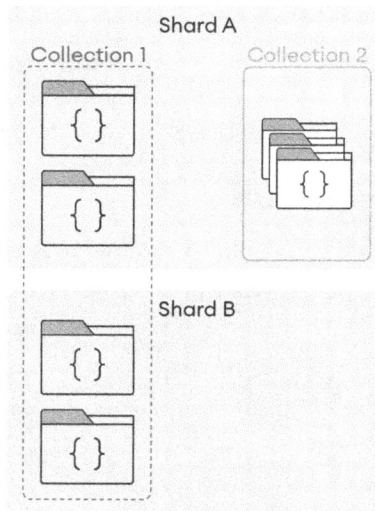

Figure 2.10: A sharded and unsharded collection

To interact with both sharded and unsharded collections in the sharded cluster, you must connect to a mongos router. Clients should *never* connect to a single shard in order to perform read or write operations.

Unsharding a collection

Starting in MongoDB 8.0, you can unshard existing sharded collections with the unshardCollection command or the sh.unshardCollection() helper method. When you unshard a collection, MongoDB moves the collection data onto a single shard and updates the metadata to reflect the unsharded state. By default, when you unshard a collection, MongoDB moves the collection's data to the shard with the least amount of data; however, you can also specify which shard to place the data on.

You can unshard a collection in the following cases:

- You can store the collection entirely on a single shard
- The collection requires resource isolation, and access patterns are better supported if the collection lives on a single shard
- The collection was previously sharded but no longer needs to be sharded

Before you unshard your collection, ensure that you meet the following requirements:

- If your deployment has access control enabled, you have been granted the enableSharding role.
- Your application can tolerate a period of two seconds where the affected collection blocks writes. During the time period that writes are blocked, your application experiences an increase in latency.
- Your database meets the following resource requirements:

  - The shard you are moving the collection to has enough storage space for the collection and its indexes. The destination shard requires at least the value of (Collection Storage Size + Index Size) * 2 bytes to be available.
  - Ensure that your I/O capacity is below 50%.
  - Ensure that your CPU load is below 80%.

To unshard a collection, follow these steps:

1. Retrieve the name of your target shard.

   You can optionally specify which shard your data will move to when you unshard a collection.

To output a list of shard names, use the `listShards` command:

```
db.adminCommand({ listShards: 1 })
```

2. Run the `unshardCollection` command.

    The following sample code unshards a collection called us_users in the `clients` database
    to shard1:

    ```
    db.adminCommand ({
        unshardCollection: "clients.us_users",
        toShard: "shard1"
    })
    ```

    If you were to omit the `toShard` field, MongoDB would move the collection data to the
    shard with the least amount of data.

3. Confirm that the collection is unsharded.

    To confirm that the `clients.us_users` collection is unsharded, use the
    `$shardedDataDistribution` aggregation pipeline stage and query for a match on the
    unsharded collection's namespace:

    ```
    db.aggregate([
        { $shardedDataDistribution: {}},
        { $match: { "ns": "clients.us_users" }}
    ])
    ```

    If the collection is unsharded, the aggregation operation doesn't return any data.

Moving an unsharded collection

Starting in MongoDB 8.0, you can move an unsharded collection to a different shard using the
`moveCollection` command. In earlier versions of MongoDB, unsharded collections only lived
on the primary shard, and you had to use the `movePrimary` command to migrate unsharded
collections. Moving an unsharded collection to any shard can help optimize performance on
larger, more complex workloads; achieve better resource utilization; and more evenly distribute
data across shards.

You might consider moving an unsharded collection in the following example scenarios:

*   You have three unsharded collections on a single shard, and one collection begins to grow
    significantly larger than the others, which causes performance degradation on the shard.

To improve performance and balance the load across the cluster, you can move the two smaller collections to a different shard.

- Your application stores data in three separate unsharded collections located in North America, Europe, and Asia on one shard. To reduce the latency of an application, you can move these collections to a shard located in each respective region in the same cluster.
- Your application frequently performs $lookup operations between two unsharded collections that reside on different shards. To improve query performance, you can move both collections to the same shard.

Before you move your collection, ensure that you meet the following requirements:

- Your application can tolerate a period of two seconds where the affected collection blocks writes. During the time period that writes are blocked, your application experiences an increase in latency.
- Your database meets the following resource requirements:
    - The shard you are moving the collection to has enough storage space for the collection and its indexes The destination shard requires at least the value of (Collection Storage Size + Index Size) * 2 bytes to be available.
    - Ensure that your I/O capacity is below 50%.
    - Ensure that your CPU load is below 80%.

Querying sharded data

Querying data from a MongoDB sharded cluster differs from querying data in a single-server deployment or replica set. Instead of connecting to the single server or replica set primary, you connect to mongos.

mongos instances provide the only interface and entry point to your MongoDB cluster. Applications connect to mongos instead of connecting directly to the shards. mongos executes queries, gathers results, and passes them to the application.

The mongos process doesn't hold any persistent state and typically doesn't use a lot of system resources. It acts as a proxy for requests. When a query comes in, mongos examines it, decides which shards need to execute the query, and establishes a cursor on all targeted shards.

Find operations

If a query includes the shard key or a prefix of the shard key, mongos performs a targeted operation, which only queries the shards that hold the keys you are looking for.

For example, assume the compound shard key for the following user collection indexes _id, email, and country:

```
db.user.find({ _id: 1 })
db.user.find({ _id: 1, "email": "packt@packt.com" })
db.user.find({ _id: 1, "email": "packt@packt.com", "country": "UK" })
```

These queries contain either a prefix or the complete shard key. A query on {email, country} or {country} would not be able to target the right shards, which would result in a broadcast operation. A broadcast operation is any operation that doesn't include the shard key or a prefix of the shard key, and results in mongos querying every shard.

sort(), limit(), and skip() operations

If you want to sort results, you have the following options:

- If you're using a shard key in the sort criteria, then mongos can determine the order in which it has to query a shard or shards. This results in an efficient and targeted operation.
- If you're not using the shard key in the sort criteria, then mongos will run a broadcast operation. To sort the results when you aren't using the shard key, the primary shard executes a distributed merge sort locally before passing on the sorted results to mongos.

A limit on the queries is enforced on each individual shard and then again at the mongos level, as there may be results from multiple shards.

A skip() operator, on the other hand, cannot be passed on to individual shards and will be applied by mongos after retrieving the results locally.

If you combine the skip() and limit() cursor methods, mongos optimizes the query by passing both values to individual shards. This can be useful in cases such as pagination. If you query without sort() and the results come from more than one shard, mongos will round robin across shards for the results.

Update and delete operations

For updateOne(), deleteOne(), and findAndModify() operations, you can use any field to match documents, similar to a non-sharded collection. You do not need to have the shard key or the _id value; however, using the shard key will be more efficient as it allows for targeted queries.

For example, the following query runs an updateOne() operation on the cities collection without having to pass the shard key, which uses the city field:

```
db.cities.updateOne({ "population": 293200}, {$set: {"areaSize": 211}});
```

The following table summarizes operations in MongoDB 8.0 that you can use for sharding:

Operation	Notes
insert()	Must include the shard key
update()	Can include the shard key, but not mandatory
Query with shard key	Targeted operation
Query without shard key	Broadcast operation
Index sorted, query without shard key	Distributed sort merge
updateOne(), deleteOne(), replaceOne(), findAndModify()	Can use any field to match on, but more efficient with a shard key

Table 2.5: Sharding Operation Behavior in MongoDB 8.0

Hedged reads

mongos instances can hedge reads that use non-primary read preferences. The mongos instances direct read operations to two members of the replica set for each queried shard, and then return the results from the first respondent per shard.

Operations that support hedged reads include the following:

- collStats
- count
- dataSize
- dbStats
- distinct
- filemd5
- find
- listCollections
- listIndexes
- planCacheListFilters

Sharding methods

To manage the distribution of data, MongoDB provides a set of helper methods. You can use these methods to enable sharding, define how data should be distributed, and monitor the state of sharding.

Some key `mongosh` shell helper methods include the following:

- `sh.shardCollection()`: Shards a collection using the specified shard key.
- `sh.status()`: Returns a formatted report of the sharding configuration and information regarding existing chunks in a sharded cluster. The level of detail can be adjusted with the verbose parameter, allowing for either a high-level overview or a detailed report. Information provided by this command includes the sharding version, details about each shard, the status of active `mongos` instances, the state of the balancer, and information about databases and sharded collections.
- `sh.reshardCollection()`: Changes the shard key for a collection and changes the distribution of your data. Starting in MongoDB 8.0, you can reshard a collection with the same shard key by passing the `forceDistribution` option.
- `sh.getBalancerstate()`: Returns a Boolean value indicating whether the balancer is presently active.
- `sh.moveCollection()`: Moves a single unsharded collection to a different shard without having to change primary shards.
- `sh.getShardedDataDistribution()`: Returns information on the distribution of data in a sharded cluster.
- `sh.unshardCollection()`: Unshards an existing sharded collection and moves the collection data onto a single shard.

Summary

In this chapter, we covered the foundational elements of MongoDB's architecture, defining replication and sharding, detailing key features that you can use in production, and introducing some new features in MongoDB 8.0 that can help maximize your deployment's performance.

Regarding replication, we learned about the critical role that it plays in ensuring data availability and fault tolerance within MongoDB, including the replica set election process, the importance of the oplog, and how you can configure your replica set to enhance read scalability. Furthermore, we introduced new features, such as background compaction and the updated TCMalloc, that help manage memory usage and, in turn, increase the efficiency of your deployment.

With sharding, this chapter provided a comprehensive overview of sharding as a strategy for horizontal scaling. We learned how sharding distributes data across multiple servers to manage large datasets and high-traffic applications. Key concepts such as shard keys and config servers helped demonstrate how sharding enables MongoDB deployments to scale efficiently while maintaining performance. Additionally, we covered new sharding commands that you can leverage to reduce the complexity of your deployment.

By the end of this chapter, you should have a solid understanding of how MongoDB's replication and sharding mechanisms work together to provide a scalable, reliable, and high-performing database solution.

In the next chapter, you will learn about MongoDB's Developer Tools, which can aid you in provisioning security measures and more for your deployment.

Get This Book's PDF Version and Exclusive Extras

UNLOCK NOW

Scan the QR code (or go to packtpub.com/unlock). Search for this book by name, confirm the edition, and then follow the steps on the page.

Note: Keep your invoice handy. Purchases made directly from Packt don't require an invoice.

3

Developer Tools

In modern software development, the efficiency and success of application creation are heavily influenced by the availability and quality of developer tools. MongoDB offers a comprehensive suite of such tools designed to streamline the development process and enhance productivity. These tools enable developers to seamlessly assemble, test, optimize, and manage the diverse components required to build robust applications.

Among the most prominent tools is MongoDB Compass, a graphical user interface that simplifies the process of constructing and executing queries against the MongoDB database. Another widely adopted utility is the MongoDB extension for **Visual Studio Code (VS Code)**, which assists developers in authoring accurate and efficient queries within their preferred integrated development environment.

Beyond query construction, MongoDB's toolset includes capabilities for data analysis, workflow automation, and environmental integration, all aimed at improving developer experience and code quality. While the full range of available tools is extensive, this chapter highlights those with the most immediate and impactful utility.

This chapter covers MongoDB's AI-enabled developer tools, which support integration with **artificial intelligence (AI)** and **machine learning (ML)** frameworks. These tools are particularly beneficial for developers working on intelligent or predictive applications, providing a seamless bridge between data infrastructure and web software.

This chapter covers the following tools:

- Integrated development environment extensions
- MongoDB Compass
- MongoDB MCP Server

Integrated development environment extensions

An **integrated development environment (IDE)** serves as the central hub for most software developers, providing a comprehensive suite of tools designed to streamline the coding process. Within the IDE, developers can efficiently write, proofread, and meticulously review their code. Beyond basic text editing, IDEs typically offer invaluable features such as syntax highlighting, which visually differentiates elements of the code to improve readability and identify errors. Autocomplete functionalities significantly accelerate coding by suggesting and automatically completing code snippets, reducing typing and potential typos.

IDEs often integrate with various other development tools, fostering a more productive and efficient workflow. These integrations can include debugging tools that allow developers to step through their code line by line, identify logical errors, and inspect variable values at different points in execution. Version control system integrations (e.g., Git) enable developers to manage changes to their code base, collaborate with team members, and revert to previous versions if needed. Built-in compilers or interpreters allow for immediate testing and execution of code, providing instant feedback on its functionality.

By consolidating these essential functionalities into a single, intuitive interface, IDEs empower developers to be significantly more productive and faster in creating robust and working applications. They minimize context switching, reduce the need for external tools, and provide a rich environment that supports the entire software development lifecycle, from initial coding to testing and deployment.

MongoDB offers three distinct IDE extensions that are worth calling out in this text. The most popular is the **VS Code extension**, which is what we will cover in more detail in the following pages, letting you work with MongoDB and your data directly within your coding environment. We'll also briefly discuss the IntelliJ plugin, which is designed to improve the development experience for Java developers working with IntelliJ IDEA.

MongoDB for VS Code extension

The **MongoDB for VS Code extension** integrates MongoDB functionalities directly into the VS Code environment. It allows you to explore and interact with your MongoDB data seamlessly while programming. Some of its key features are as follows:

- **Data exploration**: You can navigate through your databases, collections, and documents using the extension
- **Query prototyping**: It enables you to prototype queries and run MongoDB commands directly within VS Code
- **GitHub Copilot integration**: The extension includes MongoDB-specific commands to assist with GitHub Copilot, helping you generate code and interact with your MongoDB deployments

To get started, you need to install the extension from the VS Code Marketplace and connect it to your MongoDB deployment. Once set up, you can explore your data and perform various operations directly from your coding environment.

Getting started with the VS Code extension

Before you can install the MongoDB for VS Code extension, you must install VS Code. You can download VS Code from `https://code.visualstudio.com/`.

Then, here's what you can do:

1. Open the **Extensions** view in VS Code.
2. Click the **Extensions** icon in the left navigation, as shown in the following figure:

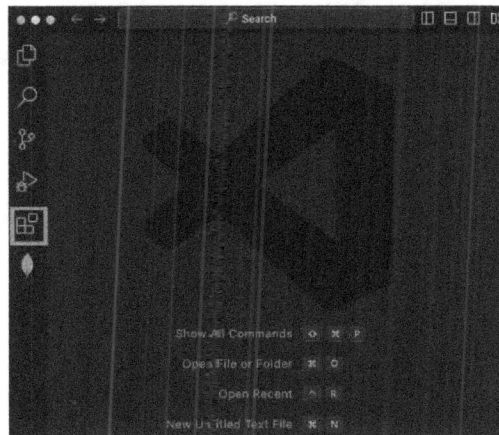

Figure 3.1: The Extensions icon in VS Code

3. Search for **MongoDB for VS Code** in the Extensions Marketplace.

4. Click **Install**.

Once the installation is complete, the **Install** button changes to the **Manage** gear button.

Data exploration

To explore your data in the VS Code extension, you'll need to first connect your VS Code environment to your MongoDB database. This is very simply done by following these steps:

1. Provide the connection string as a configuration option inside the VS Code extension in the VSCode Command Palette, as shown in *Figure 3.2*:

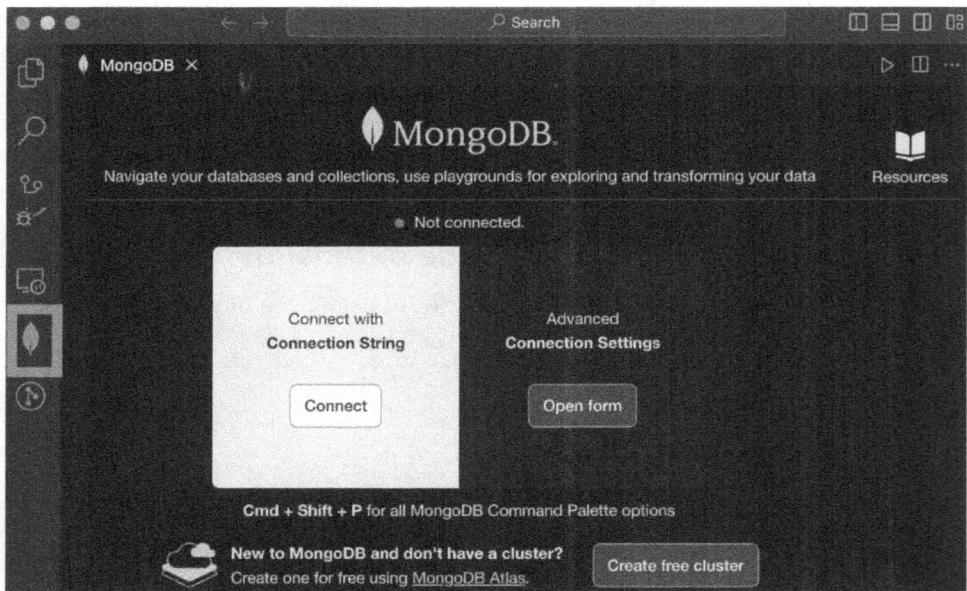

Figure 3.2: The VS Command Palette inside the MongoDB extension

2.   Click on **Connections**, then expand the **CONNECTIONS** menu:

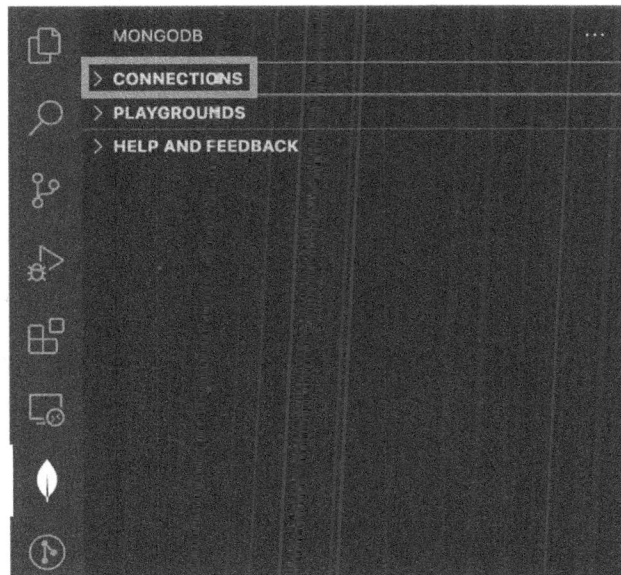

Figure 3.3: CONNECTIONS in the MongoDB VS Code extension

3.   Click the **More Actions** menu, as indicated by three dots in *Figure 3.4*:

Figure 3.4: The More Actions menu in the MongoDB VS Code extension interface

4.   Next, paste your connection string in the form entry.

Once you've properly connected to your MongoDB database, you'll be able to sift through your data and examine it more closely via the left-side navigational menu.

In this navigational bar, you can view the complete hierarchy, such as the databases, the collections within the database, the documents within the collection, and the schemas and indexes that affect those documents.

When you expand a collection's schema, the VS Code extension lists the fields of the collection's documents. If a field exists in all documents and its type is consistent throughout the collection, the VS Code extension displays an icon indicating that field's data type. You can then hover over the field name for a text description of the field's data type.

To view and edit individual fields within a document, right-click the ID of the desired document. The VS Code extension will open the document for editing. After making your desired changes, press *Ctrl + S* to save the document.

Beyond the core functionalities, the VS Code extension for MongoDB offers a suite of additional features designed to streamline your workflow and enhance productivity. You'll discover powerful tools for effortlessly managing your data, including the ability to clone existing documents with a single click, facilitating rapid iteration and testing. When it comes to data hygiene, the extension provides intuitive options for deleting documents, whether individually or in bulk, ensuring that your collections remain organized and relevant.

Furthermore, for situations requiring fresh data entry or schema creation, you can easily insert new, blank documents directly within the VS Code environment, eliminating the need to switch between applications. All these tasks, from intricate data manipulation to foundational document creation, are seamlessly integrated within the familiar VS Code interface, empowering developers to maintain a consistent and efficient development experience.

The intuitive interface makes it easy for even beginner developers to use.

Query prototyping

The VS Code extension also offers a robust feature for prototyping queries and aggregations through the MongoDB Playground. This playground is a JavaScript environment equipped with syntax highlighting and autocomplete functionalities.

This capability allows for immediate experimentation with queries, regardless of complexity, and instant verification of results against expectations. All of this can be achieved without permanent modifications to your application code. Satisfactory results can be saved instantly.

Here's how to use MongoDB Playground in VS Code:

1. Open the VS Code Command Palette. On Windows and Linux, press *Ctrl + Shift + P*. On macOS, press *⌘ + Shift + P*.

2. Select the command to create a MongoDB Playground, which will open a preconfigured default MongoDB Playground template:

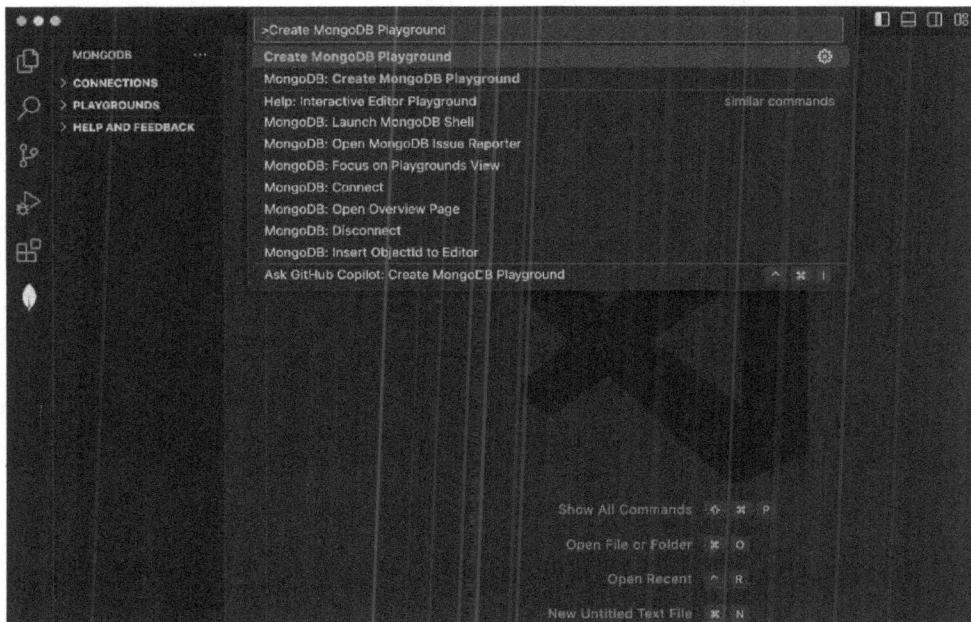

Figure 3.5: Default MongoDB Playground template in VS Code

3. To run a playground, you'll simply click the **Play** button in VS Code's top navigational bar, and your playground will run against the deployment specified in the active connection that you pasted earlier:

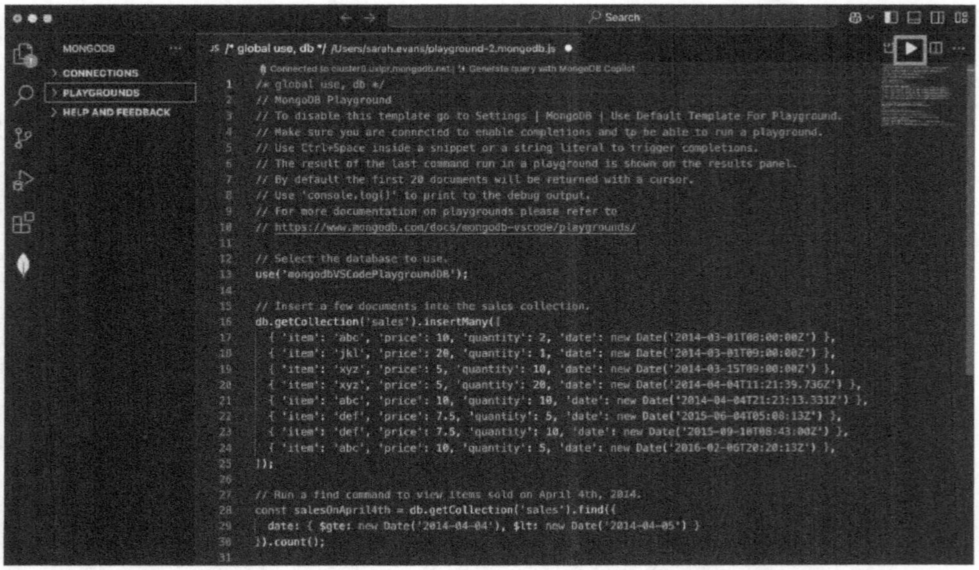

Figure 3.6: Running MongoDB Playground using the Play button in VS Code

CRUD capabilities in the MongoDB Playground for VS Code

Let's give an example of how you could perform a CRUD operation in the VS Code extension inside MongoDB Playground:

1. To start off, open the VS Code command palette.

2. Find the **Create MongoDB Playground** command from the search bar and run it.

3. Use the insertOne() method to insert one document into the collection, as in this example:

```
db.cars.insertOne(
{ "_id" : 1, "item" : "corvette", "price" : 60000, "quantity" : 1,
"dateofPurchase" : new Date("2019-03-01T08:00:00Z")}
);
```

In this example, we're inserting a new document into the cars collection.

4. To run the playground, after you've entered the code, press the **Play** button at the top right of the playground. The VS Code extension will then split your playground: on the left side, you'll see the code you just entered. On the right side, you'll see the *results* of the playground. This gives you a dynamic, real-time view of how your code is performing.

You can also read the documents in your collection in your existing database using the findOne() method or find() to find more than one document.

As before, this requires you to have already entered your connection to your MongoDB database and to have already opened the playground, and for there to be documents existing in your database already.

For example, the following code will return one document from the cars collection:

```
db.cars.findOne();
```

You can also use the updateOne() or updateMany() methods to modify existing documents in the cars collection in the MongoDB database.

Prototyping aggregations in the MongoDB Playground for VS Code

Within the VS Code extension MongoDB Playground, you can execute and test aggregation pipelines. This functionality allows for running multi-stage pipelines that manipulate data and generate computed results. These results are displayed directly in the VS Code playground, enabling immediate verification of the aggregation's output. Users can then confirm whether the results align with their expectations. Should the results be satisfactory, the aggregation query or the results generated can be saved.

If not, you can continue to refine your aggregation query until the results match your expectations. This is particularly helpful if you are learning MongoDB aggregation syntax or trying to figure out in which order certain aggregation operations should occur.

You'll want to use general best practices around the construction of MongoDB aggregation pipelines, with multiple stages defined. If you're unfamiliar with MongoDB aggregation pipelines, please see the documentation located here: https://www.mongodb.com/docs/manual/aggregation/.

For now, though, let's look at a simple example. The general syntax of an aggregation pipeline is the following:

```
db.<collection>.aggregate([
  {
   <$stage1>
  },
  {
   <$stage2>
  }
// ...
])
```

An aggregation pipeline processes data through a series of stages, with the output of one stage becoming the input for the next. A straightforward example is calculating average sales. If you have 1,000 customers, some with multiple purchases and many with none, you would determine the average sales per customer by dividing the total revenue by the total number of customers.

Alternatively, to calculate the average only for customers with at least one purchase, the initial stage would involve filtering for customers whose sales exceed $0.00.

To do this, you'll use $match to find those customers, and then $group to calculate the average value of their purchases.

The resulting aggregation would look something like this, in JavaScript:

```javascript
const pipeline = [
  // Stage 1: Match customers with purchases greater than 0.00
  {
   "$match": {
    "totalPurchases": { "$gt": 0.00 }
   }
  },
  // Stage 2: Group by customerId and calculate the average purchase amount
  {
   "$group": {
    "_id": "$customerId",
    "averagePurchaseAmount": { "$avg": "$totalPurchases" }
   }
  }
];


// Execute the aggregation pipeline
return customersCollection.aggregate(pipeline).toArray()
  .then(customers => {
    console.log(`Successfully calculated average purchase amount for
${customers.length} customers.`)
   for(const customer of customers) {
    console.log(`customer: ${customer._id}`)
    console.log(`average purchase amount: ${customer.
averagePurchaseAmount}`)
   }
   return customers
  })
```

To further your understanding of MongoDB aggregations, you can consult *Practical Aggregations* by Paul Done. This book, combined with prototyping your aggregations in the MongoDB Playground for VS Code, will allow you to quickly verify whether the results align with your expectations.

MongoDB IDE extension for IntelliJ

In 2025, MongoDB unveiled its IntelliJ IDE extension. With this plugin, developers receive enhanced autocomplete and type validation for their code. IntelliJ already had several useful features baked in:

- Connects to the MongoDB database
- Browses databases, collections, and documents
- Prototype queries

But with the extension, you receive even more capabilities. It can now indicate to the developer when a query is being run without an index, as well as tell you a more optimal query as you are writing the code, rather than after the fact. It has support for common frameworks and query patterns, such as Java Spring. To get access to the plugin, simply navigate to `https://plugins.jetbrains.com/plugin/24377-mongodb`.

At the time of this writing, the IntelliJ IDE plugin is in public preview, meaning it is not yet generally available.

Compass

Most developers would rather spend time writing code than introspecting on their database. To that end, MongoDB Compass is an invaluable developer tool, serving as a robust **graphical user interface (GUI)** that streamlines interaction with your database.

It offers a user-friendly environment where you can intuitively create and execute queries. If you're not confident in writing MongoDB queries, have no fear – its natural language querying feature will take your text descriptions and convert them to working MQL (or even Java code)!

Beyond querying, Compass provides comprehensive features for the following:

- Monitoring data quality and consistency, allowing you to easily identify and address data discrepancies or issues within your datasets
- Adding indexes and monitoring database performance, including suboptimal queries
- Constructing aggregations in a drag-and-drop visual format
- Importing and exporting data
- Creating and enforcing schemas across your database

Its visual nature and powerful functionalities make it an essential asset for developers looking to manage, analyze, and optimize their MongoDB databases efficiently.

Getting started

MongoDB Compass is free to download and is available for Linux, macOS, and Windows at this link: `https://www.mongodb.com/try/download/compass`. Once you've downloaded it, there will be an installation modal that will guide you through the process.

Then, you'll want to connect Compass to your MongoDB database so that you can begin playing with your data. Here's how you can do it:

1. Open the **New Connection** modal: In the bottom panel of the **CONNECTIONS** sidebar, click **Add new connection** to open the **New Connection** modal.

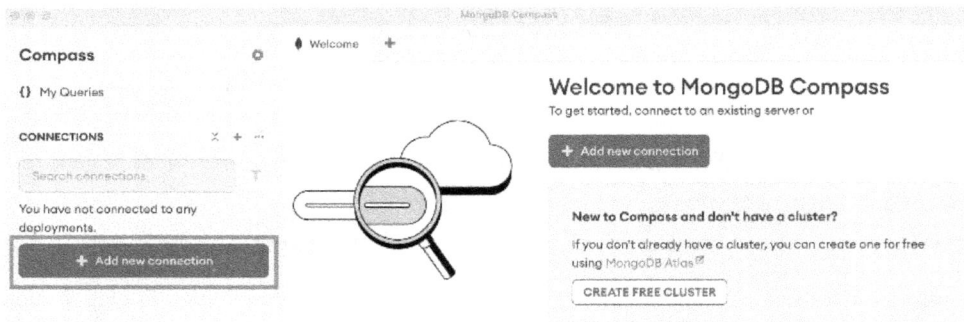

Figure 3.7: Compass Add New Connection modal

2. Paste your connection string.
3. Now, you can name your connection. This is useful if you have multiple databases that you'll be connecting to, such as production and test.

4. Connect to your cluster. The default **Save & Connect** button saves your information and connects you to your cluster.

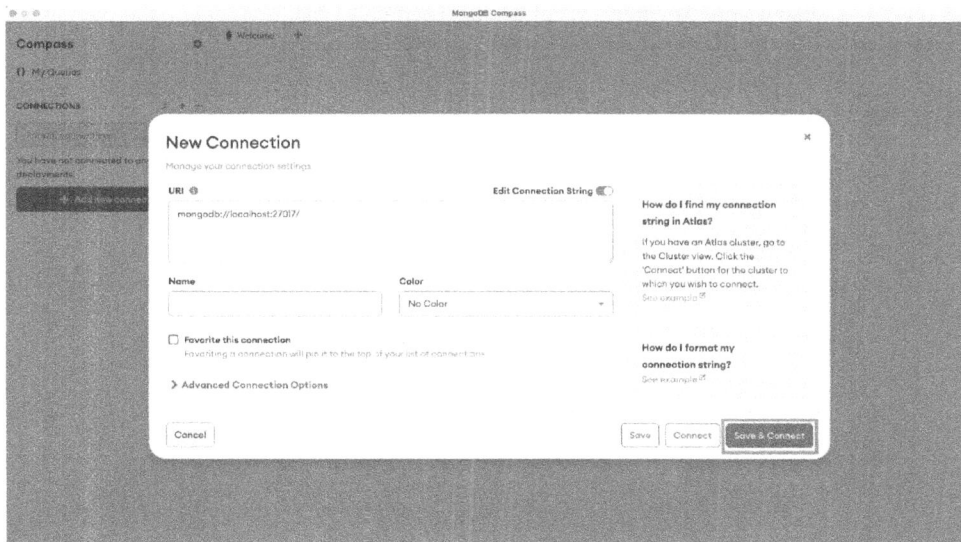

Figure 3.8: Connecting to a MongoDB cluster using Save & Connect in Compass

To access various Compass features, specific user roles may be required once connected to your MongoDB deployment. As an example, if you have read-only access to the database as an individual, you will not be allowed to edit documents via the Compass UI. If you experience issues while using Compass, the first thing to do for troubleshooting is to check your user permissions for the database.

Interacting with your data

Interacting with your data is a critical part of working effectively with MongoDB, and Compass provides an intuitive interface to help you do so. With Compass, you can easily visualize, query, and manipulate your data, enabling deeper insights and more efficient workflows. While Compass supports a wide range of activities, this section will focus on a selection of key features:

- Managing documents (viewing, inserting, updating, and deleting documents in your database)
- Querying your data
- Managing indexes
- Analyzing your schema
- Viewing real-time query performance

> To learn more about how interacting with your data helps, refer to the MongoDB documentation here: https://www.mongodb.com/docs/compass/manage-data/.

Managing documents

Within the Compass GUI, navigate to the **Documents** tab. This section allows you to view, insert, modify, and delete documents within your MongoDB database. By default, documents are displayed in a list view, showcasing each document along with some of its fields. In the following figure, you can see three example documents, shown in the List view. You can then expand these to view all the various fields and values per document:

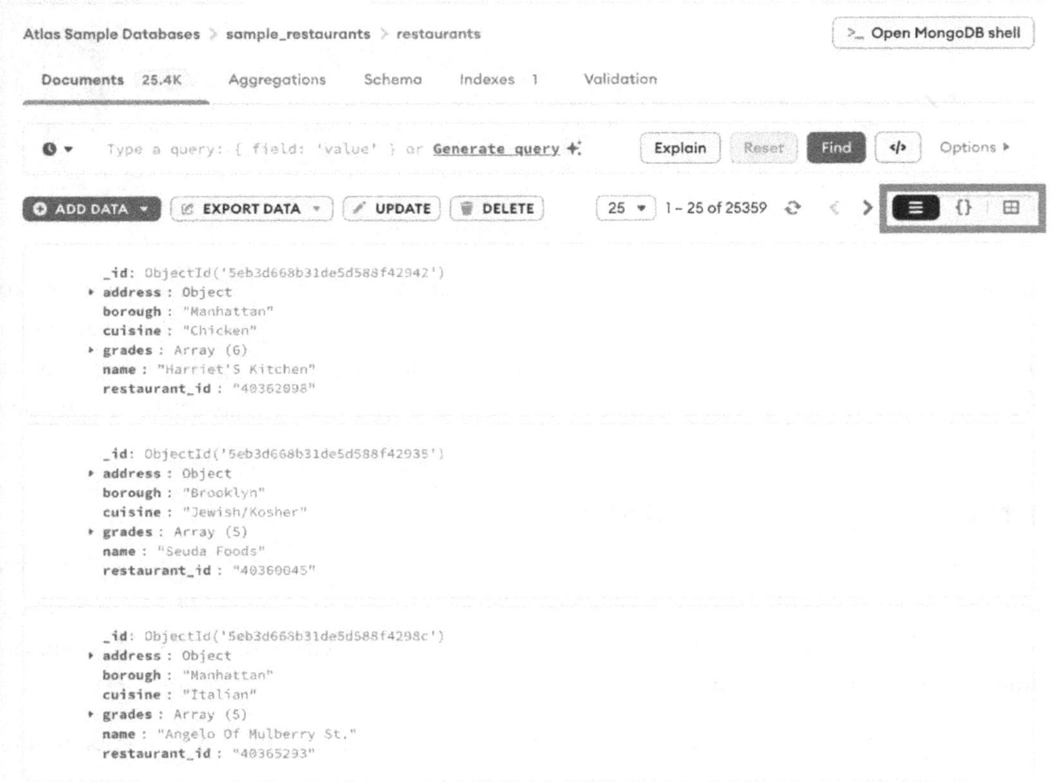

Figure 3.9: List view

For those of you who are more accustomed to tabular and relational databases, you may appreciate the Table view of your documents. The Table view can be selected on the far right:

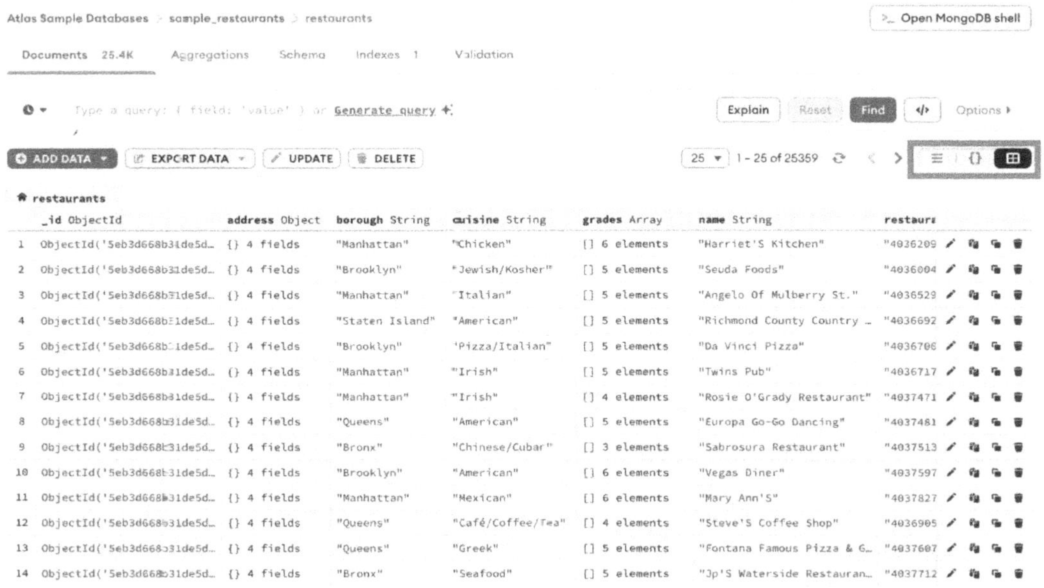

Figure 3.10: Table view of Documents

To insert data, click the **Add Data** button at the top right of the screen, as shown in *Figure 3.11*. This will take you to a new screen where you can insert a document and define its fields and values.

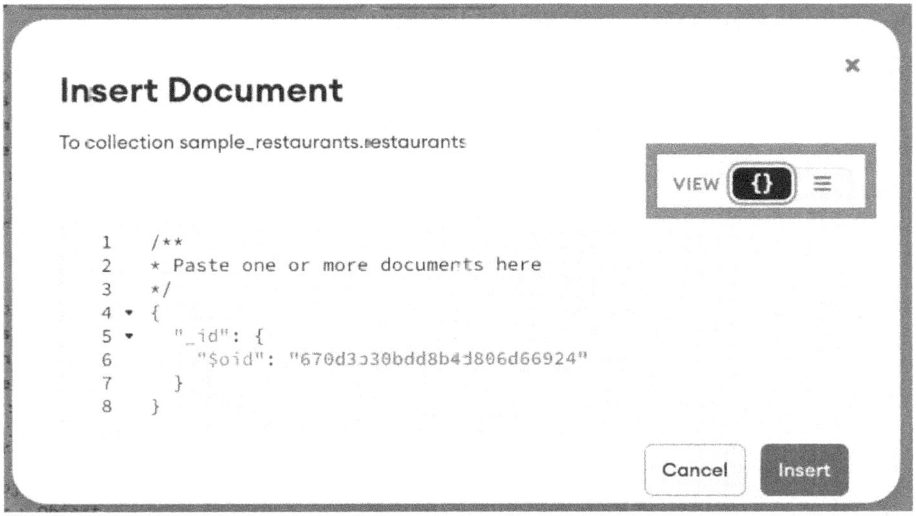

Figure 3.11: View the document in JSON

You can also modify a document by clicking the pencil icon in the List or Table view, as shown here:

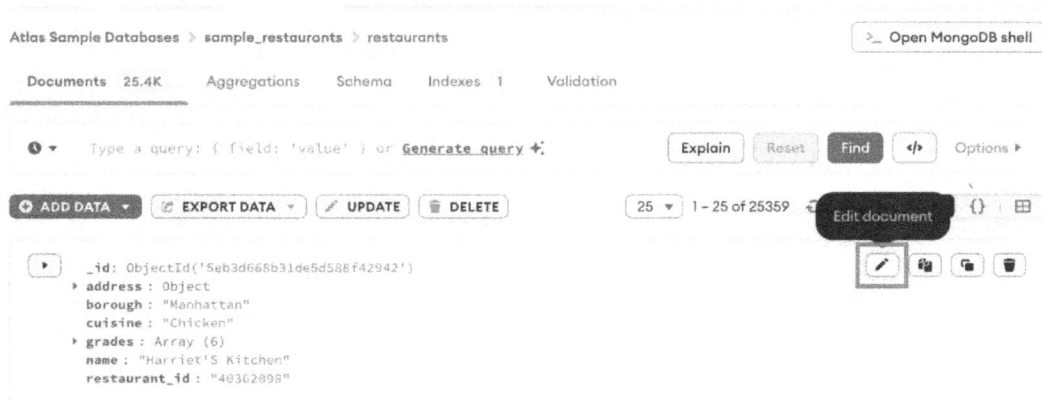

Figure 3.12: The Edit document button

Clicking the trashcan icon will delete the document, so use that particular button with caution.

As you can see, it is incredibly easy and intuitive to manage your documents in this way. Indeed, for those developers who are new to MongoDB, Compass is easily the best way to get started with learning about the database and becoming familiar with how it stores data, as well as evaluating how your documents differ from each other in a flexible schema setup.

Querying documents in MongoDB Compass

Querying documents in MongoDB Compass is also similarly easy. You simply enter the MongoDB query into the filter bar, like so:

sample_mflix.movies

Documents   Aggregations   Schema   Explain Plan   Indexes   Validation

Filter ⬚ 🕐 ▾   { "title": "Jurassic Park" }

⬇ ADD DATA ▾   ⬚ **EXPORT COLLECTION**

```
  _id: ObjectId('573a1399f29313caabcedc5d')
  fullplot: "Huge advancements in scientific technology have enabled a mogul to cre…"
> imdb: Object
  year: 1993
  plot: "During a preview tour, a theme park suffers a major power breakdown th…"
> genres: Array
  rated: "PG-13"
  metacritic: 68
  title: "Jurassic Park"
  lastupdated: "2015-08-31 00:04:50.280000060"
> languages: Array
> writers: Array
  type: "movie"
> tomatoes: Object
  poster: "https://m.media-amazon.com/images/M/MV5BMjM2MDgxMDg0Nl5BMl5BanBnXkFtZT…"
  num_mflix_comments: 148
  released: 1993-06-11T00:00:00.000+00:00
> awards: Object
> countries: Array
> cast: Array
> directors: Array
  runtime: 127
```

Figure 3.13: The document in Compass

Any properly formed MongoDB query will work within this filter bar. Once you have the results of your query, you can visually validate whether the results are as you expected. You can also export the results of your query.

Natural language querying in Compass

In case you don't know the MongoDB query language, have no fear. You can also write queries in natural language, utilizing generative AI to interpret your text and then rewrite it into properly formed query language. To do that, you'll need to first have a MongoDB Atlas account, which is the MongoDB database-as-a-service platform. Then, you'll have to enable generative AI in the Compass settings.

This can easily be accomplished by modifying the configuration file on your computer located at /etc/mongodb-compass.conf. Set this as follows:

```
{
  "enableGenAIFeatures": true,
  # ...
}
```

Return to the Compass GUI and submit your question or prompt about the collection into the query bar, such as Which movies were released in 2000?.

Harnessing the power of AI, Compass leverages Azure OpenAI's advanced capabilities for comprehensive review and in-depth analysis of your query. Furthermore, based on this thorough understanding, Azure OpenAI will intelligently rewrite and refine your query, optimizing it for clarity, efficiency, and accuracy within the MongoDB environment. This process ensures that your intentions are translated into the most effective and performant database operations.

In conclusion, MongoDB Compass is a powerful tool for developers who want a simple user interface to interact with their database.

MongoDB MCP Server

MongoDB **Model Context Protocol (MCP)** Server is a new feature introduced for public preview, designed to enhance the interaction between AI agents and MongoDB clusters using natural language prompts. Originally developed by Anthropic, MCP facilitates the connection of AI **large language models (LLMs)** to data systems, ensuring that these models have access to the most current database information. This integration allows for more intuitive and efficient data management and querying, leveraging the capabilities of AI to streamline operations.

MCP Server is particularly useful for connecting various MongoDB servers, including Atlas, Community Edition, Enterprise Advanced, and on-premises installations, to clients that support MCP. This connectivity enables users to utilize AI-driven tools to interact with their databases, making it easier to perform complex queries and data manipulations without needing deep technical expertise. By providing a bridge between AI technologies and database systems, MCP Server opens up new possibilities for data analysis and application development.

The clients that currently support MCP include Anthropic Claude Desktop, Windsurf Editor, Cursor, and VS Code GitHub Copilot.

MongoDB MCP Server allows you to perform several tasks by leveraging AI-driven tools to interact with MongoDB databases. Here are some of the things you can do through MCP:

- **Natural language queries**: You can use natural language prompts to query your MongoDB databases. This makes it easier to perform complex queries without needing to write traditional code, allowing for more intuitive data interaction.

- **Data management**: MCP facilitates efficient data management by connecting AI agents to MongoDB clusters. This integration helps streamline operations, making it easier to manipulate and analyze data using AI capabilities.

- **Enhanced application development**: By bridging AI technologies with database systems, MCP opens up new possibilities for application development. You can utilize AI-driven tools to enhance your workflows, making database interactions more accessible and efficient.

> The code is also available open sourced here: `https://github.com/mongodb-js/mongodb-mcp-server/tree/main`.

To get started with MCP Server, follow these steps:

1. **Install a supported client**: Choose a client that supports MCP, such as Anthropic Claude Desktop, Windsurf Editor, Cursor, or VS Code GitHub Copilot. For example, if you choose Claude Desktop, download and install it from the **Claude Download** page.

2. **Configure the client**: Once installed, start the client and open the configuration file. For Claude Desktop, you would go to **Settings -> Developer -> Edit Config**. In the configuration file, add the MongoDB MCP Server details. You can copy the following lines into the configuration file:

```
{
  "mcpServers": {
   "MongoDB": {
     "command": "npx",
     "args": ["-y", "mongodb-mcp-server"]
   }
  }
}
```

3. **Connect to MongoDB**: Ensure that your MongoDB server is running and accessible. MCP Server can connect to various MongoDB servers, including Atlas, Community Edition, Enterprise Advanced, and on-premises installations. Once configured, you can start interacting with your MongoDB clusters using natural language prompts through the client.

While this feature is not yet production-ready as of the time of this writing, you can find out more about it here: `https://github.com/mongodb-js/mongodb-mcp-server/blob/main/README.md`.

Summary

This chapter explored the essential developer tools provided by MongoDB, designed to enhance efficiency and streamline the development process. We began by looking at IDE extensions, then highlighting the MongoDB for VS Code extension, which seamlessly integrates MongoDB functionalities directly into the VS Code environment. This extension empowers developers with robust data exploration capabilities, query prototyping through the MongoDB Playground, and CRUD operations, all within their preferred IDE. The integration with GitHub Copilot further augments productivity by assisting with code generation and interaction with MongoDB deployments.This chapter explored the essential developer tools provided by MongoDB, designed to enhance efficiency and streamline the development process. We began by looking at IDE extensions, then highlighting MongoDB Compass, a powerful GUI that simplifies query construction, data monitoring, and schema enforcement. Its visual nature and intuitive features make it an invaluable asset for managing and optimizing MongoDB databases.

We then delved into MongoDB Compass, a powerful GUI that simplifies query construction, data monitoring, and schema enforcement. Its visual nature and intuitive features make it an invaluable asset for managing and optimizing MongoDB databases.

Finally, we introduced MongoDB MCP Server, a cutting-edge feature in public preview that bridges AI agents with MongoDB clusters. MCP enables natural language querying and data management, offering a more intuitive and efficient way to interact with databases using AI-driven tools. This technology holds significant promise for enhancing application development and data analysis by making complex database interactions more accessible.

Together, these tools (Compass, the VS Code extension, and MCP Server) form a comprehensive suite that empowers developers to build, test, optimize, and manage robust applications with MongoDB. By leveraging these tools, developers can significantly improve their workflow, enhance code quality, and efficiently tackle the complexities of modern data infrastructure.

Ultimately, the mission of MongoDB has always been to make a database that is easy to use for developers. As such, these tools aim to make life for the developer better, which is why we see such a focus on tools in developer-integrated environments such as VS Code and IntelliJ.

To read more about MongoDB developer tools, including the official drivers, integrations with web frameworks such as Spring and FastAPI, as well as AI/ML frameworks such as LangChain, please see the official MongoDB documentation for developer tools located at `https://www.mongodb.com/docs/drivers/` and `https://www.mongodb.com/docs/atlas/atlas-vector-search/ai-integrations/`.

Get This Book's PDF Version and Exclusive Extras

UNLOCK NOW

Scan the QR code (or go to `packtpub.com/unlock`). Search for this book by name, confirm the edition, and then follow the steps on the page.

Note: Keep your invoice handy. Purchases made directly from Packt don't require an invoice.

4

Data Modeling and Index Optimization

Choosing how to organize and model your data is one of the most important steps to ensuring that your application is efficient and performant. One of the main causes of poor performance in MongoDB is poor schema design. Poor schema design not only negatively impacts application performance but also makes the data model difficult to scale and maintain. By properly planning and designing your schema, you ensure that your application can quickly access the information it needs. MongoDB's flexible data model lets you store your data to match your data access patterns, meaning all necessary data can be accessed with a single query. Designing your schema based on your application's access patterns avoids the need for slow multi-table join operations commonly found in relational databases. This chapter outlines best practices to plan and maintain your MongoDB schema and how to create indexes to optimize query performance.

In this chapter, we're going to cover the following main topics:

- The MongoDB document data model and how it differs from tabular, relational data models
- How to plan your schema based on your application data access patterns
- Schema designs you can use to handle common access patterns
- How to optimize indexes to improve query performance, including new persistent query settings available in MongoDB

Document data model

The document data model is a way of structuring and storing data where information is kept in self-contained, flexible documents. The document data model provides the following benefits:

- **Self-contained documents**: You can model your schema so each document stores all related data together, which reduces the need for complex joins.
- **Flexibility**: Documents can have varying structures and data types.
- **Embedded data**: Documents can contain embedded objects and arrays, which enables you to easily model complex entity relationships such as one-to-many and many-to-many.

The following sample document illustrates MongoDB's document data structure:

```
{
  "_id": ObjectId("650d9b7fb6a6f4f8d45ce0b8"),
  "username": "johndoe",
  "email": "johndoe@example.com",
  "profile": {
    "firstName": "John",
    "lastName": "Doe",
    "birthdate": ISODate("1994-04-17T00:00:00Z")
  },
  "skills": ["JavaScript", "MongoDB"],
  "experience": [
    {
      "company": "Tech Corp",
      "role": "Software Engineer",
      "startDate": ISODate("2018-06-01T00:00:00Z"),
      "endDate": ISODate("2021-08-30T00:00:00Z")
    }
  ]
}
```

MongoDB's document model promotes a natural and intuitive way to represent data, mirroring the way developers often think about and work with information in their applications.

BSON and its data types

MongoDB stores data as BSON (Binary JSON) documents, which are collections of key-value pairs. BSON is an extension of JSON, sharing its human-readable, key-value structure and enhancing it with optimizations for storage and scanning speed.

BSON was designed to have the following three characteristics:

- **Lightweight**: BSON reduces spatial overhead, which is especially useful when sending data across a network.

- **Easy to navigate**: BSON structures can be navigated efficiently, which is critical since it's the core format MongoDB uses to represent data.

- **Efficient**: In a BSON document, large elements are prefixed with a length field. These prefixes allow queries to scan and retrieve results faster than standard JSON, especially in large-scale applications. Also, encoding data to BSON and decoding from BSON can be performed very quickly in most languages due to the use of C data types.

BSON extends the capabilities of standard JSON by supporting a broader range of data types. Notably, it includes specialized types such as the following:

- **BinData**: For efficiently storing binary data, including file contents and serialized objects.

- **MinKey** and **MaxKey**: To compare values against the absolute minimum or maximum BSON elements, typically for sorting or query range boundaries.

Additionally, BSON provides high precision decimal representation with the Decimal128 type. This allows for high-precision numerical representation, which is especially important in domains such as financial services, scientific computation, or monetary systems where exact decimal representation and rounding behavior are essential. Unlike JavaScript's Number type, which is a double-precision 64-bit binary format IEEE 754 value, Decimal128 avoids rounding errors in high-precision use cases.

The following example document shows the various data types available in BSON, including data types not available in standard JSON:

```
{
  "_id": ObjectId("507f1f77bcf86cd799439013"),
  "doubleField": 87.9,
  "stringField": "Greetings!",
  "objectField": {
    "name": "Sarah",
    "age": 28
  },
  "arrayField": [10, 20, 30, 40, 50],
  "binaryField": BinData(0, "different-binary-data"),
  "booleanField": false,
  "dateField": ISODate("2024-12-15T14:30:00Z"),
```

```
    "nullField": null,
    "regexField": /^xyz/,
    "javascriptField": Code("function () { print('hello world!'); }"),
    "int32Field": 128,
    "timestampField": Timestamp(1701410400, 2),
    "int64Field": NumberLong("1234567890"),
    "decimal128Field": NumberDecimal("9.876543210987654321"),
    "minKeyField": MinKey(),
    "maxKeyField": MaxKey()
}
```

In this document, each field shows a unique BSON data type. This highlights the flexibility of MongoDB when it comes to representing data. The data types are summarized in the following table:

Type	Alias	Explanation
Double	`double`	Floating-point decimal number with roughly 16-decimal-digit precision.
String	`string`	String of characters that represent text.
Object	`object`	Represents a document.
Array	`array`	List of elements.
Binary data	`binData`	Arbitrary raw binary data.
ObjectId	`objectId`	Unique identifier for an object.
Boolean	`bool`	Represents `true` or `false`.
Date	`date`	Represents a specific point in time.
Null	`null`	Represents a null value.
Regular Expression	`regex`	Represents pattern-matching rules for strings.
JavaScript	`javascript`	Stores executable JavaScript code.
32-bit integer	`int`	Whole number.
Timestamp	`timestamp`	Represents a point in time relative to the epoch.
64-bit integer	`long`	Whole number with a wider range of values than `int`.
Decimal128	`"decimal"`	High-precision decimal number with up to 34-decimal-digit precision.

Type	Alias	Explanation
MinKey	"minKey"	Represents a value less than all other possible BSON values. Typically used to represent a lower bound.
MaxKey	"maxKey"	Represents a value greater than all other possible BSON values. Typically used to represent an upper bound.

Table 4.1: BSON data types

As you design and model your databases, having a solid grasp of BSON types will help you make smarter, more informed choices about how your data is stored and retrieved.

Embedded data

One of the key features of the document data model is embedding related data in a hierarchical structure, which lets you keep related data in a single document. Embedding data lets you easily model relationships between different data entities. By employing these denormalized data models, applications can access and modify correlated data through just one database operation.

The following example shows a book document in MongoDB with embedded author details:

```
{
  "_id": ObjectId("65a1b2c3d4e5f6789abccef0"),
  "title": "The Digital Revolution",
  "isbn": "978-0-123456-78-9",
  "publication_date": ISODate("2024-03-15T00:00:00Z"),
  "pages": 342,
  "genres": ["Technology", "History"],
  "price": NumberDecimal("29.99"),
  "author": {
    "name": "Sarah Johnson",
    "bio": "Dr. Sarah Johnson is a professor of Computer Science at
  Stanford University and expert in digital transformation.",
    "nationality": "American",
    "previous_works": [
      "AI and Society",
      "The Future of Computing"
    ]
  },
```

```
   "description": "An exploration of how digital technology has changed
society over the past three decades.",
   "average_rating": 4.7,
   "in_stock": true
}
```

If the application always returns the book details and author details together, embedding those entities in a single document allows the application to return all of the required data with a single read operation. In contrast, the same relationship in a relational database would require the book and author entities to be stored in separate tables, which would need to be joined together and likely have worse performance.

In the document data model, using references can still be a valid design pattern. Later in this chapter, you will learn how to determine whether embedding data or using references is the best choice based on your application's data access patterns.

Schema design

Designing an effective schema is crucial for optimizing your application's performance and scalability. To design an effective schema, you first need to understand the data your application needs and how frequently it needs to access that data. This lets you design your schema so that data that is accessed together is stored together, which leads to efficient queries and optimal performance.

The process of designing a schema that best meets your application requirements consists of the following steps:

1. Identify your application's workload.
2. Map relationships between your data entities.
3. Apply schema design to improve application performance and reduce schema complexity.

By taking schema design seriously, you leverage MongoDB's strengths while mitigating potential pitfalls that come from its flexible, non-relational structure. This results in a robust database that supports efficient application operation and development.

Identify the application workload

To begin designing your database schema, first determine your application's most frequent operations. Understanding these common queries is crucial for creating efficient indexes and reducing the number of database calls your application needs to make.

As you analyze your application's workload, consider both its current functionalities and potential future features. Design your schema to remain effective throughout all phases of your application's development.

To create a clear view of your application's requirements, you can create a workload table with the queries that your application needs to run. Each row of the table should contain an action that the application needs to handle, how frequently that action occurs, and how critical it is that the action succeeds.

For example, a workload table for a blog application might look something like the following:

Action	Query Type	Information	Frequency	Priority
Submit a new article	Write	author, text	10 per day	High
Submit a comment on an article	Write	user, text	1,000 per day (100 per article)	Medium
View an article	Read	article id, text, comments	1,000,000 per day	High
View article analytics	Read	article id, comments, clicks	10 per hour	Low

Table 4.2: Workload table for a blog application

After you complete this step of the schema design process, you should have a solid understanding of your application's workload and the data required by your application. In the next step, you will learn how to map relationships between related data to return the required information in a single query.

Map schema relationships

The way you model relationships between different data entities significantly impacts your application's performance and ability to scale.

MongoDB's document data model lets you embed related information as sub-documents. Embedding allows your application to fetch necessary data with a single read operation, preventing the performance overhead associated with $lookup operations. However, in certain situations, particularly when frequent updates are required, storing related data in separate collections and using references might be more suitable.

To decide whether to embed data or use references, weigh the importance of these factors for your application:

- **Improving queries on related data**: If your application frequently retrieves data from one entity to access information about a related entity, embedding the related data can optimize query performance by eliminating the need for frequent $lookup operations.

- **Improving data returned from different entities**: If your application commonly returns data from related entities together, embedding this data within a single collection can streamline data retrieval.

- **Improving update performance**: If your application performs frequent updates to related data, storing this data in separate collections and using references can be advantageous. This approach avoids data duplication and reduces the write workload by requiring updates in only one location.

For this step of the schema design process, create a schema map that shows the type of relationship between those fields (one-to-one, one-to-many, many-to-many). For example, consider the following schema map for a blog application:

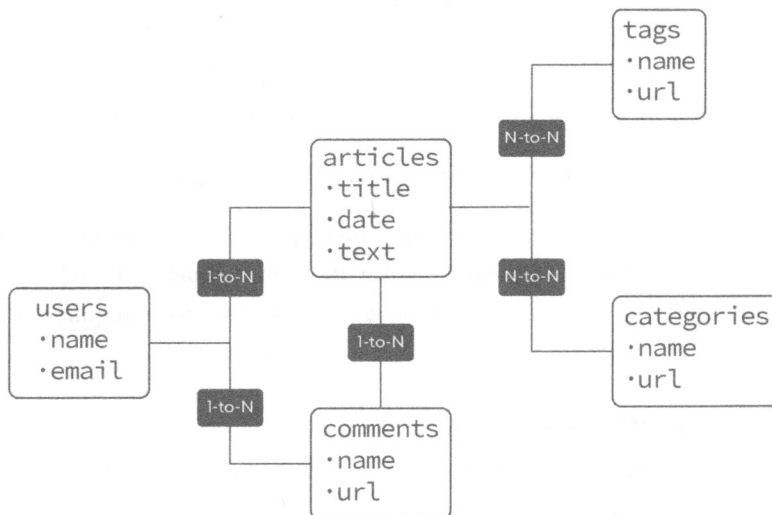

Figure 4.1: Blog application schema showing different relationships

Given these data entities, you are now presented with a choice of whether to embed related data in the same collection or store data in separate collections and use references when you need to return data from multiple entities. The best choice depends on the data users need when they use your application.

Optimizing queries for articles

In a blog application, you have two key data entities to connect: blog posts and authors. Imagine your application's users mainly search for blog posts on title keywords and rarely search by author. Your application still needs to return the author information and blog post information together. In this scenario, you should design your schema to embed author information inside the blog post document. This way, the application can retrieve all necessary information with a single read operation. A sample document with this schema design would look something like the following:

```
{
  title: "My Favorite Vacation",
  date: ISODate("2023-06-02"),
  text: "We spent seven days in Italy...",
  tags: [
    {
      name: "travel",
      url: "<blog-site>/tags/travel"
    },
    {
      name: "adventure",
      url: "<blog-site>/tags/adventure"
    }
  ],
  comments: [
    {
      name: "pedro123",
      text: "Great article!"
    }
  ],
  author: {
    name: "alice123",
    email: "alice@mycompany.com",
    avatar: "photo1.jpg"
  }
}
```

Optimizing queries for articles and authors

Imagine a different data access pattern where users want to see blog posts and author information separately. For example, if blog posts do not contain author information, and instead, author information exists on a separate profile page. In this scenario, it would be best to store articles and authors in separate collections. This schema design reduces the work required to return the required information and does not include unneeded fields.

The following schema design uses two collections. The `articles` collection contains an `authorId` field, which is a reference to the `authors` collection:

```
// articles collection

{
    title: "My Favorite Vacation",
    date: ISODate("2023-06-02"),
    text: "We spent seven days in Italy...",
    authorId: 987,
    tags: [
       {
          name: "travel",
          url: "<blog-site>/tags/travel"
       },
       {
          name: "adventure",
          url: "<blog-site>/tags/adventure"
       }
    ],
    comments: [
       {
          name: "pedro345",
          text: "Great article!"
       }
    ]
}

// authors collection

{
```

```
    _id: 987,
    name: 'alice123",
    email: "alice@mycompany.com",
    avatar: "photo1.jpg"
}
```

With this schema, in the event that the application needs to return article information and author information together, it can run a $lookup operation to join the data from the different collections. This design will be less performant than a read operation on a single collection, but it is optimized for the typical access pattern of reading each entity's data separately.

Modeling relationships

The types of entity relationships that your schema contains can significantly impact how you design your schema. Entity relationships can be **one-to-one**, **one-to-many**, or **many-to-many**.

One-to-one relationships

In a one-to-one relationship, a single element of one entity can only be linked to a single element of another entity. For example, country to capital city is a one-to-one relationship because each country only has one capital city, and that capital is of only one country. For one-to-one relationships, embedding is the preferred way to model data, especially if the data from the two entities is returned together.

One-to-many relationships

In a one-to-many relationship, a single element of one entity can be linked to multiple elements of another entity. For example, car owner to cars is a one-to-many relationship because the owner may own multiple cars, and each car only has a single owner. To model one-to-many relationships, either embedding or references can be valid schema design choices depending on your access patterns.

Many-to-many relationships

In a many-to-many relationship, multiple elements of one entity can be linked to multiple elements of another entity. For example, books to authors is a many-to-many relationship because a book may be written by multiple authors, and an author may have written multiple books. Generally, references are useful to represent many-to-many relationships because references are well-suited to model complex hierarchical data structures.

Embedding versus references

A key decision for your schema design is whether to model your data with embedding or references. Embedding data means storing related data in a single document where it can be retrieved with a single read operation. For example, the following document embeds contact and address data in a single document:

```
// users collection
{
  _id: <ObjectId1>,
  username: "user1",
  contact: {
    phone: "123-456-7890",
    email: "abc@example.com"
  },
  access: {
    level: 5,
    group: "dev"
  }
}
```

Embedded data models can be useful in the following scenarios:

- You have contains relationships between entities. For example, a contacts document that contains an address.

- You have one-to-many relationships between entities. In these relationships, the many or child documents are viewed in the context of the one or parent documents. For example, a single order that contains many items.

References, on the other hand, store data in separate collections and use certain fields as links between entities. For example, in the following schema, the contacts and address documents contain references to the users document:

```
// users collection
{
  _id: <ObjectId1>,
  username: "user1"
}

// contacts collection
{
```

```
  _id: <ObjectId2>,
  user_id: <ObjectId1>,
  phone: "123-456-7890",
  email: "abc@example.com"
}

// access collection
{
  _id: <ObjectId3>,
  user_id: <ObjectId1>,
  level: 5,
  group: "dev"
}
```

References result in normalized data models because data is split into multiple collections and not duplicated. References can be useful in the following scenarios:

- Embedding would result in duplication of data but would not provide sufficient read performance advantages to outweigh the implications of the duplication. For example, when the embedded data frequently changes.

- You need to represent complex many-to-many relationships or large hierarchical datasets.

- The related entity is frequently queried on its own. For example, if you have employee and department data, you could consider embedding department information in the employee documents. However, if you often query for a list of departments, your application will perform best with a separate department collection that is linked to the employee collection with a reference.

Applying schema design patterns

Schema design patterns are ways to optimize your data model for your application's access patterns. They improve application performance and reduce schema complexity. Before you implement schema design patterns, consider the problem that you are trying to solve. Each schema design pattern has different use cases and trade-offs for data consistency, performance, and complexity. For example, some schema design patterns improve the write performance, while others improve the read performance. Implementing a pattern without understanding your application and the data it needs can degrade the application performance and cause unnecessary complications to your schema design. This section provides an overview of various MongoDB design patterns.

The bucket pattern

The bucket pattern separates long series of data into distinct objects. This pattern is most effective for managing streaming data, such as time-series, real-time analytics, or **Internet of Things (IoT)** applications. It reduces the overall number of documents in a collection, simplifies data access, and improves the index performance.

Consider an IoT application where a sensor sends temperature readings every day. Instead of creating a new document for every reading, the data can be bucketed together in monthly intervals. In the following example, the month is indicated by the document ID:

```
{
  "_id": "sensor_001_2023_10", // Unique ID (sensor_id + month year bucket)
  "sensor_id": "sensor_001",             // Sensor identifier
  "location": {
    "latitude": 37.7749,
    "longitude": -122.4194
  },
  "month": "October",
  "year": 2023,
  "readings": [
    {
      "timestamp": ISODate("2023-10-01T10:15:00Z"),
      "temperature": 72.5
    },
    {
      "timestamp": ISODate("2023-10-01T12:30:00Z"),
      "temperature": 74.1
    },
    {
      "timestamp": ISODate("2023-10-02T08:45:00Z"),
      "temperature": 68.9
    }
    // Additional readings for the bucket go here...
  ]
}
```

The attribute pattern

The attribute pattern groups documents in the same collection that have different fields but share common characteristics for sorting and querying. This pattern is especially effective when these differing fields appear in a limited number of documents.

Consider an e-commerce platform with a catalog of products. Each product has a set of attributes that can vary based on the type of product:

```
{
    "_id": ObjectId("652f89b8ac11b816a4cd1234"),
    "name": "Wireless Headphones",
    "type": "Electronics",
    "price": 99.99,
    "attributes": [
        {
            "key": "battery_life",
            "value": "30 hours"
        },
        {
            "key": "connectivity",
            "value": "Bluetooth 5.0"
        },
        {
            "key": "warranty",
            "value": "1 year"
        },
        {
            "key": "noise_cancellation",
            "value": true
        }
    ]
}
```

The polymorphic pattern

The polymorphic pattern utilizes MongoDB's flexible data model to let you access documents that have different fields or data types together in the same query.

Consider a collection that stores financial information and keeps accounts and customer data in the same collection. Each document has a docType field that indicates whether the document is an account or a collection. While it is not necessary to create a field to signify document type in a polymorphic collection, doing so can help with organization and schema validation.

```
// Customer document
{
     "customerId": "CUST-123456789",
     "docType": "customer",
     "name": {
        "title": "Mr",
        "first": "Andrew",
        "middle": "James",
        "last": "Morgan"
     },
     "address": {
        "street1": "240 Blackfriars Rd",
        "city": "London",
        "postCode": "SE1 8NW",
        "country": "UK"
     },
     "customerSince": ISODate("2005-05-20")
  }


// Account document
{
     "accountNumber": "ACC1000000890",
     "docType": "account",
     "accountType": "savings",
     "customerId": [
        "CUST-123456789"
     ],
     "dateOpened": ISODate("2003-12-15"),
     "balance": NumberDecimal("10341.89")
  }
```

The extended reference pattern

If your application often needs to perform repetitive `$lookup` operations across multiple collections, the extended reference pattern can help reduce `$lookup` operations by moving frequently accessed fields into the main document. As a result, your application can achieve faster reads by only needing to access a single collection.

Consider an e-commerce platform with products and orders. A simple reference between these collections would be on the `_id` field. With the extended reference pattern, the schema includes the product name and price in addition to the `_id` field. With this schema design, when the application displays an order, it can show the product name and price without fetching all the product details:

```
// products collection
{
  "_id": ObjectId("652f89b8ac22b816a4cd0011"),
  "name": "Wireless Headphones",
  "price": 99.99,
  "category": "Electronics",
  "in_stock": 250
},
{
  "_id": ObjectId("652f89b8ac22b816a4c0022"),
  "name": "Gaming Mouse",
  "price": 49.99,
  "category": "Accessories",
  "in_stock": 500
}

// orders collection:
{
  "_id": ObjectId("652f89d9ac33b816a4cd1234"),
  "order_date": ISODate("2023-10-01T14:32:00Z"),
  "customer_id": ObjectId("652f89b8ac22b816a4cd5678"),
  "products": [
    {
      "product_id": ObjectId("652f89b8ac22b816a4cd0011"),
      "name": "Wireless Headphones",  // Extended reference field
      "price": 99.99,                 // Extended reference field
```

```
      "quantity": 2
    },
    {
      "product_id": ObjectId("652f89b8ac22b816a4cd0022"),
      "name": "Gaming Mouse",   // Extended reference field
      "price": 49.99,           // Extended reference field
      "quantity": 1
    }
  ],
  "total": 249.97
}
```

The approximation pattern

Use the approximation pattern when you have values that change frequently, but users don't need to know precise values. Instead of updating values every time data changes, the approximation pattern updates data based on a larger granularity, which results in fewer updates and a lower application workload.

Consider a website that tracks the number of views and visitors on its articles. Due to high traffic, updating the exact metrics in real time for each view can be taxing. Instead, you can track a daily aggregate of your key metrics to maintain an approximate view of the values:

```
{
    "_id": ObjectId("652f89d9ac33b816a4cd1234"),
    "date": ISODate("2023-10-01"),
    "page": "/home",
    "aggregates": {
        "page_views": 15432,
        "unique_visitors": 5432,
        "avg_time_spent": 215
    }
}
```

The computed pattern

The computed pattern involves precomputing the results of certain calculations and storing those results in the document, rather than calculating values as part of the read operation. If a computed value is requested often, it can be more efficient to save that value in the database ahead of time. When the application requests data, only one read operation is required.

Consider inventory data where the application stores the total value of items held in stock. The client could perform this calculation by multiplying the price of each item by the number in stock, but if this data is requested frequently, it can be helpful to calculate this value on the server side and store it as part of the document itself:

```
{
    "_id": ObjectId("652f89b8ac11b816a4cd1234"),
    "name": "Wireless Headphones",
    "price": 99.99,
    "in_stock": 250,
    "stock_value": 24997.5  // Computed field
}
```

The outlier pattern

If your collection stores documents of generally the same size and shape, a drastically different document (an outlier) can cause performance issues for common queries. Use the outlier pattern to isolate documents that don't match the expected shape from the rest of your collection.

Consider an application that tracks book sales. Most books have around 50 sales, but an outlier has 2,000 sales. Depending on the schema design, this could potentially create a large document that would negatively impact performance for regular queries. Instead, you can separate the sales documents into separate collections to avoid huge arrays:

```
// sales collection
{
    "_id": 2,
    "title": "The Wooden Amulet",
    "year": 2023,
    "author": "Lesley Moreno",
    "customers_purchased": [ "user00", "user01", "user02", ... "user49"
],
    "has_extras": true
}

// sales_extra collection
{
    "book_id": 2,
    "customers_purchased_extra": [ 'user50', "user51", "user52", ...
"user999" ]
}
```

The subset pattern

The subset pattern improves data access for applications that return a predetermined number of elements, such as a set number of product reviews. This pattern is particularly useful when handling large documents that have many embedded elements.

Consider a library system where each book has hundreds of reviews. However, when displaying a list of books, the application only shows the latest five reviews for quick browsing. Those five reviews can be embedded in the book document, and other reviews can be stored in a separate collection and retrieved as required by using a $lookup operation.

```
{
  "_id": ObjectId("549f1faabcf88cd799433037"),
  "title": "The Great Gatsby",
  "author": "F. Scott Fitzgerald",
  "subset_reviews": [
    {
      "user": "coolreader123",
      "rating": 5,
      "comment": "Great!",
      "date": ISODate("2023-10-01T10:00:00Z")
    },
    {
      "user": "cozyreading",
      "rating": 4,
      "comment": "Good read.",
      "date": ISODate("2023-09-29T08:30:00Z")
    }
    // ... 3 more recent reviews
  ]
}
```

The document versioning pattern

The document versioning pattern provides a way to keep a history of older versions of data. For example, an insurance company might use the document versioning pattern to keep a record of modifications a customer makes to their policy. In this example, the most current version of the policy is stored in its own collection, and the policy history is stored in a separate collection:

```
// currentPolicies collection

{
     _id: ObjectId("6626c9832a98aba8ddec31d3"),
     customerName: 'Michelle',
     dateSet: ISODate("2024-04-22T20:32:43.232Z"),
     itemsInsured: [ 'car', 'watch' ],
     policyId: 1,
     revision: 3
 }


// policyRevisions collection

{
  _id: ObjectId("6626c8f02a98aba8ddec31d1"),
  policyId: 1,
  customerName: 'Michelle',
  revisior: 1,
  itemsInsured: [ 'golf clubs', 'car' ],
  dateSet: ISODate("2024-04-22T20:30:42.809Z")
},
{
  _id: ObjectId("6626c92b2a98aba8ddec31d2"),
  customerName: 'Michelle',
  dateSet: ISODate("2024-04-22T20:31:03.000Z"),
  itemsInsured: [ 'golf clubs', 'car', 'watch' ],
  policyId: 1,
  revision: 2
},
{
  _id: ObjectId("6626c9832a98aba8ddec31d3"),
  customerName: 'Michelle',
  dateSet: ISODate("2024-04-22T20:32:43.232Z"),
  itemsInsured: [ 'car', 'watch' ],
  policyId: 1,
  revision: 3
}
```

The schema versioning pattern

The schema versioning pattern lets you account for changes in application requirements by storing multiple versions of a schema in the same collection. Each document has a field that indicates its schema, which can be incorporated into the query logic to query for the correct fields.

```
{
    _id: 1,
    schemaVersion: 1,
    name: 'Taylor',
    home: '209-555-7788',
    work: '503-555-0110'
},
{
    _id: 2,
    schemaVersion: 2,
    name: "Cameron",
    contactInfo: {
        cell: "903-555-1122",
        work: "670-555-7878",
        instagram: "@camcam9090",
        linkedIn: "CameronSmith123"
    }
}
```

The tree pattern

The tree pattern uses arrays to store the full path from a node to the top of the hierarchy. This pattern is useful to represent hierarchical structures such as an employee chart or a product database with nested categories.

```
{
  _id: <ObjectId>,
  name: "Samsung EVO",
  price: {
    value: NumberDecimal("169.99"),
    currency: "USD"
  },
  parent_category: "Solid state drives",
  ancestor_categories: [
```

```
    "Solid state drives",
    "Hard drives",
    "Storage",
    "Computers",
    "Electronics"
  ]
}
```

Schema design anti-patterns

Schema design anti-patterns are inefficient ways to structure your database schema. They can create unnecessary complexity and cause performance issues. Recognizing and avoiding schema design anti-patterns can help create applications with better performance. This section describes common schema anti-patterns and how to avoid them.

- **Unbounded arrays**: Unbounded arrays occur when your schema design causes an array field to grow indefinitely. One common pattern that can lead to unbounded arrays is if you embed reviews for a product in the product document. Without additional schema logic, as more reviews for the product are written, the array grows indefinitely, which leads to large documents that worsen performance. A common way to avoid unbounded arrays is to use the subset pattern described earlier in this chapter.

- **Unnecessary indexes**: If you create an index for every possible query your application runs, you might end up with unnecessary indexes, which can degrade database performance. To evaluate index use, use the $indexStats aggregation stage. You can also hide indexes to evaluate the impact on the database before fully removing them.

- **Too many collections**: Every collection you create in MongoDB comes with a default _id index, which takes up additional storage. While the _id index is small, having excessive collections can cause unnecessary strain on your system storage. To reduce the number of collections, consider implementing embedding or data access patterns such as the bucket pattern, as suitable for your application.

- **Bloated documents**: Storing data fields that are related to each other but not accessed together can create bloated documents that lead to excessive RAM and bandwidth usage. To prevent bloated documents, restructure your schema into multiple collections and use document references to separate fields that aren't returned together. This approach reduces the working set size and improves performance.

- **Excessive $lookup operations**: While the $lookup operation is useful when used infrequently, it can be slow and resource-intensive compared to operations that only query a single collection. If you often use $lookup operations, consider restructuring your schema to store related data in a single collection.

Indexes

Every database system relies on indexing to improve query performance. Index optimization is the process of creating and refining indexes to best meet the needs of your application. Optimizing indexes is crucial for using MongoDB to its full speed and potential. MongoDB features a powerful, granular indexing system that can improve the overall performance of the database.

An index is a special data structure that enables faster access to data in a collection, much like an encyclopedia index. It is an ordered list of references to the actual contents (the documents), which allows MongoDB to query much faster. Indexes store ordered values of a specific field or a set of fields. MongoDB can return sorted results using the ordering of the index itself, which means indexes not only can improve performance when reading data, but also when sorting it.

MongoDB indexes use a data structure known as **B-tree**. B-trees are self-balancing, which allows efficient operations such as search, insertion, deletion, and sequential access, all in logarithmic time. You can think of an index as a sorted map of key-value pairs, where each key corresponds to an indexed field's value, and the value points to the associated document. Like an index of a book, the keys are stored in order and associated with one or more fields.

This tree-based structure helps minimize the number of comparisons needed during searches. Without an index, every new document added to a collection increases the work required to scan for matching results. But with a B-tree, new entries are placed in a way that preserves order and balance, so queries remain efficient without adding unnecessary overhead.

Determining whether a query used an index

Before you create an index, populate a database with some test data. You will use this data to determine whether your queries use an index. Run the following script in the MongoDB Shell to populate the companies collection inside of the test database with sample documents:

```
use test

for (i = 0; i < 1000; i++) {
  db.companies.insertOne({
    "i": i,
```

```
      "name": "Company_" + i,
      "ticker": "CMPY_" + i,
      "revenue": Math.floor(Math.random() * 1000000),
      "created": new Date(),
      "meta": {
        "employees": Math.floor(Math.random() * 100),
        "acquisitions": Math.floor(Math.random() * 5)
      },
      "info": "Lorem ipsum dolor sit amet"
    })
  }
```

The script inserts 1,000 companies with some fake data: name, revenue, and some embedded meta fields for the number of employees and acquisitions.

You can run a query with the explain command to see how MongoDB performs a query without any indexes. In MongoDB Shell, run the following command:

```
db.companies
  .find({name: 'Company_456'})
  .explain('executionStats')
```

To analyze index usage, the most important fields in the output to examine are the following:

- totalKeysExamined, which is the number of indexes used to fulfill the query
- totalDocsExamined, which is the number of documents examined during query execution
- The query's winning plan, which contains IXSCAN if an index was used

Without an index, totalKeysExamined is 0, totalDocsExamined is the number of documents in the collection, and the winning plan is a COLLSCAN stage. These attributes indicate that the query performed a collection scan, which isn't very performant.

Generally, you want to create indexes so they align with your expected query shape. More precisely, an index supports a query when it contains all the fields scanned by the query. In this case, you can create your first index on the company name field:

```
db.companies.createIndex( { "name": 1 } )
```

This command creates a single-field index on the name field, where the number 1 indicates the sort order. This example index is in ascending order. If you want your application to access data in descending order, you can set the sort order to -1.

After you create the index, if you rerun the previous query, you should see the following values in the executionStats:

- totalKeysExamined: 1

- totalDocsExamined: 1

- winningPlan.inputStage.stage: IXSCAN

Now, the query uses the index and only needs to examine a single document to return results. The query returns results faster, and the performance improves even further as the number of documents in the collection increases.

In a database with many complex documents, indexes are necessary. However, indexes make write performance worse, so be careful when creating indexes on fields that are frequently updated. Understanding your application's read:write ratio is critical to creating effective, performant indexes. The proper choice of indexes is an important part of mastering MongoDB. Later in this chapter, you will receive guidelines on how and where to create indexes.

Index types

The following section describes different index types available in MongoDB and explains the different types of queries they support.

Single-field indexes

Single-field indexes store information from a single field in a collection. By default, all collections have a unique index on the _id field. This index prevents documents with duplicate _id values from being inserted into the collection.

In the previous section, you learned how to create a single-field index on a top-level document field. You can also create a single-field index on an embedded document field. When you do, you must put the field name in quotation marks. For example, the following command creates an index on the meta.employees field:

```
db.companies.createIndex( { "meta.employees": 1 } )
```

You can also create a single-field index on embedded documents as a whole, as shown in the following example:

```
db.companies.createIndex( { "meta": 1 } )
```

However, only queries that specify the entire embedded document use the index. Queries on a specific field within the document do not use the index. This can lead to unexpected behaviors if your schema model changes and you add or remove fields from your indexed document. Before you create an index on an embedded document, consider whether you should instead index specific fields in that document.

Compound indexes

Compound indexes collect and sort data from two or more fields in each document in a collection. Data is grouped by the order in which fields appear in the index.

The compound index is often the best solution for cases where you expect several fields to be used in your queries. For example, building on our companies example from this section, you can create an index composed of the name and ticker fields:

```
db.companies.createIndex( { "name": 1, "ticker": 1 } )
```

With compound indexes, the order of the index determines whether the index can support a sort operation. Compound indexes support sort operations that match either the sort order of the index or the reverse sort order of the index.

The previous compound index supports sorts on the following field combinations:

```
db.companies.find().sort({ "name": 1,"ticker": 1 })
db.companies.find().sort({ "name": -1,'ticker": -1 })
```

The index is not used for the following sorts, because the sort order does not match the order of the index:

```
db.companies.find().sort({ "name": 1, 'ticker": -1 })
db.companies.find().sort({ "name": -1,"ticker": 1 })
```

Index prefixes

Index prefixes are the beginning subsets of indexed fields. Compound indexes support queries on all fields included in the index prefix. For example, the compound index from the previous example can support a query on the author and ISBN fields, or on just the author field because it is part of the index prefix. Querying just by the ISBN code will not use the index and will instead perform a collection scan.

To help remove redundant indexes, check for any indexes that are contained in another index's prefix. For example, consider the following indexes:

- `{ "name": -1,"ticker": 1 }`
- `{ "name": -1 }`

The preceding indexes have a common prefix of `{ "name": -1 }`. If neither index has a sparse or unique constraint, you can remove the index on the prefix `{ "name": -1 }`. MongoDB uses the compound index in all of the situations that it would have used the prefix index.

ESR guideline

When choosing the order in which to place the fields in your compound index, following the **Equality, Sort, Range (ESR)** guideline helps create an efficient compound index.

- **Equality** refers to an exact match on a single value. Index searches make efficient use of exact matches to limit the number of documents that need to be examined to complete a query. Put the fields that require exact matches first in your index.
- **Sort** determines the order of results. Sort follows equality matches because the equality matches reduce the number of documents that need to be sorted. Sorting after the equality matches also allows MongoDB to do a non-blocking sort.
- **Range** filters scan fields. The scan doesn't require an exact match, which means range filters are loosely bound to index keys. To improve query efficiency, limit the range bounds and use equality matches to reduce the number of documents to scan. Put fields that are used for range matches last in your index.

Using the company example from earlier in this section, imagine that the application needed to perform a query with the following shape:

```
db.companies.find( {
   "meta.employees": { $gte: 20 },
   "name": "Company_45"
} ).sort( { "revenue": -1 } )
```

If we follow the ESR guideline, the following index would be optimal to support this query:

```
db.companies.createIndex( {
   "name": 1,
   "revenue": -1,
   "meta.employees": 1

} )
```

- The query performs an **equality** match on the name field, which means it should be the first field in the index
- The query performs a **sort** on the revenue field, which means it should be the next field in the index
- The query contains a **range** filter on meta.employees, which means it should be the last field in the index

Multikey indexes

MongoDB's ability to store arrays of values extends to indexing as well. To improve performance for queries on array values, you can create a multikey index.

The example database doesn't have any arrays; however, you can insert the following document:

```
db.companies.insertOne({
  "name": "Company with tags",
  "ticker": "TAGS",
  "revenue": 23000,
  "tags": ["Finance", "Insurance", "Banking"]
})
```

To create a multikey index, use the same command as a single-field index and specify an array field in the index key:

```
db.companies.createIndex( { "tags": 1 } )
```

You can also create compound multikey indexes, with the limitation that only one field in the index can be an array field. Here's an example:

```
db.companies.createIndex( { "name": 1, "tags": 1 } )
```

Text search

MongoDB supports full-text searching through text indexes, which are special indexes on string value fields. All MongoDB deployments support standard text indexes; however, with MongoDB Atlas, you can create Atlas Search indexes, which are an improved full-text query solution.

Text indexes

Text indexes support text search queries on fields that contain string content. Text indexes improve performance when you search for specific words or strings within string content. A collection can only have one text index, but that index may include multiple fields.

To create a text index, set the value of the index key to text. Here's an example:

```
db.companies.createIndex( { "info": "text" } )
```

Text indexes will apply word stemming (removing common suffixes and stop words, such as a, an, the). When you create a text index on multiple fields, you can specify the importance of each text field. For instance, you can apply more weight to matches in the title or subtitle of a document compared to the same matches in a body paragraph of an article.

Since MongoDB performs a full index search for every single search term, text index performance is directly proportional to the number of search terms. To improve the performance of a text query, limit the number of documents by using a compound index. For example, you can include the author of the document or a date range in the index, thus partitioning the documents and speeding up the text index search by reducing the search space.

Consider the following additional factors when building text indexes:

- Text indexes can use high amounts of RAM because they create a separate index entry for every unique, stemmed word in each indexed field of every inserted document.

- Building a text index takes longer than building a simple ordered (scalar) index on the same data.

- Text indexes break down text strings into individual words, without storing phrases or information about how close words are to each other in the original document. Therefore, queries with multiple search terms run more efficiently when the entire collection can be held in memory.

Atlas Search indexes

MongoDB Atlas has a full-text search index based on Apache Lucene, which has additional capabilities compared to MongoDB text indexing. Atlas Search indexes create mappings between terms and documents containing those terms, which enables fast retrieval of documents using identifiers.

TTL indexes

Time-to-live (TTL) indexes are special indexes that automatically delete documents after a specified length of time. These indexes are useful for deleting documents that represent data such as user sessions or logs, where typically only the most recent data is useful.

Using the sample companies collection, you could create an index on the created field, and specify 60 * 60 * 24 = 86,400 seconds, which is equivalent to one day:

```
db.companies.createIndex(
  { "created": 1 },
  { expireAfterSeconds: 86400 }
)
```

The preceding index deletes all companies with a created datetime value that is older than the expireAfterSeconds period of 86,400 seconds or one day. The deletion check runs as a background job and runs every 60 seconds. Note that if you expect to delete a large number of documents with a TTL index, you may want to schedule the deletion in batches.

TTL indexes and capped collections have similar properties in that they both delete old data to make room for new data. Generally, TTL indexes offer better performance and more flexibility than capped collections and should be preferred over capped collections when possible.

Partial indexes

Partial indexes only index the documents in a collection that meet a specified filter expression. By indexing a subset of the documents in a collection, partial indexes have lower storage requirements and reduced performance costs for index creation and maintenance.

For instance, you can create an index on the employees and name fields of your documents, but only for companies with more than 50 employees:

```
db.companies.createIndex(
  {
    "meta.employees": 1,
    "name": 1
  },
  {
    partialFilterExpression: {
      "meta.employees": { $gt: 50 }
    }
  }
)
```

For queries that might use only a subset of the data, such as the most recent social network status or the latest news, a partial index can be an efficient way to return results.

> MongoDB also provides sparse indexes, which only contain entries for documents that have the indexed field. Partial indexes provide a superset of the functionality of sparse indexes and should generally be preferred over sparse indexes.

Geospatial indexes

Geospatial indexes support queries on location data – either GeoJSON or MongoDB legacy coordinate pairs. Use these indexes to create geo-aware applications.

- 2d indexes support queries on data that is stored as points on a 2d plane. Potential use cases for 2d indexes include calculations on a 2d graph or analyzing visual similarities between two art pieces.

- 2dsphere indexes support geospatial queries on an earth-like sphere. They can determine points within a specified area, calculate proximity to a specified point, and many other useful calculations.

MongoDB provides several query operators for use with geospatial indexes to perform geospatial queries. Here are some examples:

- $near: Returns points or shapes that are near a specified geolocation
- $nearSphere: Returns geospatial objects that are near a point on a sphere
- $geoWithin: Returns all points within a specified area
- $geoIntersects: Determines whether a specified area intersects with other geospatial areas and objects

Wildcard indexes

Wildcard indexes let you create an index on unknown or arbitrary fields. They are useful when you don't know the exact fields that'll be present in the document, or if you expect document fields to change over time.

To create a wildcard index on all document fields, you can use the following command:

```
db.companies.createIndex( { "$**": 1 } )
```

However, wildcard indexes don't perform as well as targeted indexes on specific fields. The preceding wildcard index may work on a small dataset, but on a large dataset with many document fields, performance might not be optimal.

Instead, a common use case for wildcard indexes is to index a specific embedded object where the subfields may vary between documents. For example, we can imagine that the meta field in the sample data might contain different subfields for different companies. It would make sense to create a wildcard index on the meta field to support queries on all possible meta subfields:

```
db.companies.createIndex( { "meta.$**": 1 } )
```

Wildcard indexes are helpful alternatives in scenarios where your application would require a large number of individual indexes to cover all possible queries. However, wildcard indexes do not effectively replace workload-based index planning. If your collection contains arbitrary field names that prevent targeted indexes, consider remodeling your schema to have consistent field names.

Hidden indexes

Hidden indexes are not visible to the query planner and can't be used to support a query. As you iterate your schema design and indexes, hiding indexes is useful to evaluate the impact of deleting an index before fully committing to deleting it.

To hide an existing index, use the hideIndex command. Here's an example:

```
db.companies.hideIndex("name_1_tags_1")
```

The argument for the hideIndex command can either be the index name or the index key specification document. Indexes are fully maintained while they are hidden, so hidden indexes still negatively impact write performance.

Hashed indexes

Hashed indexes are used in sharded deployments to distribute data across shards based on the hashes of shard key values. The field you choose for your hashed shard key should have a high cardinality, meaning a large number of different values. Hashed indexing is ideal for shard keys with fields that change monotonically, such as ObjectId values or timestamps.

To create a hashed index on the _id field, run the following command:

```
db.orders.createIndex( { _id: "hashed" } )
```

Clustered indexes

Clustered indexes are used to create clustered collections, which store indexed documents in the same WiredTiger file as the index specification. This storage pattern provides performance benefits compared to regular indexes because inserts, updates, and deletions only require a single write operation. The only allowed clustered index key is { _id: 1 }.

The following example creates a clustered collection called events:

```
db.createCollection("events", {
  clusteredIndex: {
    key: { _id: 1 },
    unique: true
  }
})
```

Identifying common queries

There are multiple tools available to analyze your cluster's workload and identify common queries. Identifying common queries helps you decide which queries would be best supported by indexes.

- The database profiler collects detailed information about database commands run on your cluster, including CRUD, configuration, and administration commands. Enabling the profiler and analyzing its output can provide an overview of common read operations that would benefit from an index.

- MongoDB 8.0 introduces the $queryStats aggregation stage, which returns runtime statistics for recorded queries. The queries are grouped by query shape, which helps you identify common fields used for querying and sorting.

  The following example shows how to use the $queryStats stage. Note that the command must be run on the admin database:

  ```
  db.getSiblingDB("admin").aggregate( [
    {
      $queryStats: { }
    }
  ] )
  ```

Persistent query settings for indexes

MongoDB 8.0 introduces a new feature that lets you enforce stricter control on how your queries execute. Specifically, you can force your queries to use a specific index for all queries that match a particular query shape. A query shape is a set of specifications that group similar queries together, such as filters, sorts, and projections.

The idea of forcing a query to use a particular index is called "index hinting." An index hint overrides MongoDB's default index selection process and causes the query to use a specific index, assuming that index is eligible to support the query.

In most scenarios, queries do not require index hints because the default index selection results in the most efficient query. However, if the query can choose from multiple possible indexes, an index hint can be useful to ensure optimal performance.

Consider the following index and query:

```
db.companies.createIndex( { i: 1, revenue: 1 } )


db.companies.find( {
  i: { $gte: 30 }
} ).sort( { revenue: 1 } )
```

The following example shows how to set your cluster's query settings so that queries that match the preceding shape always use the same index:

```
db.adminCommand( {
  setQuerySettings: {
    find: "companies",
    filter: {
      i: { $gte: 30 }
    },
    sort: {
      revenue: 1
      },
      $db: "test"
  },
  settings: {
    indexHints: {
     ns: { db: "test", coll: "companies" },
     allowedIndexes: [ "i_1_revenue_1" ]
    },
    queryFramework: "classic",
    comment: "Index hint for i_1_revenue_1 index to improve query
performance"
  }
} )
```

Covered queries

A covered query is a query that can be satisfied entirely using an index and does not have to examine any documents. An index covers a query when all the following conditions are met:

- All the fields in the query are part of an index.

- All the fields returned in the results are in the same index.

- No fields in the query are equal to null.

For example, consider the following index:

```
db.companies.createIndex( { i: 1, name: 1 } )
```

The index covers the following query:

```
db.companies.find(
  {
    i: 30,
    name: "Company_30"
  },
  { name: 1, _id: 0 }
).explain("executionStats")
```

This index covers the query because it only queries on the indexed fields, i and name. Also, the query only returns the title field. For the query to be covered, the query projection must explicitly omit the _id field because _id is not included in the index.

To confirm that the query was covered, examine the query's executionStats and observe that totalKeysExamined is 1 and totalDocsExamined is 0.

Remember that queries always return _id by default. To achieve a covered query, you need to explicitly exclude the _id field from query results or add it to the index.

Indexing strategies

To help create effective indexes, review the following strategies and best practices:

- Make sure that your indexes support your most common queries. Use the explain plan regularly to analyze your queries and determine whether and how they are using indexes.

- When creating compound indexes, follow the ESR guidelines described earlier in this chapter to best inform the order of the index fields.

- When possible, enable your application to run covered queries.

- Wildcard indexes do not replace workload-based index planning. For workloads with many ad hoc query patterns or that handle highly polymorphic document structures, wildcard indexes provide extra flexibility. However, they come with increased storage and performance overhead. If your application's query patterns are known in advance, then you should use more selective indexes on the specific fields accessed by the queries.

Summary

In this chapter, you learned how to optimize your data model and use indexes to ensure efficient and performant applications. Effective schema design and index optimization are critical to the success of a MongoDB deployment. One of the most important benefits of MongoDB's flexible data model is how it enables you to iterate on your schema design. As your application grows over time and business requirements change, you have options to seamlessly redesign your schema without downtime to ensure that your schema model best matches your data access patterns.

Through careful data modeling and index optimization, you can harness MongoDB's capabilities to build scalable and high-performing applications. The chapter provided detailed guidance on aligning application requirements with database architecture for maximum efficiency.

In the next chapter, you will learn about queries in MongoDB, including new query features available in MongoDB 8.0. Now that you've learned how to create effective indexes, you can ensure that the queries you'll learn about are efficient and performant.

5

Queries

MongoDB offers a powerful and flexible query system designed for working with semi-structured, hierarchical data stored in BSON format. As a document-oriented NoSQL database, MongoDB allows for expressive and dynamic queries that go well beyond simple key-value lookups. Its query engine is optimized for a wide range of workloads, including operational data access, analytical processing, and real-time application use cases.

At its foundation, MongoDB supports standard **create, read, update, and delete (CRUD)**, executed through an intuitive, JSON-like syntax that makes working with nested documents and arrays straightforward. Queries can be composed using field-level operators, logical expressions, regular expressions, and geospatial criteria, among others.

This chapter covers the following topics:

- MongoDB CRUD operations
- CRUD operations with mongosh and PyMongo
- Batch operations with mongosh
- Advanced queries and aggregations
- Query shapes
- Database commands introduced in MongoDB

Technical requirements

To follow along with the code in this chapter, you must either connect to an on-premises deployment or connect to a MongoDB Atlas database.

To connect to an on-premises deployment, you must install MongoDB locally. You can download the on-premises MongoDB Community Edition from www.mongodb.com, free of charge. As an alternative to MongoDB Community Edition, the fully managed **database-as-a-service (DBaaS)**, MongoDB Atlas, also has a free tier as well as the opportunity to seamlessly upgrade.

The code examples in this chapter use mongosh and PyMongo:

- mongosh is a JavaScript and Node.js REPL environment for interacting with MongoDB deployments. You can download mongosh from https://www.mongodb.com/docs/mongodb-shell/.

- PyMongo is the official MongoDB driver for Python. You can download PyMongo or another MongoDB driver of your choice at https://www.mongodb.com/docs/drivers/.

MongoDB CRUD operations

CRUD operations are the foundation of interacting with a MongoDB deployment. These operations require you to connect to the MongoDB server before you can query the relevant documents, adjust the specified properties, and subsequently, transmit the data back to the database for updates. Each CRUD operation serves a distinct purpose:

- The create operation creates and inserts new documents into the database
- The read operation queries a document or documents in the database
- The update operation modifies existing documents in the database
- The delete operation removes documents from the database

Basic CRUD with mongosh

mongosh, also known as the MongoDB Shell, is an environment for hosting MongoDB deployments. It is equivalent to the administration console that relational databases use. You can download mongosh at https://www.mongodb.com/docs/mongodb-shell/install/.

This section explains how to connect to your deployment with mongosh, insert a document into a database, query your database for a specified document, update a document, and delete a document. For more in-depth information and examples, you can also refer to the CRUD operations section of the MongoDB database manual at https://www.mongodb.com/docs/manual/crud/.

Connecting to MongoDB

Before you can perform CRUD operations, you must connect to your MongoDB deployment. To connect to mongosh, you must specify your deployment connection string as well as any specified parameters.

For example, enter a variation of the following code block in your terminal to connect to a MongoDB deployment with mongosh:

```
mongosh "mongodb+srv://mycluster.packt.mongodb.net/myDatabase"
--username myUsername --password myPassword
```

Creating documents

To create a document in mongosh, you can use the db.collection.insertOne() command. This mongosh command creates a new document and inserts the created document into the specified collection.

For example, the following db.collection.insertOne()command creates and inserts a new document into the library collection of the database. The new document has a title field set to Mastering MongoDB 8.0 and an isbn field set to 101:

```
db.library.insertOne(
   { title: 'Mastering MongoDB 8.0', isbn: '101' }
)
```

When you successfully create and insert a document, MongoDB returns a confirmation output that contains the ObjectID value of the new document:

```
{
   acknowledged: true,
   insertedId: ObjectId("652024e7ab44f3bf77788a3d")
}
```

You can also use the following mongosh commands to update documents:

- db.collection.insertMany()
- db.collection.updateOne() with the upsert: true option
- db.collection.updateMany() with the upsert: true option
- db.collection.findAndModify() with the upsert: true option
- db.collection.findOneAndUpdate() with the upsert: true option
- db.collection.findOneAndReplace() with the upsert: true option

Reading documents

Read operations in MongoDB are also called **queries**. To perform a basic read operation, or query, for a single document, use the db.collection.findOne() method and specify the selection criteria of the document that you want to read.

For example, the following operation queries for a document in the library collection that contains the isbn field value of 101:

```
db.library.find( { isbn: '101' } )
```

If the library collection contains a document that matches your specified selection criteria, MongoDB returns an array that contains the document that matches:

```
[ {
  _id: ObjectId("652024e7ab44f3bf77788a3d"),
  title: 'Mastering MongoDB 8.0',
  isbn: '101'
} ]
```

You can also use the following mongosh commands to read documents:

```
db.collection.findOne()
```

Updating documents

To update a document, you can use the db.collection.updateOne() command. This command finds a document that matches the specified criteria and updates the found document.

For example, the following code finds the document in the library collection that has an isbn field value of 101 and updates that document so that it contains a price field with a value of 30:

```
db.library.updateOne( { isbn: '101' }, { $set: { price: 30 } } )
```

When you successfully update a document, MongoDB returns the following confirmation summary:

```
{
  acknowledged: true,
  insertedId: null,
  matchedCount: 1,
  modifiedCount: 1,
  upsertedCount: 0
}
```

You can also use the following mongosh commands to update documents:

- `db.collection.updateMany()`
- `db.collection.replaceOne()`
- `db.collection.findOneAndReplace()`
- `db.collection.findOneAndUpdate()`
- `db.collection.findAndModify()`

MongoDB 8.0 also introduces the ability to sort documents within an update operation. If you specify a sort parameter in an operation that uses db.collection.updateOne(), db.collection. replaceOne(), or update, MongoDB sorts documents before updating to be able to select a specific document for the operation when multiple documents match the query.

For example, the following update operation sorts all books by price and updates the lowest price book to be on sale for 25% off:

```
db.library.updateOne(
   { },
   [
     { $set: { price: { $multiply: ["$price", 0.75] } } }
   ],
   { sort: { price: 1 } }
)
```

Deleting documents

To delete a document, you can use the db.collection.deleteOne() command. This command queries for a document that matches specified criteria and deletes the found document.

For example, the following operation deletes a document in the library collection that has an isbn field value of 101:

```
db.library.deleteOne( { isbn: '101' } )
```

When you successfully delete a document, MongoDB returns the following output:

```
{
   acknowledged: true,
   deletedCount: 1
}
```

You can also use the following mongosh commands to delete documents:

- `db.collection.deleteMany()`
- `db.collection.remove()`
- `db.collection.findOneAndDelete()`
- `db.collection.findAndModify()`

Basic CRUD with the Python driver

As an alternative to mongosh, MongoDB provides official drivers to interact with your MongoDB deployment. For a full list of official MongoDB driver libraries, see `https://www.mongodb.com/docs/drivers/`.

The following sections walk you through performing CRUD operations with the MongoDB Python driver, PyMongo. PyMongo provides a seamless bridge between the dynamic world of Python programming and the efficient, document-oriented NoSQL database of MongoDB.

Installing and connecting to PyMongo

You can use `pip` to install PyMongo. You must have Python installed prior to installing PyMongo.

For example, the following operation installs PyMongo through your terminal:

```
$ python -m pip install pymongo
```

> If your machine uses Python 3, replace `python` in your installation command with `python3`.

To connect to your MongoDB deployment with PyMongo, you must use your connection string. For example, the following code snippet in a `.py` file connects to a MongoDB deployment:

```python
from pymongo import MongoClient
uri = "<connection string>"

client = MongoClient(uri)

try:
    client.admin.command('ping')
    print("Pinged your deployment. You successfully connected to
MongoDB!")
```

```
except Exception as e:
    print(e)
```

If you run the preceding code in a .py file and successfully connect to your deployment, MongoDB returns the following confirmation:

```
"Pinged your deployment. You successfully connected to MongoDB!"
```

You can test your connection to your MongoDB deployment on Atlas with the following code block in a .py file. This code block uses the asyncio asynchronous framework:

```
import asyncio
from motor.motor_asyncio import AsyncIOMotorClient
from pymongo.server_api import ServerApi

async def ping_server():
    uri = "<connection string>"
    client = AsyncIOMotorClient(uri, server_api=ServerApi('1'))

    try:
        await client.admin.command('ping')
        print("Pinged your deployment. You successfully connected to
MongoDB!")
    except Exception as e:
        print(e)
asyncio.run(ping_server())
```

If you run the preceding code in a .py file and successfully connect to your deployment, MongoDB returns the following confirmation:

```
"Pinged your deployment. You successfully connected to MongoDB!".
```

Creating documents

To create and insert documents with PyMongo, use the insert_one command.

For example, the code block that follows performs the following operations:

- Specifies the library collection within the resources database
- Defines a new document that represents a book titled Python and MongoDB
- Inserts the new document into the library database
- Prints the ObjectId value of the new document

```
library = client.resources.library

book = {
  'isbn': '301',
  'name': 'Python and MongoDB',
  'meta': {'version': 'MongoDB 8.0'},
  'price': 60
}

insert_result = library.insert_one(book)
print(insert_result)
```

If you successfully insert a document with this script, MongoDB prints the ObjectId value of the inserted document.

Reading documents

You can read documents from your database with queries.

To read a document, specify the condition(s) of the document you want to read with a find_one command.

For example, the code block that follows performs the following actions:

- Specifies the library collection in the resources database
- Finds documents with the name value of Python and MongoDB
- Prints the found document

```
library = client.resources.library

result = library.find_one( {"name": "Python and MongoDB"} )
print (result)
```

Updating documents

To update a document with PyMongo, use the update_one command. This command finds a document based on specified criteria and updates the found document.

For example, the code block that follows performs the following operations:

- Finds the document where the name field is Advanced MongoDB Techniques
- Sets the price field of the found document to the value of 75

- Prints the result of the update_one operation
- Prints the updated document

```python
update_result = library.update_one(
  { "name": "Advanced MongoDB Techniques"},
  { "$set": { "price": 75 } }
)


print(update_result.raw_result)


updated_document = library.find_one(
  {"name": "Advanced MongoDB Techniques"}
)


print(updated_document)
```

Deleting a document

To delete a document with PyMongo, use the delete_one command. For example, the code block that follows performs the following operations:

- Specifies the isbn value of the book to delete as 303
- Uses the delete_one command to delete a book from the library collection with the desired isbn value
- Prints the result of the delete_one operation

```python
isbn_to_delete = '303'


delete_result = library.delete_one({"isbn": isbn_to_delete})


print(delete_result.raw_result)
```

If the operation successfully deleted the desired document, MongoDB returns the following confirmation:

```python
{'n': 1, 'ok': 1.0}
```

The n value indicates the number of documents that MongoDB deleted. In this case, MongoDB deleted one document. The ok value indicates whether the operation caused any errors. The 1.0 value in the preceding confirmation signifies that MongoDB did not encounter an error with this operation.

Bulk operations

To perform more complex CRUD operations, MongoDB 8.0 introduces a new `bulkWrite` database command that can create, update, and delete operations on multiple collections in one request. `bulkWrite` expands the functionality of the existing `db.collection.bulkWrite()` command, which only allows you to modify one collection at a time.

Syntax

The `bulkWrite` command takes the following commonly used fields:

Field	Type	Necessity	Description
`insert`	Integer	Required	Namespace ID index for an `insert` operation, which must match the namespace ID index in the `ns` field in the `nsInfo` array. Indexes start at 0.
`document`	Document	Required	Document to insert into the collection.
`update`	Integer	Required	Namespace ID index for an `update` operation, which must match a namespace ID index in the `ns` field in the `nsInfo` array. Indexes start at 0.
`filter`	Document	Optional	Query selector to limit the documents for the `update` or `delete` operation.

Table 5.1: Common Fields in bulkWrite Command

See the MongoDB documentation page on `bulkWrite` for a list of all `bulkWrite` parameters, in-depth examples, and behavioral considerations: `https://www.mongodb.com/docs/manual/reference/command/bulkWrite/`.

There are some additional considerations for the `bulkWrite` command, as discussed in the following subsections.

The multi field and retryable writes

`bulkWrite` can take an optional `multi` field that specifies whether an `update` or `delete` operation impacts all documents that match the document filter. If you set `multi` to `true`, the operation updates or deletes all operations that match the filter. If `multi` is `false`, MongoDB only updates or deletes the first document that matches the filter.

You can enable retryable writes to automatically retry write operations that may encounter network errors or cannot find a healthy primary to address. Retryable writes are compatible with some bulkWrite operations:

- You can enable retryable writes with bulkWrite insert operations that set multi to true
- If multi is true, you cannot enable retryable writes with bulkWrite update or delete operations
- If multi is false, you can enable retryable with bulkWrite update or delete operations

Performance

bulkWrite operations that insert documents may produce a single operation log entry (or oplog entry) for multiple insert operations. Accordingly, bulkWrite improves the performance of multi-document inserts and removes possible lags in replication that are usually the result of multiple oplog writes. However, a database shutdown immediately following a bulkWrite insert operation may take a longer time due to the extra data that is flushed to disk.

In general, using a bulkWrite command for multiple operations improves database performance and reduces the number of round trips to the database server. bulkWrite may be especially optimal for high-throughput applications.

Aggregations in MongoDB

MongoDB offers a rich set of advanced query features that extend beyond basic data retrieval and manipulation. These features allow you to optimize query performance, create aggregation pipelines, and perform complex aggregations.

Introduction to the aggregation framework

MongoDB's aggregation framework is a data processing tool for performing complex data transformations and computations. You can use the framework to filter, transform, and analyze data within MongoDB.

The aggregation framework centers around **aggregation pipelines**, which are data processing pipelines that take in data and transform the data as it passes from one aggregation stage to the next. With different aggregation stages, you can filter, group, and reshape entire documents. Aggregation stages are represented by operators preceded by $. For example, a $group aggregation stage groups documents by specified parameters.

The following diagram illustrates how data flows through an aggregation pipeline that contains $match, $sort, $group, and $set aggregation stages:

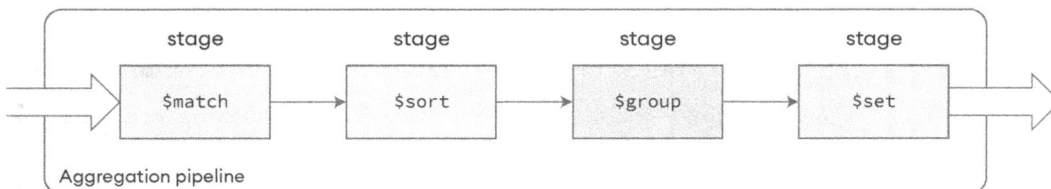

Figure 5.1: A diagram illustrating how data is passed through an aggregation pipeline

With over 150 operators and expressions, the MongoDB ecosystem offers a vast range of possibilities, enabling you to perform incredibly complex and useful data operations through relatively simple steps. All MongoDB language-specific drivers (JavaScript, Python, etc.) fully support the aggregation framework, making it convenient for you to write aggregations in any language. The examples in this section show aggregation pipelines that use mongosh.

Aggregation pipeline example

A university might use an aggregation pipeline to compute the final grade for each student. Consider a university database that contains a student_grades collection. Each document in the collection has the following data structure:

```
{
  "_id": ObjectId("5f4b7de8e8189a46aaf6e3ad"),
  "student_id": ObjectId("5f4b7de8e7139a46aaf5e4a5"),
  "course_id": ObjectId("5f4b7de8e7179a56aaf6e1b2"),
  "grade": 76,
  "semester": "Fall 2025"
}
```

To calculate final grades using multiple steps, the university can use an aggregation pipeline to perform the following operations:

- **Filter grades:** If the university wants to specify that final grades only take certain semesters into account, they can use a $match aggregation stage to filter grades by the semester field

- **Group grades:** To group documents by student_id, they can use a $group aggregation stage

- **Compute the average grade:** To compute the average grade of the filtered grades by student, they can use a $project aggregation stage

The following aggregation pipeline achieves these operations using mongosh:

```
db.student_grades.aggregate( [
  { $match: { semester: "Fall 2025" } },
  { $group  {
        _id: "$student_id",
        averageGrade: { $avg: "$grade" }
     } },
    { $prcject: {
          _id: 0,
          student_id: "$_id",
          averageGrade: 1
    } }
 ] )
```

The result of this aggregation pipeline displays the average grade for each student, where each student is identified by their student ID.

Benefits of the aggregation framework

MongoDB's aggregation framework provides a robust way to process and analyze your data. It enables you to perform complex transformations, computations, and combinations of documents within your collections. This makes it easier to extract insights, summarize information, and support analytical queries directly within the database.

Aggregating in MongoDB provides a range of benefits, such as the following:

- **Performance**: Native database operations within MongoDB are often faster than extracting data and processing it with an external tool
- **Flexibility**: The aggregation framework provides a wide range of tools and operators to transform data in complex ways, often reducing the need for external data processing logic
- **Data integrity**: Data processing at the database level ensures consistency and integrity compared to external processes, which may encounter synchronization or transactional issues

Aggregation stages

MongoDB provides a wide range of aggregation stages that process and output data. An aggregation stage represents a specific step in the pipeline where the data transformation process takes place. Each stage processes data and outputs documents that can be further processed by the subsequent stages.

A complete, up-to-date list of all MongoDB aggregation stages is available on the MongoDB documentation website: `https://www.mongodb.com/docs/manual/reference/operator/aggregation-pipeline/`.

Compatibility

You can use aggregation pipeline stages in the following environments:

- **MongoDB Atlas:** The fully managed service for MongoDB cloud deployments
- **MongoDB Enterprise:** The subscription-based, self-managed version of MongoDB
- **MongoDB Community:** The source-available, free, and self-managed version of MongoDB

Common aggregation stages

The following list shows commonly used aggregation stages:

- **`$match`:** Filters documents and outputs the filtered document set to the next pipeline stage
- **`$limit`:** Limits the number of documents output to the next stage
- **`$sort`:** Sorts documents by a specified order
- **`$project`:** Reshapes data to output only the specified fields
- **`$set`:** Specifies a new field to add to documents for the new stage
- **`$unwind`:** Flattens array fields and outputs a new document for each array element
- **`$lookup`:** Performs a left outer join within another collection

MongoDB 8.0 aggregation stage enhancements

MongoDB 8.0 makes several enhancements and improvements to MongoDB's aggregation stage offerings.

$convert

The `$convert` aggregation stage converts a value to a specified data type. The `input` field of a `$convert` aggregation stage can be any valid expression. The `to` field specifies the type that MongoDB converts the `input` value to. For a full list of `$convert` parameters, see the MongoDB documentation at `https://www.mongodb.com/docs/manual/reference/operator/aggregation/convert/`.

For example, the following aggregation stage converts the $price field of documents in an inventory collection to a string:

```
db.inventory.aggregate( [
  {
    $set: {
      price: {
        $convert: {
          input: "$price",
          to: "string",
        }
      }
    }
  }
] )
```

MongoDB 8.0 extends the $convert capabilities to perform the following conversions, which were not previously available:

- String values to binData values
- binData values to string values

Additionally, MongoDB 8.0 introduces a new helper expression, $toUUID, which provides a simpler syntax for converting strings to UUID values.

For a full list of conversion abilities, see the MongoDB documentation.

$denseRank and $rank

The $denseRank and $rank aggregation pipeline operators return the document position (rank) relative to other documents within a window (document range) specified by a $setWindowFields operation.

For example, consider a sales collection that contains documents that represent individual sales and the state in which the sale was made. The following aggregation stage uses $rank within the $setWindowFields aggregation stage to rank the quantity of sales for each state:

```
db.sales.aggregate( [
  {
    $setWindowFields: {
      partitionBy: "$state",
      sortBy: { quantity: -1 },
```

```
        output: {
          rankQuantityForState: {
            $rank: {}
          }
        }
      }
    }
  ] )
```

While $denseRank and $rank have several differences in the way they rank documents, starting in MongoDB 8.0, $denseRank and $rank treat null and missing field values equivalently when calculating rankings.

$queryStats

MongoDB 7.1 introduces the $queryStats aggregation stage, which returns runtime statistics for recorded queries on Atlas deployments. $queryStats returns metrics for aggregate(), find(), and distinct() queries on the admin database and must be the first stage in an aggregation pipeline.

> The $queryStats aggregation stage is unsupported by MongoDB and is not guaranteed to be stable in a future server release.

$queryStats outputs an array of query stats entries. Some query stats entry properties contain literal values, and MongoDB normalizes other properties to group similar queries. MongoDB normalizes $queryStats properties by user-provided fields to their data types. For example, MongoDB normalizes a { item: 'card' } filter to { item: '?string' }.

Each query stats entry in the output contains the following top-level documents:

Document Field	Description
Key	The unique combination of attributes that define an entry, such as the query shape, client information, read concern, or collection type.
asOf	The time, in UTC, that $queryStats read the corresponding entry.
metrics	Aggregated runtime metrics of the corresponding query stats entry.

Table 5.2: Top-Level Fields in $queryStats Output

For more in-depth descriptions of nested documents in the output array, see the full MongoDB documentation: `https://www.mongodb.com/docs/manual/reference/operator/aggregation/queryStats/`.

For example, the following aggregation pipeline outputs query stats on the `admin` database:

```
db.getSiblingDB("admin").aggregate( [
    {
        $queryStats: { }
    }
] )
```

Advanced aggregation pipelines

While the previous examples in this chapter use single-stage aggregation pipelines to demonstrate basic functionalities of stages, you can use multiple stages to perform complex data processing.

For example, consider an application that uses a collection of users where each user document contains the user's age. The following multi-stage aggregation pipeline uses $sort to first sort users from oldest to youngest and then uses $limit to output the three oldest users:

- Here is the input:

    ```
    [
      { "_id": 1, "name": "Justin", "age": 28 },
      { "_id": 2, "name": "Sydney", "age": 23 },
      { "_id": 3, "name": "Lauren", "age": 26 },
      { "_id": 4, "name": "Sophie", "age": 19 }
    ]
    ```

- This is the aggregation pipeline:

    ```
    db.users.aggregate([
      { $sort: { age: -1 } },
      { $limit: 3 }
    ])
    ```

- Here is the output:

    ```
    [
      { _id: 1, name: 'Justin', age: 28 },
      { _id: 3, name: 'Lauren', age: 26 },
      { _id: 2, name: 'Sydney', age: 23 }
    ]
    ```

With the same collection of users, consider an application that sorts users into age groups.

The aggregation pipeline that follows performs the following operations:

- Uses the $addFields aggregation stage to add an age_group field
- Uses the $group aggregation stage to group users by age group
- Uses the $sort aggregation stage to sort in ascending order
- Uses the $project aggregation stage to output the age group, number of users in each age group, and the names of the users in each age group

Here is the input:

```
[
  { "_id": 1, "name": "Justin", "age": 28 },
  { "_id": 2, "name": "Sydney", "age": 23 },
  { "_id": 3, "name": "Lauren", "age": 26 },
  { "_id": 4, "name": "Sophie", "age": 19 },
]
```

This is the aggregation pipeline:

```
db.users.aggregate([
  {
    $addFields: {
      age_group: {
        $switch: {
          branches: [
            { case: { $lt: ["$age", 18] }, then: "18 and under" },
            { case: { $lt: ["$age", 25] }, then: "19 to 25" },
          ],
          default: "26 and Older"
        }
      }
    }
  },
  {
    $group: {
      _id: "$age_group",
      count: { $sum: 1 },
      names: { $push: "$name" }
```

```
      }
    },
    {
      $sort: { count: 1 }
    },
    {
      $project: {
        _id: 0,
        ageGroup: "$_id",
        count: 1,
        names: 1
      }
    }
])
```

Here is the output:

```
[
  { count: 2, names: [ 'Lauren', 'Justin' ], ageGroup: '26 and Older' },
  { count: 2, names: [ 'Sophie', 'Sydney' ], ageGroup: '19 to 25' }
]
```

Best practices

In this section, we'll cover some key principles for writing efficient and robust aggregation pipelines.

Code modularity

Even the most complex aggregation pipelines should be structured as a series of clear, focused stages. Breaking your pipeline into logically separated parts not only improves readability but also makes it easier to test and debug each stage individually. For example, if you're using MongoDB Compass to prototype pipelines, you can temporarily disable specific stages without deleting them, which helps with iterative development. When working in a code editor, keeping stages clearly separated (often by commenting them out as needed) can improve maintainability. For example, the MongoDB extension for Visual Studio Code offers tools to help visualize, debug, and refine your pipelines. In the MongoDB Shell, where JavaScript is available, defining each stage as a separate variable and then assembling them into an array can make the pipeline structure easier to manage and modify.

Streaming and blocking stages of a pipeline

Aggregation stages generally fall into two categories: **streaming** and **blocking**. Streaming stages process batches of documents as they arrive, allowing data to flow continuously through the pipeline. In contrast, blocking stages must collect all incoming documents before performing their operation. Common blocking stages include $group and $sort, as well as others such as $bucket, $count, $sortByCount, and $facet, which also rely on full input accumulation.

Although blocking stages are sometimes necessary, placing them carelessly can negatively impact performance by increasing latency and limiting concurrency. To mitigate these issues, consider the following strategies:

- **Filter before sorting**: Whenever possible, use $match stages to reduce the working set before introducing expensive operations such as $sort. Early filtering can shrink the data volume significantly.

- **Sort early on indexed fields**: If $sort is required, try to sort on fields that are indexed and positioned near the start of the pipeline. This can substantially reduce the processing burden.

- **Combine $sort with $limit**: When only a subset of sorted documents is needed, placing $limit after $sort allows MongoDB to optimize the operation internally, reducing memory usage by narrowing the scope of documents early.

- **Avoid the $unwind + $group antipattern**: If you're modifying or summarizing arrays, prefer using array expression operators instead. They often provide better performance and clarity.

- **Defer field transformations**: When sorting or grouping, it's best to do so on fields that haven't yet been altered within the pipeline. Relying on existing indexed fields prior to mutation improves efficiency.

Query shapes

A **query shape** is a set of specifications that group similar queries. Queries that match the specifications have the same query shape. If you frequently run queries that have the same shape, you can take advantage of their shared qualities to optimize performance.

The following terms are also useful for this section:

- **Query plan**: A query plan is a method for executing a query. A single query can have multiple query plans that all produce the same results.
- **Query optimizer/planner**: The MongoDB query optimizer, also called the query planner, evaluates query plans and determines which plan to execute. Most often, the query plan that produces the most results during the evaluation plan while performing the least amount of work is the winning plan that MongoDB executes. The query optimizer evaluates queries with the same query shape as equivalent.

> Previously, MongoDB used the term *query shape* to specifically describe queries with shared qualities that the MongoDB query planner evaluates. MongoDB 8.0 renames the pre-existing query shapes to *plan cache query shapes*. The plan cache query shape (formerly, the query shape) supports query planning, deprecated index filters, and a subset of the aggregation pipeline.

With MongoDB 8.0, the new query shape supports the following features:

- Query settings
- `$queryStats` statistics
- Most fields and operands that are available for the `find`, `distinct`, and `aggregate` database commands
- The entire aggregation pipeline

Notably, the new query shape extends the aggregation capabilities of the plan cache query shape.

Queries also have a queryShapeHash, which identifies query shapes. Queries with the same query shape have the same queryShapeHash value.

Query settings

MongoDB 8.0 introduces the ability to specify query settings for query shapes. The MongoDB query optimizer takes query settings into account when it determines how to execute a query. Query settings are useful for specifying indexes or execution settings. To add query settings, use the setQuerySettings database command.

For example, you can use a query setting to specify the index that you want a query to use to optimize query performance.

Consider a users collection that contains the following data:

```
[
  { "_id": 1, "name": "Justin", "age": 28 },
  { "_id": 2, "name": "Sydney", "age": 23 },
  { "_id": 3, "name": "Lauren", "age": 26 },
  { "_id": 4, "name": "Sophie", "age": 19 },
]
```

This users collection also contains an ascending index on the age field, called age_1. The following command specifies a query setting for a find operation that uses filter and sort:

```
db.adminCommand({
  setQuerySettings: {
    find: "users",
    filter: {age: {$gt: 23 }},
    sort: {age: 1},
    $db: "test"
  },
  settings: {
    indexHints: {
      ns: {db: "test", coll: "users"},
      allowedIndexes: ["age_1"]
    },
    queryFramework: "classic",
    comment: "Index hint for age_1 index to improve performance"
  }
})
```

The following queries have the same shape and, therefore, the specified query setting applies to both queries:

```
db.users.find( { age: { $gt: 23 } } ).sort( { age: 1 } )
db.users.find( { age: { $gt: 21 } } ).scrt( { age: -1 } )
```

When MongoDB runs queries with this shape, the query optimizer takes the query settings into account as additional input.

Query settings commands

You can use the following database commands to manage your query settings:

- To add query settings, use the setQuerySettings command
- To delete query settings, use the removeQuerySettings command
- To retrieve query settings, use a $querySettings stage in an aggregation pipeline

Operation rejection filters

MongoDB 8.0 also introduces **operation rejection filters,** which temporarily reject operations that are associated with a specified query shape. An operation rejection filter is also known as a **rejected query shape.**

The query planner takes operation rejection filters into account when it determines how to execute a query. Operation rejection filters can be useful if an application has an inefficient query that leads to an excessive workload.

For example, if an application has a users collection and wants to prevent find operations that use filter and sort, a query setting with an operation rejection filter can prevent those operations.

Consider a users collection with the following data:

```
[
  { "_id": 1, "name": "Justin", "age": 28 },
  { "_id": 2, "name": "Sydney", "age": 23 },
  { "_id": 3, "name": "Lauren", "age": 26 },
  { "_id": 4, "name": "Sophie", "age": 19 }
]
```

The following setQuerySettings operation rejects find operations on the users collection that have filter and sort:

```
db.adminCommand({
    setQuerySettings: {
        find: "users",
        filter: {
            age: { $gt: 24 }
        },
        sort: {
            age: 1
        },
        $db: "test"
    },
    settings: {
        reject: true
    }
})
```

The output of this command shows the queryShapeHash field of the query shape that the query setting blocks.

If you attempt to run a query with the specified query shape, MongoDB returns the following error:

```
MongoServerError: Query rejected by admin query settings
```

To view your operation rejection filters, you can use the $querySettings and $match aggregation stages in an aggregation pipeline.

For example, the following aggregation pipeline on the users collection outputs the queryShapeHash of blocked queries:

- Here is the aggregation pipeline:

```
db.aggregate([
  { $querySettings: { showDebugQueryShape: true } },
  { $match: { "settings.reject": true } }
])
```

- This is the output:

```
[
  {
    queryShapeHash: 'AB8ECADEE8FCEB0F447A30744EB4813AE7E0BFEF523',
    settings: { reject: true },
    representativeQuery: {
      find: 'users',
      filter: { age: { '$gt': 24 } },
      sort: { age: 1 },
      '$db': 'test'
    },
    debugQueryShape: {
      cmdNs: { db: 'test', coll: 'users' },
      command: 'find',
      filter: { age: { '$gt': 24 } },
      sort: { totalNumber: 1 }
    }
  }
]
```

$queryStats statistics

$queryStats operations return a key field that contains the query shape and attributes that group similar queries. The key.queryShape nested document contains fields related to the query shape. The fields vary depending on the type of command that outputs the query stats entry. For example, the following table illustrates some of the fields that may appear in a key.queryShape nested document for a find command:

Field	Type	Literal or Normalized
key.queryShape.filter	Document	Normalized
key.queryShape.sort	Document	Literal
key.queryShape.projection	Document	Normalized
key.queryShape.skip	Integer	Normalized

Table 5.3: Fields in key.queryShape for Find Commands in $queryStats Output

Fields, operands, and aggregation pipelines

The MongoDB 8.0 query shape supports all of the fields and operands that the plan cache query shape supports. For example, the query shape supports `filter`, `sort`, and `project` operations. In other words, you can specify query settings on `filter`, `sort`, and `project` operations.

Additionally, the query shape supports most of the fields and operands that the `find`, `distinct`, and aggregate commands support.

The MongoDB 8.0 query shape also supports the entire aggregation pipeline. Prior to MongoDB 8.0, query shapes did not take entire aggregation pipelines into account. For example, in MongoDB 7.0, a `find` operation and an aggregate operation might share the same query shape if the operations are semantically similar. However, in MongoDB 8.0, query shapes take all stages of an aggregation pipeline into account to further differentiate query shapes.

New database commands

MongoDB 8.0 also provides new database commands with driver-level support to extend prior database capabilities. These commands are typically ad-hoc administrative tasks.

Collection database commands

MongoDB 8.0 introduces the following collection-level database commands:

- `abortMoveCollection`: Halts an in-progress `moveCollection` operation
- `unshardCollection`: Unshards an existing sharded collection
- `abortUnshardCollection`: Halts an in-progress `unshardCollection` operation
- `moveCollection`: Moves a single unsharded collection to a different shard

Server database commands

MongoDB 8.0 introduces the following server-level database commands:

- `transitionFromDedicatedConfigServer`: Transitions a config server from a dedicated config server to a config shard
- `transitionToDedicatedConfigServer`: Transitions a config server from a config shard to a dedicated config server

Summary

This chapter explored how to interact with your MongoDB data with basic CRUD operations, advanced queries, and aggregation pipelines. You learned about ways to create, read, update, and delete documents with both mongosh and PyMongo. To build on these basic database interactions, we looked at bulk operations that can perform multiple operations on multiple collections within the same request. You also learned about MongoDB's aggregation framework and explored several basic and advanced aggregation pipelines, using commonly used aggregation stages. This chapter also included information on aggregation best practices and query shapes, both of which can be used to enhance your data performance.

In the next chapter, we'll shift our focus from querying and data manipulation to the operational side of working with MongoDB. You'll learn how to monitor performance, set up secure deployments, configure backups, and implement auditing strategies. These tools and practices are essential for building reliable, scalable, and production-ready MongoDB systems.

6

Database Operations

Reliability and security are key factors that distinguish a production-ready database system from one in development. With the appropriate tools, you can optimize performance, troubleshoot potential disruptions, scale resources, update workflows, and ward off threats all before they impact your users. Ensuring you have these tools in place from the outset of development is the surest path to smooth deployment.

MongoDB and its attendant managed deployment services provide robust suites of monitoring, backup, and auditing to make operational maintenance simple. In this chapter, you will explore the importance of operational tooling; strategies to ensure consistent performance, accurate backups, and quick restores and how to configure, troubleshoot, and analyze auditing and logging.

This chapter will cover the following topics:

- The importance of database monitoring
- Key metrics to monitor in MongoDB
- Reporting and monitoring tools
- Cluster backup and recovery methods
- Database authentication principles
- Advanced monitoring and backup

Technical requirements

In order to follow along, you'll need to have a MongoDB cluster. Your MongoDB cluster can be either a self-managed installation or one managed by MongoDB Atlas, MongoDB Cloud Manager, or MongoDB Ops Manager. Where a specific tool is expected, the instructions will specify.

Monitoring

"What is not measured cannot be improved." – William Thomson, Lord Kelvin"

Monitoring is the foundation of any proactive database performance strategy. However rigorous and nuanced your initial system design may be, the usage patterns of real people will always surprise you. In the absence of careful, consistent monitoring, you will have to adopt a reactive posture, only reallocating resources and redesigning workflows once they have already impacted users.

MongoDB enables a proactive approach with a featureful suite of monitoring tools that offer granular insights into how your system is used in the real world, how effectively your architecture accounts for this, and where it has room for improvement.

Why monitor?

Before discussing specific aspects of monitoring, let's establish what we want to achieve with our monitoring tools. This will help motivate our specific strategic suggestions and give you a framework within which to devise your own use-case-specific refinements. Our goals are as follows:

- **Early detection**: Think of the monitoring suite as your early warning system. Keeping a weather eye on key metrics lets you anticipate issues and intervene before they impact users. Proactivity saves time, effort, and user frustration down the road.

- **Preemptive scaling**: If the load on your system increases without a corresponding increase in resource allocation, your users will experience service disruptions that can lead to attrition. Incorporate metrics to plan and execute upscaling in advance.

- **Cost management**: The same monitoring that tells you when to scale up can tell you when your system is overprovisioned and it's time to scale down, optimizing costs.

- **Performance optimization**: Efficient database operation is about more than just sufficient computational resources; it's also about indexes and retrieval operations themselves. Monitoring helps identify and remediate specific query bottlenecks.

- **Data integrity**: Regular monitoring ensures backup processes are behaving as expected and that data remains consistent, accurate, and available.

With these goals in mind, let's see how MongoDB helps achieve them.

Cluster monitoring

Monitoring in MongoDB happens primarily at the level of the cluster, the fundamental building block of any MongoDB-backed database deployment. When you design and first deploy your application, your cluster usage reflects your assumptions about user behavior and requirements; a robust monitoring strategy can validate or correct these assumptions and serve as the basis for future design adjustments.

Figure 6.1 illustrates various metrics of cluster performance as seen in MongoDB Atlas.

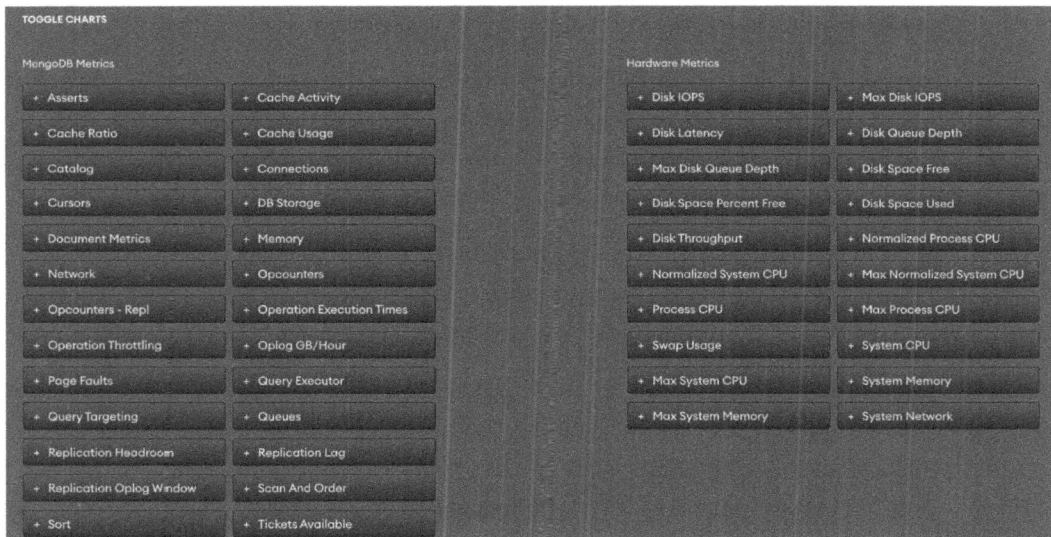

Figure 6.1: MongoDB Atlas metrics

Memory metrics

One of the most important metrics in MongoDB is memory usage. Like all database systems, MongoDB leverages system memory to boost performance, making it a top priority for monitoring. This section aims to provide high-level overviews of key memory concepts and common issues related to each concept, as well as monitoring and remediation strategies for those issues.

Page faults

The majority of data on a given system typically resides "on disk," that is, on **Hard Disk Drives (HDDs)** or **Solid-State Drives (SSDs)**. This is a sensible default, as these media are significantly more affordable per GB of storage, and they are non-volatile, meaning the data written on them persists unless explicitly deleted. However, reading data from disk is prohibitively slow for systems that receive thousands or millions of requests per second.

In contrast, RAM provides access speeds appropriate to such heavy-traffic applications, but it is much costlier per GB and is volatile, meaning it doesn't persist data during the disruption of service. Consequently, MongoDB employs a hybrid strategy for retrieving data:

1. Receive a query.
2. Search RAM for the requested data.
3. If found, return data to the application, or else continue.
4. Search the disk for the requested data.
5. If found, load data into RAM and return it to the application.

When your system has to fetch data from your disk, it's called a *page fault*, referring to data in RAM being structured in pages. With each page fault, newly loaded data consumes your reserve of free RAM. When your application exhausts this reserve, the operating system discards pages, called a *page eviction event*, to free up space for additional data later.

Page evictions can increase your system's I/O burden; the next time a page that was evicted is needed for a query, the database has to perform a slow read from disk again. This, in turn, can cause query latency to spike and CPU throughput to drop as the system waits for disk reads to complete.

While it's impossible to wholly eliminate page faults, especially with dynamic datasets, you should reduce their occurrence as much as you can. One powerful strategy is **stress testing**. In this approach, you create a test environment that mirrors your live setup and use this environment to push your system to its limits. Track how many page faults your system can handle before performance degrades and compare the stress test data with the actual page fault metrics in your live system to determine your available resource margin.

To gather the relevant data from a self-managed deployment, you can use the following:

```
db.adminCommand({ "serverStatus" : 1 })['extra_info']
```

Then, you can consult `extra_info.page_faults`. If you're using MongoDB Ops Manager, MongoDB Cloud Manager, or MongoDB Atlas, navigate to your deployment's metrics page and consult the **Page Faults** metric chart.

You can also reduce page faults by ensuring that the *working set*, that is, your most frequently accessed data, remains in RAM as much as possible. A practical strategy to achieve this is to refine your schema so that individual documents are smaller. If you observe excessive page faults in a cluster hosting a collection of very large documents, consider decomposing the large documents into multiple smaller documents according to which fields need to be accessed together, and using document references to embed the relationships between the resulting collections.

Resident memory

Resident memory, that is, the portion of available RAM that MongoDB actively uses, is one of the strongest indicators of the fitness of your database architecture. While leveraging the high-speed operations of RAM is the easiest way to improve database performance, you should take care to spare enough RAM for other system processes.

As a rule of thumb, resident memory should comprise no more than 80% of total available memory. The risk with using more is that you force the operating system to rely on swap space, operating on data on disk, rather than in memory, drastically slowing down your system. If you find your database regularly approaching or ever exceeding that 80% threshold, consider allocating more RAM and investigating your database design for possible memory savings.

To gather the relevant data from a self-managed deployment, you can use the following:

```
db.adminCommand({ "serverStatus" : 1 })['mem']
```

Then, you can consult mem.resident. If you're using MongoDB Ops Manager, MongoDB Cloud Manager, or MongoDB Atlas, navigate to your deployment's metrics page and consult the **Memory metrics** chart.

Virtual memory

Virtual memory is an allotment of space corresponding to some amount of physical RAM, disk space, or a combination of the two, with virtual addresses for accessing the underlying data. This is an abstraction of your operating system to put an overall cap on how much memory your applications can use. In addition to using virtual memory for ordinary operations, MongoDB allocates a separate virtual address for journaling when enabled.

Your operating system will refuse requests for further virtual memory if your current application workload has reached the cap. Consequently, monitoring your virtual memory consumption is an important part of your deployment strategy.

To gather the relevant data from a self-managed deployment, you can use the following:

```
db.adminCommand({ "serverStatus" : 1 })['mem']
```

Then, you can consult mem.virtual. If you're using MongoDB Ops Manager, MongoDB Cloud Manager, or MongoDB Atlas, navigate to your deployment's metrics page and consult the **Memory metrics** chart. If your usage patterns are pushing the limits of available virtual memory, you should scale up your system RAM to increase the available virtual memory.

We strongly recommend *against* deactivating journaling; while this can reduce your virtual memory footprint significantly, it compromises data integrity and system recoverability. Unless you have thoroughly analyzed these risks and developed and tested a specific mitigation strategy, this should not be considered a viable option.

Likewise, we recommend against raising your virtual memory cap at the operating system level as a long-term strategy. While it can serve as an emergency remediation in the short term if you are unable to scale up your hardware for any reason, an elevated virtual memory cap introduces the following challenges:

- **Increased swap activity**: An increased virtual memory allocation will come chiefly from disk space, meaning your system will swap operations to disk more frequently. This results in significant performance degradation.
- **Thrashing**: Under heavy workloads, the system may have to allocate more resources to managing memory pages than the desired operations.
- **Process killing**: Operating systems under extreme memory demand and heavily reliant on swapping can kill processes in unpredictable ways.
- **Transaction timeouts**: Long-running transactions are more likely to time out under heavy swap conditions.

If you must adopt this strategy to respond to spikes in user activity, you should prioritize hardware scaling as soon as possible.

WiredTiger

Storage engines are the components of database systems responsible for the reading, writing, and manipulation of data, including indexing, querying, updating, and transaction processing. Because storage engines determine the physical shape of data in memory and on disk, different storage engines can be optimized to produce physical access patterns more suitable for specific workloads.

By default, MongoDB uses the WiredTiger storage engine. WiredTiger establishes an internal memory cache, which is typically equal to half of your available RAM less 1 GB. For example, if you have a 16 GB RAM host machine, the WiredTiger cache would be (16 - 1)/2, or 7.5 GB, using the default settings. MongoDB then preallocates memory for handling connections and sort operations. You can adjust the WiredTiger cache using the `storage.wiredTiger.engineConfig.cacheSizeGB` parameter.

For most use cases, the default cache size is best. However, if you handle a large proportion of heavily compressed data, you can consider reducing the cache allocation to free up memory for other processes. Carefully monitor usage and performance patterns before making such an adjustment to determine an appropriate cache size and continue observing after the adjustment to determine its long-term viability.

In-memory storage engine

As an alternative to WiredTiger, 64-bit builds of MongoDB also support an in-memory storage engine, which, as its name suggests, does not maintain data on disk. This allows you to sidestep disk I/O, resulting in more predictable latency. Similar to WiredTiger's cache, this storage engine defaults to using half of the available RAM less 1 GB.

This storage engine does not persist data in any way; consequently, it is best on instances that serve as the user's point of contact with frequently accessed data. These instances can then be supported by another instance in the same cluster that runs the WiredTiger storage engine and handles data persistence.

I/O metrics

I/O metrics can often serve as helpful bellwethers for emerging memory-related issues. Closely monitoring these can allow you to anticipate performance degradation and implement remediation strategies as early as possible.

Waits and queues

I/O wait refers to how long an operating system waits for a given I/O operation to complete and can correlate with page faults. I/O wait increasing over time likely indicates that your system is dealing with a growing volume of page faults. You can use monitoring tools built into your operating system, such as top, to check your I/O wait time.

In turn, these I/O wait periods can cause backlogs of accumulating read and write requests. While memory monitoring is the heart of your proactive monitoring strategy, these I/O metrics can be considered the heart of your reactive monitoring strategy. A sustained increase in I/O wait times and read-write queues is a clear signal that active intervention is required.

To gather data on your read and write queues from a self-managed deployment, you can use the following:

```
db.adminCommand({ "serverStatus" : 1 })['queues']
```

If you're using MongoDB Ops Manager, MongoDB Cloud Manager, or MongoDB Atlas, navigate to your deployment's metrics page and consult the **Queues metrics** chart.

Free disk space

Databases commonly run low on free disk space as user data accumulates. Setting up alerts for when you reach disk use milestones such as 40%, 60%, and 80% is crucial for helping you stay on top of your hardware scaling, especially for systems that add large amounts of data quickly.

In addition to pure storage needs, free disk space is also essential for proper indexing. MongoDB automatically terminates index builds if you have insufficient disk space. You can view MongoDB's disk usage in MongoDB Ops Manager, MongoDB Cloud Manager, or MongoDB Atlas by navigating to your deployment's metrics page and consulting the **Disk Space Used metrics** chart.

To specifically check whether limited disk space is causing index builds to fail, you can use the following:

```
db.adminCommand({ "serverStatus" : 1 })['indexBuilds']
```

Then, you can consult the `indexBuilds.killedDueToInsufficientDiskSpace` property.

You should consider making compaction part of your disk space management strategy. Over time, delete and update operations, along with index rebuilds, can render storage blocks in your collection unused. MongoDB and MongoDB Atlas provide the `compact` command, which analyzes your database for obsolete blocks that have not been released back to the operating system, consolidates your data into contiguous blocks, and releases unused blocks.

Monitoring replication

Replication is an essential part of ensuring continuity of service in a database system. Replica sets store their synced state in the **operations log (oplog)**. As each operation takes place, it is written to the primary node's oplog, which takes the form of a capped collection. Secondary nodes asynchronously stream this oplog, writing operations to their own in the same order.

High volumes of write operations can hamper your primary node's ability to replicate events to the oplog in real time, which in turn slows down replication to secondary instances. The time it takes to replicate a write operation from the primary to a secondary is called *replication lag*.

If the time is 4:30 P.M. and your secondary node just applied an operation that was applied on your primary node at 4:25 P.M., you have a replication lag of five minutes.

In a production cluster, the replication lag should be close or equal to 0.

If you're using MongoDB Ops Manager, MongoDB Cloud Manager, or MongoDB Atlas, navigate to your deployment's metrics page and consult the **Replication Oplog Window** and **Oplog GB/Hour** charts.

Oplog size

The oplog contains a history of the operations performed on your MongoDB cluster that is used primarily to reconstruct the state of your cluster in the event of a service interruption. Every member in your cluster replica set stores a copy in db.oplog.rs(), so if your primary node fails or steps down, a secondary can be elected and ensure it's in an appropriate state. The oplog size doesn't affect memory usage.

Ensure you set aside enough storage space on disk for your oplog, and that the size limit you set for the oplog allows you to capture sufficient operation history for robust replication to protect against the consequences of replication lag. Given sufficient replication lag, your system can reach a state where the earliest record remaining in your primary node's oplog is newer than the most recent record that the secondary node has processed. Such a gap in the continuity between the oplogs represents a loss of track of operations that may have occurred, causing the secondary to halt replication. The smaller the oplog, the more likely this situation is to arise.

As a general rule, you should size your oplog to hold at least two days' worth of operations. It should also be longer than the time it takes for the initial sync given your current I/O and network bandwidth.

To set your oplog size in a self-hosted deployment, you can use the following:

```
db.adminCommand({ "replSetResizeOplog": 1, size: Double(<num>)})
```

Here, <num> is the size in megabytes to which you want to set the oplog. On MongoDB Atlas, you can set the oplog size using the following Atlas CLI command:

```
atlas clusters advancedSettings update <clusterName> --oplogSizeMB
```

Network monitoring

Network activity patterns provide another angle of insight into user behavior and system performance. Irregular network usage may indicate a need to redesign your data storage and distribution architecture to better service geographically diverse user bases. Additionally, time-dependent usage patterns can help you schedule maintenance and deployment windows to minimize service disruption.

For information about network activity in a self-hosted deployment, use the following:

```
db.adminCommand({ "serverStatus" : 1 })['network']
```

If you're using MongoDB Ops Manager, MongoDB Cloud Manager, or MongoDB Atlas, navigate to your deployment's metrics page and consult the **Network** chart.

Cursors and connections

Connection and cursor counts can act as proxies for overall user traffic and system responsiveness under load. This makes them helpful metrics to track when evaluating and refining your deployment architecture. Too many connections and open cursors can degrade database performance, and increases in timed-out cursors reflect already-occurring performance bottlenecks. Too few connections suggest an underutilized database, which may warrant downscaling your system to avoid overspending.

For information about cursors in a self-hosted deployment, use the following:

```
db.adminCommand({ "serverStatus" : 1 })['metrics.cursor']
```

If you're using MongoDB Ops Manager, MongoDB Cloud Manager, or MongoDB Atlas, navigate to your deployment's metrics page and consult the **Connections** and **Cursors** charts.

Replication opcounters

Tracking CRUD operations is obviously useful for discerning database utilization patterns but can also be a powerful tool for analyzing your system's network behavior. Specifically, the opcountersRepl metric, which tracks replication of operations from the primary oplog to the secondaries, can be used to identify desynchronization between nodes. If the two secondary nodes in a replica set display a significant disparity in replication operation counts, it could indicate network bandwidth or configuration issues between the lagging node and the primary.

For information about replication opcounters in a self-hosted deployment, use the following:

```
db.adminCommand({ "serverStatus" : 1 })['opcountersRepl']
```

If you're using MongoDB Ops Manager, MongoDB Cloud Manager, or MongoDB Atlas, navigate to your deployment's metrics page and consult the **Opcounters - Repl** chart.

Working set considerations

We briefly touched on the concept of the working set earlier, but it deserves further discussion due to its pivotal influence over your database's performance. Ensuring that your working set, that is, your most commonly accessed data, fits entirely within RAM should be a priority when designing your system to minimize page faults, evictions, and thrashing. This facet of your system will require constant observation, but as your application grows and the user base takes definite shape, the adjustments required should get smaller and smaller.

The obvious challenge in working this knowledge into your design is that, before you have a wealth of production environment data to work with, it may not be immediately apparent what the working set will look like and, by extension, what your RAM needs will be. You can form a rough estimate to begin planning your implementation by adding up the following:

- Enough data to satisfy 95% of user requests
- MongoDB logs
- Cached query plans
- An additional 50% margin above the sum of the former to account for indexes

Indexes and the working set

Indexes are crucial to fast data access. If you are unable to design your deployment such that your entire working set resides in RAM, prioritizing your indexes to reside in RAM can still go a long way to improving performance. Even if the actual data has to be fetched from disk, MongoDB can quickly locate it with the aid of in-RAM indexes.

Considerations for sharded clusters

In addition to the techniques described thus far, your monitoring strategy for sharded clusters should incorporate regular checks for config server health, data distribution, and locking.

Config server health

Your sharded cluster's config server orchestrates operations such as chunk distribution and mongos instance initialization. If your config server becomes inaccessible, your shards will gradually fall out of balance as some become overloaded with incoming data and others underutilized. For a self-hosted deployment, you can check connectivity to the config server using the following line:

```
db.adminCommand({ "serverStatus" : 1 })['sharding']
```

`sharding.lastSeenConfigServerOpTime` indicates the last time a given mongos instance or shard has seen an operation on the config server. If there is a discrepancy between this value and the last known operation time on the config server, this may indicate a connectivity issue.

MongoDB Ops Manager, MongoDB Cloud Manager, and MongoDB Atlas monitor config servers by default, and you can configure alerts pertaining to config server health through any of these tools.

Data distribution

A key advantage of sharded cluster deployments is the automatic, balanced distribution of chunks of data among the constituent shards. This is handled by a background balancer process that watches sharded collections and migrates data between shards when migration thresholds are met, attempting to reach as even a distribution of data across shards as possible. Monitoring this process can provide valuable insights into the fitness of your system design.

Data migration creates additional system overhead. If you observe reduced performance on your sharded clusters, use the `sh.isBalancerRunning()` command in mongosh to check whether it's due to an active migration. If frequent migrations consistently impact your sharded cluster, you can do either of the following:

- Increase the range size of the cluster, which reduces the frequency of migrations in exchange for a less even data distribution
- Set a shard balancing window, which limits the balancer to running migrations only during specific hours

You should carefully monitor range deletion as well. Range deletions are costly operations, and if they are too frequent or affect too many documents at once, they can degrade sharded cluster performance. If you notice degradation following range migrations, consider limiting the range deletion batch size and implementing time delays between deletions.

When you perform bulk data ingestion or export for a specific sharded collection, consider disabling the balancer for the duration of the operation; bulk operations are more likely to trigger migrations, diverting cluster resources. By disabling the balancer, you allow the bulk operation to proceed efficiently while mitigating the impact on users. Reenable the balancer when the operation is complete.

Monitoring disk usage across all shards is crucial to ensure that the balancer always has space to allocate data when running migrations. Furthermore, unexpectedly large discrepancies in disk usage between shards may indicate connectivity issues within your sharded cluster, or issues with the balancer process itself.

Locks

To prevent conflicts between migrations, the balancer registers a special database lock to the config database of a sharded cluster. If you observe that expected migrations aren't starting, use this command to check the status of the balancer lock and determine whether it's stale:

```
db.locks.find({ _id: "balancer"})
```

Data consistency

Manual manipulation of your config server or maintenance operations such as upgrades or downgrades can result in inconsistent sharding metadata if you do not properly prepare your sharded cluster beforehand. Inconsistent metadata can lead to incorrect query results or data loss. A proper maintenance strategy prevents this problem from emerging, but if you suspect a sharded cluster is suffering from metadata inconsistency, run the following:

```
db.runCommand({ checkMetadataConsistency: 1 })
```

MongoDB reporting tools

Now that you know what to look for, let's discuss how to look for it. MongoDB reporting tools can be divided into three broad categories: local tools, first-party-hosted tools, and third-party-hosted tools.

Local tools

Local tools for metrics reporting include dedicated command-line utilities and database commands. These are ideal options for quick feedback and provide performance data in easily digestible formats for custom analytics workflows.

Examples of local MongoDB reporting tools include:

- **mongostat**: Provides frequency and memory use information on a by-operation basis, enabling you to analyze user behavior and needs
- **mongotop**: Reports read-write activity levels on a by-collection basis, revealing utilization patterns and bottlenecks that can inform your data architecture

Database commands provide greater granularity than the dedicated utilities and are recommended for users who know the metrics with which they are most concerned:

- **serverStatus**: Provides comprehensive reporting on all facets of your database server. As detailed throughout this chapter thus far, you can isolate specific facets of your system operation by passing in arguments corresponding to subdocuments of the overall report.

- `dbStats`: Provides storage and capacity reports for a given database.
- `collStats`: Provides reports on collection-level metrics. This command is an essential part of monitoring indexing.
- `replSetGetStatus`: Provides a report on the status of the replica set as a whole.

First-party tools

In addition to the monitoring tools built directly into the MongoDB database server, MongoDB provides monitoring tools out of the box with each of its hosted database solutions:

- **MongoDB Cloud Manager**: A cloud-hosted suite for managing MongoDB deployments, providing monitoring, backup, and automation
- **MongoDB Ops Manager**: An on-premises equivalent to Cloud Manager
- **MongoDB Atlas**: A fully cloud-hosted and managed MongoDB deployment solution, offering several extensions to MongoDB functionality, such as Atlas Search, Atlas Vector Search, and Atlas Stream Processing

Third-party tools

MongoDB also supports a variety of third-party monitoring tools that interface with your MongoDB database to provide enriched metrics and/or helpful interfaces such as dashboards and mobile interfaces:

- **VividCortex**: An agent that analyzes MongoDB database statistics and network traffic to provide second-by-second performance insights.
- **Scout**: A fully cloud-hosted and managed MongoDB deployment solution, offering several extensions to MongoDB functionality such as Atlas Search, Atlas Vector Search, and Atlas Stream Processing.
- **Server Density**: Provides a MongoDB-specific dashboard, alerts, replication failover timeline, and mobile apps.
- **Application Performance Management**: A **software-as-a-service (SaaS)** offering from IBM that monitors application performance. This includes monitoring tools for MongoDB.
- **Datadog**: Infrastructure monitoring tool for visualizing the performance of MongoDB deployments. This integrates with MongoDB Ops Manager, MongoDB Cloud Manager, or MongoDB Atlas.
- **SPM Performance Monitoring**: Monitors all crucial MongoDB metrics and provides a correlation of metrics and logs.
- **Pandora FMS**: Provides the `PandoraFMS-mongodb-monitoring` plugin for MongoDB monitoring.

Monitoring with the Atlas CLI

In addition to monitoring tools similar to those offered in MongoDB Ops Manager and MongoDB Cloud Manager, MongoDB Atlas provides several commands for inspecting your deployment's performance through the Atlas CLI. For programmatic monitoring workflows, consider the following commands:

- **Atlas alerts**: A family of commands for interacting with metrics alerts you've configured for your Atlas deployment. The `describe` and `list` commands retrieve information about existing alerts, while the `settings` subfamily allows you to create and configure alerts.

- **Atlas metrics**: A family of commands for fetching performance metrics at either the database, disk, or process level.

Common monitoring pitfalls

A powerful monitoring suite is only as useful as the strategy you build around it. In addition to the general guidelines described so far, let's explore some common usage anti-patterns and how to avoid them:

- **Neglecting replica set status**: MongoDB's replica sets offer redundancy and high availability. However, not keeping an eye on the status of your replica set can lead to potential data loss or availability issues:

  - **How to avoid it**: Regularly check the health and status of each member in your replica set. Set up alerts for any changes in the replica set's status.

- **Using default configuration**: MongoDB provides a default configuration intended to offer sane defaults for most scenarios, but not optimized for particular ones. Relying on this configuration for production deployments can lead to performance bottlenecks:

  - **How to avoid it**: Regularly analyze middle- and long-term usage trends for your applications, and adjust your deployments to accommodate these trends

- **Ignoring storage warnings**: Running out of storage can bring your MongoDB server to a halt. Storage warnings may seem less important than memory-related warnings due to the difference in urgency, but neglecting these will lead to cascading performance degradations:

  - **How to avoid it**: Configure alerts for your storage metrics, and incorporate storage scaling and data archiving into your long-term deployment strategies from the beginning

- **Ignoring connection limits**: Each MongoDB instance has a limit to the number of simultaneous client connections it can maintain. Ignoring this limit can lead to refused connections, the consequences of which can be significantly more complex to remediate than preemptively responding to your increased connectivity demands would have been:

  - **How to avoid it**: Adjust your connection pool settings or scale your MongoDB deployments in advance of workloads that push your existing connection limits

MongoDB backups

"An ounce of prevention is worth a pound of cure."

One of the easiest and surest ways to improve the data integrity of your system is to implement a backup strategy. Unforeseen events compromise your data, up to and including outright data loss. While the replication built into the MongoDB cluster model can mitigate most such issues, physical or digital security breaches, human error, and natural disasters such as fires, floods, and earthquakes can impact all replicas in a set simultaneously. To truly protect against these scenarios, we turn to backups. MongoDB provides several methods for capturing and restoring backups.

Backing up with Atlas

MongoDB Atlas provides the Cloud Backups feature. This backup management service leverages the snapshot capabilities of your chosen cloud provider, AWS, Azure, or GCP, to back up your data, and provides intuitive controls through the GUI, API, or CLI. Atlas supports the following conveniences for backup management:

- Users can initiate on-demand backups and configure automatic, continuous backups. Continuous backups operate according to user-defined backup policies, allowing you to set the granularity, frequency, and retention time of snapshots.
- Users can configure multi-region clusters to automatically copy snapshots from one region to other regions, allowing you to restore data even in the event of region-scale service outages within your cloud provider.
- Users can enforce strict data protection by setting up a backup compliance policy. This greatly restricts the ability of users to manually scale down various backup settings or delete backup data.

- Atlas can apply encryption at rest to your data using a **Key Management Service (KMS)** provider.
- Users can export snapshots to AWS S3 buckets or Azure Blob Storage.
- Atlas automatically archives infrequently accessed data to object storage devices.
- Users can restore databases to Atlas using snapshots, continuous backups, locally downloaded snapshots, Cloud Manager snapshots, and even self-managed MongoDB deployments (with the mongoimport tool).

Additionally, you can manage Atlas backups either through Atlas CLI with the Atlas backups family of commands or with the Cloud Backups OpenAPI endpoint.

Self-managed platform backup

For those managing MongoDB on their own infrastructure, both MongoDB Ops Manager and MongoDB Cloud Manager provide backup tooling:

- **MongoDB Ops Manager:** For organizations that have reservations about connecting their servers to an external SaaS due to security or other concerns, Ops Manager is the go-to solution. It can be configured to write snapshots to blockstores, AWS S3 buckets, or a filesystem. It also supports regional backup, where each cluster or shard in your deployment reads from and writes to snapshot stores in a region of your choosing to support data isolation.
- **MongoDB Cloud Manager:** A cloud equivalent to the on-premises functionality of Ops Manager, with the same support for backup and restore conveniences.

Both of these services also provide queryable backups. These are provisioned as read-only MongoDB instances with 24-hour lifespans during which you can query the contents of the backup without restoring it to your deployment directly. This allows you to restore a subset of the data contained within, or else to determine the best point in time to which to restore a system by comparing data across snapshots.

Local backups

For those with entirely self-managed MongoDB deployments, several methods exist for creating a copy of the underlying MongoDB data files. Before we discuss specific approaches, let's examine a few practical considerations.

Consistency requirements

Your deployment must meet certain prerequisites in order to take a valid snapshot of a mongod instance. The most basic is that you must have journaling enabled, and the journal must reside on the same logical volume as all other data files relevant to your MongoDB deployment. You can't guarantee your snapshot's consistency or validity without first meeting these conditions.

Sharded clusters require a few additional considerations to ensure consistency. First, you must disable the balancer process to ensure that no chunk migrations initiate during the snapshot process, or else you run the risk of either duplication or data loss. You should also run the fsync command, which is discussed in more detail later in this chapter, against your mongos instance to help ensure cluster-wide consistency. This command blocks incoming write operations to the cluster, ensuring that your backup captures a single, stable state.

Full versus incremental backup

As your MongoDB deployments grow, there comes a point where executing full backups each time is impractical due to the time and resource requirements. Fortunately, MongoDB supports incremental snapshots: after you take the first snapshot of a given deployment, subsequent snapshots capture only data that has changed in the intervening period. This reduces disk use, network use, and memory use, though these incremental snapshots are dependent on underlying full snapshots for restore functionality.

Strategically, you should evaluate your application's usage pattern to determine an appropriate frequency for full backups and complement these with a nightly incremental snapshot policy. Consider beginning with a monthly full backup, adjusting as you develop a clearer understanding of what your users need and what your system can handle.

Ops Manager, Cloud Manager, and Atlas all provide robust support for incremental backups and heavily streamline the process. You can still perform incremental backups using a self-managed MongoDB deployment leveraging the oplog. To do so, follow this procedure:

1. Make an initial full backup using any of the supported local backup methods described later.
2. Temporarily lock writes on the secondaries of your replica set.
3. Identify the most recent entry in the oplog.
4. Export the subsequent oplog entries.
5. Unlock writes on the secondaries of your replica set.

If you wish to restore from this manual incremental snapshot, use mongorestore with the --oplogReplay option, utilizing the exported oplog.rs file.

Backing up with mongodump

mongodump is a command-line utility that creates a binary backup of the data in your MongoDB cluster. It is meant to be paired with the mongorestore utility to restore from an existing snapshot.

mongodump is non-blocking, meaning you write data to your cluster while running it; to add these writes to the output oplog, simply pass the --oplog flag. You can then restore from this composite backup using the --oplogReplay flag when you run mongorestore. This does not apply to sharded clusters, which must be write-locked using fsync before you initiate a mongodump.

While this approach is effective for smaller deployments, as your system scales up, you will likely encounter performance limitations using these tools. When you restore a database with mongorestore, you need to kick off a rebuild of all your indexes, which can place significant demands on system resources for a long time. Additionally, these operations force the database to read all data through memory, which can result in evictions of data in your working set, slowing performance beyond the duration of the operation.

Filesystem snapshots

If your storage system supports snapshots, leveraging this functionality can be one of the fastest approaches for a local backup. The following table describes a few storage systems that support filesystem snapshots:

Operating System Solutions	Cloud Storage Solutions
Logical Volume Manager (LVM)	Amazon EC2 Elastic Block Store (EBS)
ZFS	Azure Disk Storage
BTRFS	Oracle Cloud Block Volumes
Microsoft Storage Spaces	Google Cloud Persistent Disk

Table 6.1: Filesystem snapshot-enabled storage solutions

Each of these systems comes with its own tooling for interacting with logical volumes, but the basic workflow for creating filesystem snapshots can be summarized as follows:

- Ensure journaling is enabled for your MongoDB deployment.
- Determine to which logical volumes on the target storage system your dbPath is linked.
- Target your snapshot creation to those logical volumes.
- Validate your backup by mounting the snapshot and initiating a mongod process against the data. Establish a connection to that mongod instance and inspect the dataset.

Backing up with cp or rsync

If your storage system does not support snapshots, you can copy the files directly using cp, rsync, or a similar tool. Since copying multiple files is not an atomic operation, you must stop all incoming writes to the target mongod before copying the files. Otherwise, you will produce an invalid backup.

Backups produced by copying the underlying data do not support point-in-time recovery for replica sets and can be cumbersome for large and/or sharded clusters. Furthermore, these backups take up considerable storage space because they include indexes and duplicate underlying storage padding and fragmentation.

Cluster-to-cluster sync

MongoDB supports data replication across clusters using the mongosync utility. While not strictly a form of backup, this operation holds an important place in your redundancy and continuity strategy, allowing you to automate the process of transferring data and indexes between clusters. The sync process takes place in two phases: the sync phase and the commit phase. During the sync phase, mongosync alters various properties of indexes and capped collections to facilitate writes to the target cluster; these alterations are only reversed during the commit phase, meaning you cannot ensure idempotency of data across the clusters if you interrupt the process during the sync phase. mongosync doesn't support rolling index builds, so ensure that you plan to perform an index build either on the source cluster before the sync or on the target cluster after the sync as part of your migration.

Common backup pitfalls

Backups are a crucial tool for protecting data integrity, but don't let the peace of mind they provide turn into complacency. Backups themselves need to be managed with care to ensure they actually serve their intended purpose. Let's examine some common problems that can arise in backup strategies:

- **Backing up without oplog data:** The oplog tracks all operations that modify data. It's the basis of point-in-time restores, as well as a crucial part of self-managed incremental backups; without the oplog, these features won't function:
    - **How to avoid it:** Ensure that your oplog data is backed up as rigorously as your actual application data
- **Not verifying backups:** Unverified backups can turn temporary disruptions of access into permanent data loss:
    - **How to avoid it:** Verify backups by performing test restorations in controlled environments and inspecting the contents to ensure they match your expectations

Monitoring and backup are essential to the reliability of MongoDB deployments. The former lets you plan and design for optimal performance, while the latter safeguards against data loss. MongoDB provides methods ranging from the command line to the extensive suite of GUI tools in Atlas, allowing users to choose how they conceptualize and implement their strategies. Whether on-premises or in the cloud, you will have the information and reliability needed to get the most out of your data.

Just as important as being able to analyze current system behavior and recover from current service interruptions is the ability to trace the history of events within your system. This is where auditing comes into play.

Auditing

Database auditing is the tracking and recording of operations, whether read-write operations on data, user authentications, or other administrative actions. Maintaining such a history helps to ensure that your system provides the user with security, compliance, diagnostics, and accountability.

Audit logs can reveal suspicious patterns of activity that point to compromised authentication or authorization, allowing you to remediate existing security threats and adjust your system design to prevent further threats. Hand in hand with strengthening your security posture, proper auditing ensures that user data protection and access requirements match the strictest regulatory standards, fulfilling your organization's obligations to users and regulators.

System administrators can read audit logs to diagnose issues of performance and data integrity with extreme granularity above and beyond even the finest time-bound metrics. This same granularity ensures the accountability of being able to attribute all database operations to specific users.

Given its importance, your auditing strategy warrants a thoughtful approach that balances system performance and capacity with selective retention policies. Before you implement your strategy, ensure that you have a clear sense of which types of activity warrant this level of granularity.

System logging versus auditing

Logging and auditing are closely related concepts in MongoDB, but they are not interchangeable. Both serve different but equally important purposes as part of your monitoring and administration strategy and produce different outputs. There is some overlap between the concepts, but a look at some examples should help clarify the differences.

First, we have an example of a typical log message:

```
{
  "t": {
    "$date": "2020-05-01T15:16:17.180+00:00"
  },
  "s": "I",
  "c": "NETWORK",
  "id": 12345,
  "ctx": "listener",
  "svc": "R",
  "msg": "Listening on",
  "attr": {
    "address": "127.0.0.1"
  }
}
```

This entry tells you that the MongoDB server started with the specified parameters, as shown in the attr attribute. In this case, the attribute contains parameters from the configuration file (mongod.conf).

In comparison, here is a typical audit record:

```
{
  "atype": "createCollection",
    "ts": {
      "$date": "2025-04-21T16:09:33.810-04:00"
    },
    "uuid": {
      "$binary": "ZF9aa2odPqSg74C/Lf1yJk==",
      "$type": "04"
    },
    "local": {
      "ip": "127.0.0.1",
      "port": 27017
    },
    "remote": {
      "ip": "127.0.0.1",
      "port": 56292
    },
```

```
    "users": [
      {
        "user": "admin",
        "db": "admin"
      }
    ],
    "roles": [
      {
        "role": "root",
        "db": "admin"
      }
    ],
    "param": {
        "ns": "audit.coll1"
    },
    "result": 0
}
```

This entry tells us what happened, when it happened, where it happened, and who took the action.

With these examples in hand, we can see the key distinctions between general logging and auditing:

	System Logging	**Auditing**
Goal	Facilitate monitoring, diagnosis, and performance optimization by capturing server events and state	Facilitate compliance, security, and investigation by capturing data access and modification events
Granularity	Less granular, focusing on a breadth of different activities and facets of system state	More granular, tracking at the level of specific actions, users, or even documents
Nature of data	Structured as JSON	Structured as JSON, with additional support for the OCSF schema built in
Retention	Intended to be rotated at regular intervals to prevent the overconsumption of storage capacity	Intended to be retained for arbitrarily long periods to uphold data security and access regulations and facilitate investigations
Destiny	Typically stored locally; may be consumed by analysis and monitoring tools	Forwarded to **Security Information and Event Management (SIEM)** systems and/or long-term storage media

Table 6.2: Differences between general logging and auditing

In summary, system logging provides comprehensive monitoring and diagnosis of the system state. It provides the breadth to your logging strategy. In contrast, auditing observes specific actions for security and compliance purposes. It provides the depth.

System logging

While we will focus mostly on audit logging, a few aspects of system logging are worth considering to get the most value out of them.

Verbosity

MongoDB system logs can be configured for different levels of verbosity, increasing or decreasing the volume of logging done by MongoDB. Verbosity levels correspond to the severity categories of the log entries: a higher verbosity level shows messages for lower-severity items, while a lower verbosity level limits the output to only higher-severity items. When determining the verbosity level of your system logging, consider the following:

- For which components of your system do you want the most or least detailed logging?

  MongoDB allows you to set different verbosity levels for various components, such as `ACCESS`, `COMMAND`, and `ELECTION`.

- How confident are you in the correctness of your system?

  When you are still developing your database in a staging environment, a higher verbosity level improves the utility of your logs for general debugging. However, logs do take up storage space and require write operations, so for a fully vetted production deployment, consider setting a low verbosity level to minimize resource consumption.

To view your current verbosity levels, you can use the following:

```
db.getLogComponents()
```

You can set your verbosity levels by editing the `systemLog.verbosity` setting in your `mongod.conf` file.

Redaction

MongoDB provides built-in log redaction with the `redactClientLogData` parameter. If you enable this setting in your `mongod.conf`, everything except metadata, source files, and line numbers is redacted in your log messages. This adds an additional layer of data security to your system, though it reduces the diagnostic utility of your logs. If your system handles sensitive data, consider implementing this as part of your compliance strategy.

Logging on managed deployments

In addition to the MongoDB process logs available to self-managed MongoDB deployments, MongoDB Atlas logs authentication attempts made against your clusters, which you can view with the `atlas accessLogs list` command in the Atlas CLI, or by visiting the **View Database Access History** page for your cluster.

MongoDB Ops Manager and MongoDB Cloud Manager provide logs for each MongoDB agent in your deployment, as well as logs of access, backup, operations, and startup events. These can be found by navigating to the **Deployment** pane, selecting the **Agents** tab, and then clicking **Agent Logs** in your Cps Manager or Cloud Manager GUI.

Audit logging

By configuring auditing, administrators can filter events that are relevant to their needs, ensuring they have a detailed view of critical activities while minimizing information clutter.

Audit log formats

The example audit log message shown previously used the mongo schema. While MongoDB defaults to this schema, it also supports the OCSF schema, a widely used standard format compatible with many log-processing tools. You can set the schema used for auditing with the `auditLog.schema` option in `mongod.conf`.

The following example message describes an authenticate action according to the OCSF schema:

```
{
    "activity_id" : 1,
    "category_uid" : 3,
    "class_uid" : 3002,
    "time" : 1710715316123,
    "severity_id" : 1,
    "type_uid" : 300201,
    "metadata" : {
        "correlation_uid" : "20ec4769-984d-445c-aea7-da0429da9122",
        "product" : "MongoDB Server",
        "version" : "1.0.0"
    },
```

```
    "actor" : {
      "user" : {
        "type_id" : 1,
        "groups" : [ { "name" : "admin.root" } ]
      }
    },
    "src_endpoint" : { "ip" : "127.0.0.1", "port" : 56692 },
    "dst_endpoint" : { "ip" : "127.0.0.1", "port" : 20040 },
    "user" : { "type_id" : 1, "name" : "admin.admin" },
    "auth_protocol" : "SCRAM-SHA-256",
    "unmapped" : { "atype" : "authenticate" }
}
```

Due to the broader compatibility of the OCSF schema, we strongly recommend you consider adopting this schema for your audit logs.

Types of auditable events

The following is a nonexhaustive list of the types of events MongoDB audits:

- **Authentication and authorization events:**

    - authenticate and authCheck: Events related to user authentication

    - logout: User logout events

- **User management events:**

    - createUser, dropUser, dropAllUsersFromDatabase, and updateUser: Events associated with creating, modifying, and managing users

    - createRole, dropRole, grantRolesFromUser, and revokeRolesFromUser: Events associated with creating, modifying, and managing roles

- **Data operation events:**

    - createCollection, dropCollection, and renameCollection: Events associated with collection management

    - createDatabase and dropDatabase: Events associated with database management

    - createIndex and dropIndex: Events associated with index management

- **Administrative operation events**:

  - enableSharding, addShard, removeShard, and shardCollection: Events related to sharding operations

  - replSetReconfig: Events associated with the configuration of replica sets

- **Startup and shutdown events**:

  - startup and shutdown

Enabling auditing in self-managed deployments

Before you enable auditing in MongoDB, you must choose where and how to store your audit logs. MongoDB supports a variety of output formats to suit different organizational requirements. Each of the following examples uses the storage.dbPath.auditLog parameter for configuration:

- **Console**:

  - Write audit logs directly to your console's standard output (stdout).

  - This output method does not persist your audit log data and is not suitable as a standalone solution. This is useful for testing or to pass the logs directly to another tool for additional processing before writing the logs to disk:

    ```
    storage:
      dbPath: data/db
    auditLog:
      destination: console
    ```

- **JSON**:

  - Write audit logs as JSON-formatted files.

  - This output method is a highly compatible approach to storing your audit logs. In addition to supporting the many tools that have built-in methods for ingesting and processing JSON data, it allows you to import records directly into a MongoDB collection, or a collection in any other document-model database:

    ```
    storage:
      dbPath: data/db
    auditLog:
      destination: file
      format: JSON
      path: data/db/auditLog.json
    ```

Note that this format requires two additional parameters, one to specify the type of file output and the other to specify the file path to which you want to write the log.

- **BSON:**

  - Write audit logs as a binary representation of JSON-like data
  - This option optimizes for integration with MongoDB, trading generic compatibility for efficiency:

    ```
    storage:
      dbPath: data/db
    auditLog:
      destination: file
      format: BSON
      path: data/db/auditLog.json
    ```

- **Syslog:**

  - Write audit logs directly to syslog, a standard UNIX/UNIX-like logging tool
  - This facilitates integration with a class of log management and monitoring tools built around the ingestion of syslog events:

    ```
    storage:
      dbPath: data/db
    auditLog:
      destination: syslog
    ```

The most suitable choice for you depends on a balance of regulatory compliance, the suite of tools you want to build around your audits, and the degree of system lock-in with which you are comfortable.

MongoDB Ops Manager and MongoDB Cloud Manager support auditing as well, offering convenient GUI options for configuring it through a given MongoDB process's *advanced configuration options*.

Enabling auditing in Atlas

Atlas also facilitates MongoDB auditing for all clusters at the M10 tier or higher. Follow this procedure to enable auditing:

1. Log in to your Atlas project, and select **Advanced** from the **SECURITY** section of the left-hand nav menu:

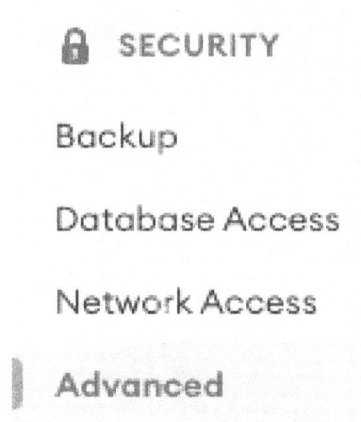

Figure 6.2: Advanced security configuration

2. Toggle the **Database Auditing** button to the *On* position:

Database Auditing

Database auditing allows you to customize log downloads with the users, groups, and actions you want to audit.

Figure 6.3: Enabling database auditing

3. After enabling the feature, configuration options appear below. These options allow you to set up audit filters using a selection menu by default.

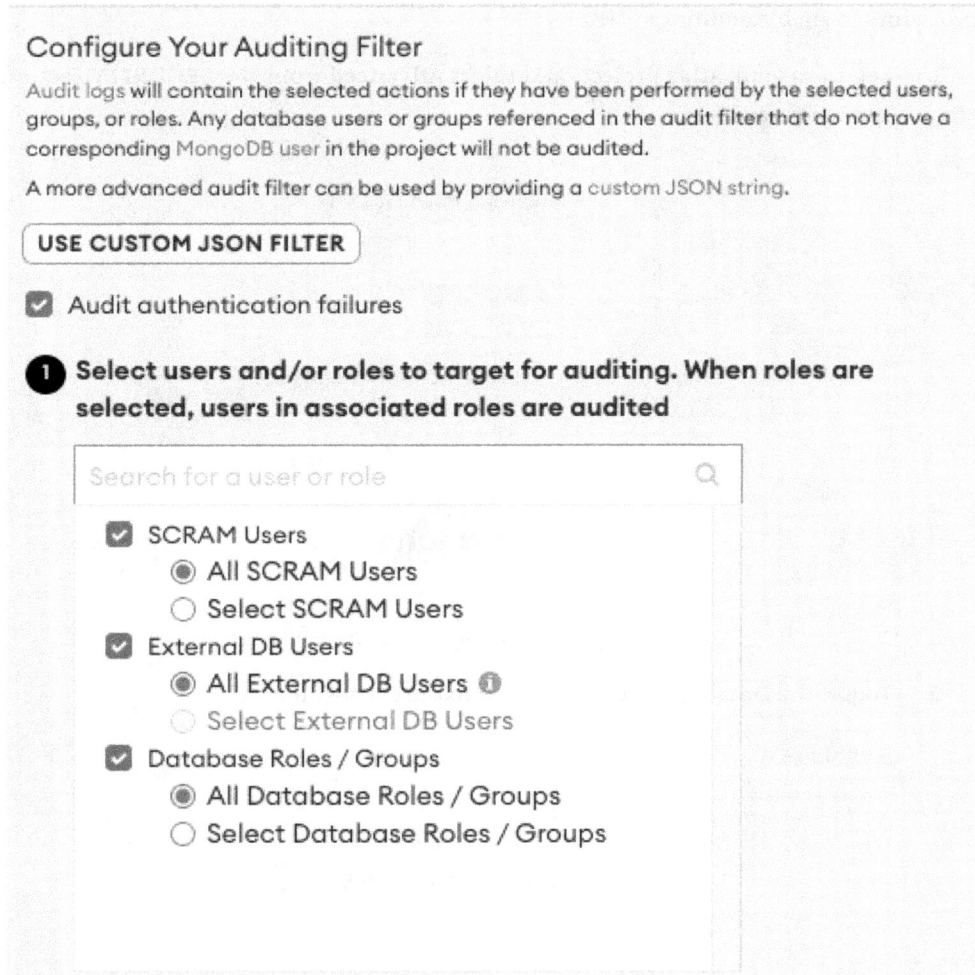

Figure 6.4: Using the filter builder

4. Alternatively, you can click the **USE CUSTOM JSON FILTER** button to manually define your filter via a JSON expression.

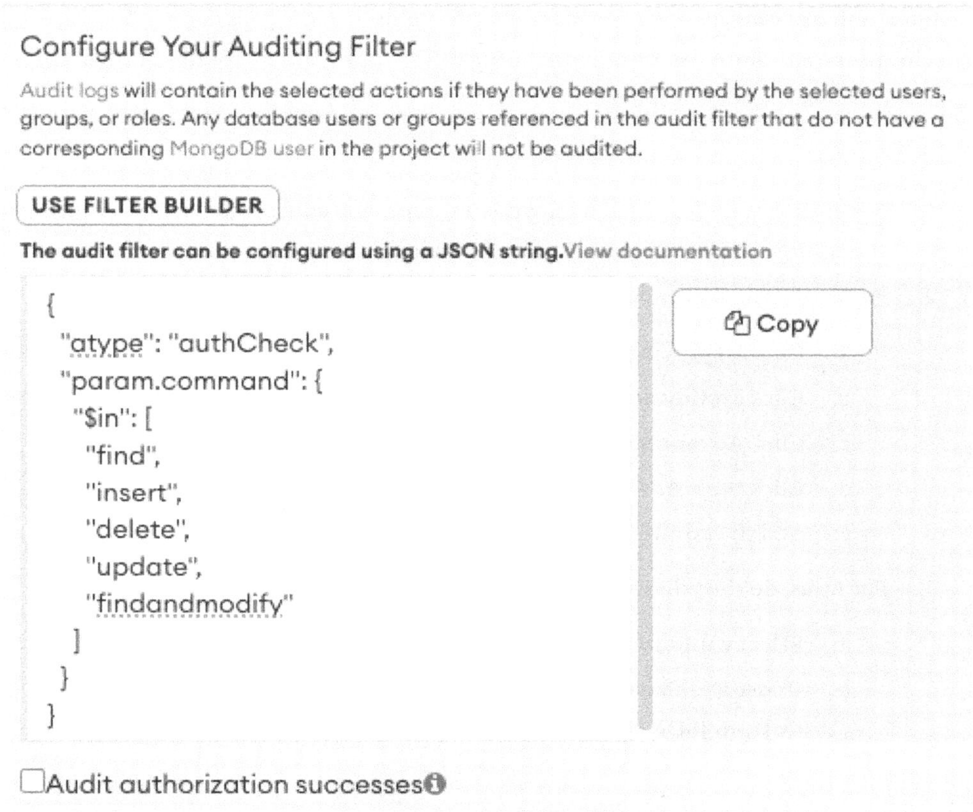

Configure Your Auditing Filter

Audit logs will contain the selected actions if they have been performed by the selected users, groups, or roles. Any database users or groups referenced in the audit filter that do not have a corresponding MongoDB user in the project will not be audited.

USE FILTER BUILDER

The audit filter can be configured using a JSON string. View documentation

```
{
  "atype": "authCheck",
  "param.command": {
    "$in": [
      "find",
      "insert",
      "delete",
      "update",
      "findandmodify"
    ]
  }
}
```

Copy

☐Audit authorization successes❶

Figure 6.5: Defining a custom JSON filter

5. Regardless of which option you choose, click the **Save** button to apply the changes.

In addition to these generally available MongoDB audit logs, Atlas keeps a log of trigger, function, and change stream events, which it publishes to your Atlas project's activity feed. These logs are retained for 10 days, after which they are deleted. To retain these logs beyond 10 days, download your currently available logs as described later in this chapter.

Audit filters

Auditing all of the event traffic on your system would rapidly consume your storage and incur significant performance penalties. Just as importantly, the overwhelming volume of data thus captured could make investigations or any kind of meaningful analysis more onerous by drowning the signal in noise. Audit filters allow administrators to avoid these pitfalls by specifying which events they want to audit and which they don't.

To filter your auditing, define criteria for specific fields in audit documents. Criteria can filter on specific users, specific collections, specific operation types, or any combination of these.

Once you have enabled auditing in your deployment as described previously, how you define audit filters varies by deployment type:

1. For entirely self-managed deployments, manually edit `mongod.conf` according to one of the configuration patterns described previously.

2. For Ops Manager or Cloud Manager, do the following:

    a. Click **Deployment**, then **Processes**.

    b. Click **Modify** next to the mongod process for which you want to configure auditing.

    c. Click **Advanced Configuration Options**.

    d. Click the **+ Add** option.

    e. Add the **auditLogFilter** property.

3. For Atlas, do the following:

    a. Select your project and click **Advanced**.

    b. Under **Database Auditing**, select **Configure Your Auditing Filter**, then click **Use Custom JSON Filter**.

Filters take the form of JSON documents. For example, to audit all actions of the user `jim` authenticating against the `admin` database, use the following filter:

```
{ "users" : [ { "user" : "jim", "db": "admin" } ] }
```

Here are a few examples of audit filter patterns:

*   **Audit read operations for any user in the collA collection of the db1 database:**

    ```
    {
      "atype": "authCheck",
      "param.ns": "db1.collA",
      "param.command": {
        "$in": [
          "find"
        ]
      }
    }
    ```

- **Audit all update operations for any user in any collection:**

```
{ "atype": "update" }
```

- **Combine auditing criteria:** By combining multiple audit criteria, you can refine your filter, making it more granular. The following example captures only delete operations against the collA collection made by the user jim:

```
{
  "users": [
    {
      "user": "jim",
      "db": "admin"
    }
  ],
  "atype": "delete",
  "param.ns": "db1.collA"
}
```

- **Change parameters at runtime:** The db.adminCommand command, when called with the setAuditConfig argument, allows you to alter filters at runtime:

```
db.adminCommand(
  {
    setAuditConfig: 1,
    filter: {
      "atype": "authCheck",
      "param.command": {
        "$in": [
          "find",
          "insert",
          "delete",
          "update",
          "findAndModify"
        ]
      }
    }
  }
)
```

This example reconfigures audit filters for CRUD operations on any database. Note that when you change settings at runtime in this manner, they revert to those defined in your mongod.conf when you restart the server. If you want these changes to be permanent, always persist them by writing them in mongod.conf.

- **Check current audit parameters:**

```
db.adminCommand({ getAuditConfig: 1 })
```

It's important to remember that auditing can introduce performance overhead. You can mitigate this concern with the careful use of audit filters to capture only the events you need. You should also test your filters in a development environment before rolling them out to a production deployment, verifying the following:

- Acceptable performance impact
- Capture of expected events
- No unwanted side effects

Database profiling

To round out your system analysis strategy, MongoDB provides the database profiler, which logs detailed information about database commands against a running mongod instance to a capped collection called system.profile. This feature is off by default but can be activated by setting the operationProfiling.mode parameter to the appropriate integer value in your mongod.conf.

When activated, the profiler introduces some performance and storage overhead. When you use the profiler as part of your testing strategy in a staging environment, these considerations can be balanced on the fly. If you want to perform database profiling in a production environment, it's important to carefully evaluate your needs and priorities before enabling the profiler.

For most use cases where database profiling is desirable, consider setting the profiling level to 1. If you use a slowms time threshold, set it to the maximum value your system can wait on a given event. If you use a filter, select only those events that are of greatest interest.

A profiling level of 2 captures *all* events and thus introduces the heaviest overhead. This profiler level is only recommended for testing environments.

Viewing and downloading logs

There are multiple ways to access logs depending on the nature of your MongoDB deployment. For self-managed MongoDB, Ops Manager, or Cloud Manager deployments, your deployment writes logs to a file path of your choice, in a format of your choice.

In MongoDB Atlas, you can do the following:

- **Download logs through the GUI**: On your project overview page, for a given cluster, click the ellipsis icon (**...**) and select **Download Logs** from the drop-down menu:

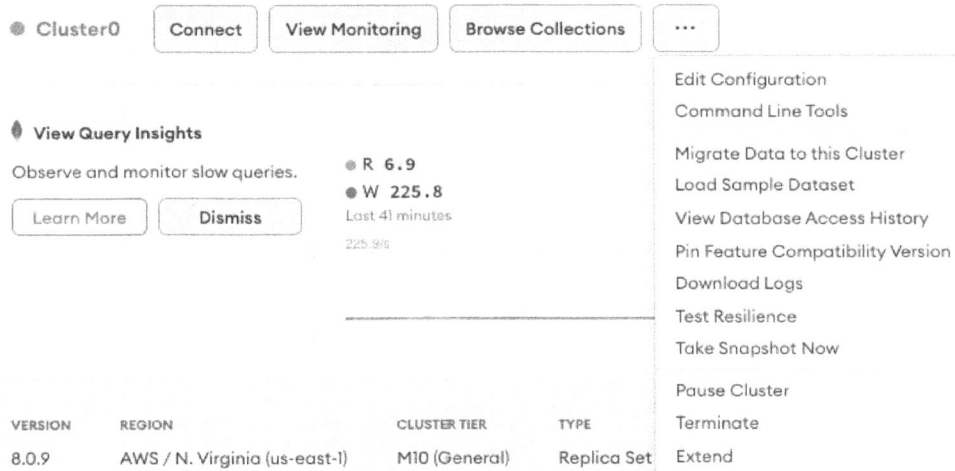

Figure 6.6: The Download Logs action

- **Download logs with an API call**:

  - Create or retrieve your public and private Atlas API keys through your organization's **Access Manager** page

- Retrieve your project ID using the **Copy Project ID** action on the **Projects** page:

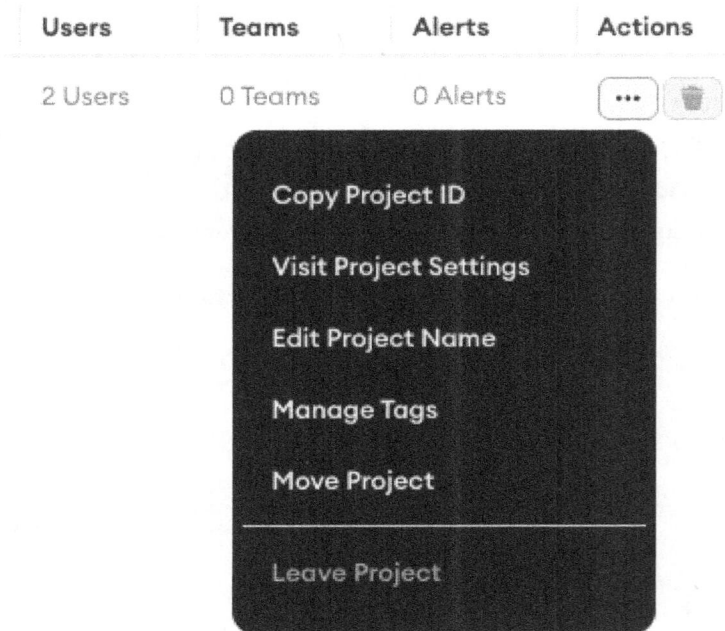

Users	Teams	Alerts	Actions
2 Users	0 Teams	0 Alerts	··· 🗑

Copy Project ID

Visit Project Settings

Edit Project Name

Manage Tags

Move Project

Leave Project

Figure 6.7: Retrieving your project ID

- Retrieve your MongoDB cluster hostname from your **Clusters** page

Once you have all four parameters, make an API call of the following form:

```
curl --user "{public_key:private_key}" \
     --digest \
     --header "Accept: application/gzip" \
    GET  "https: //cloud.mongodb.com/api/atlas/v2/groups/{groupId}/
clusters/
{hostname}/logs/{logName}.gz"
```

Here, groupId is your projectId and hostname is the cluster hostname.

Alternatively, you can download cluster logs with the Atlas CLI using atlas logs download.

Log rotation

Over time, your deployments will accrue large volumes of logging data, even with aggressive filtration. The storage and memory requirements to retain or read very large log files can interfere with system performance, so a fully fleshed-out logging strategy will involve regular log rotation. Broadly speaking, you have three approaches to log rotation for self-hosted MongoDB deployments:

- You can use the MongoDB built-in logRotate command. It archives the current log file, appending an ISODate-formatted timestamp to the name for easy reference, then opens a new log file.

- You can set the systemLog.logRotate parameter to reopen in your mongod.conf, in which case MongoDB will leverage the Linux/UNIX logrotate utility. This utility closes your current log file and reopens a log file with the same name, expecting that another process renamed the file prior to rotation.

- You can configure mongod to write log data to the syslog. In this case, you can use any log rotation utilities that you would use with an ordinary syslog.

Regardless of which method you choose, be aware that log rotation is not replicated. You must ensure each instance in a replica set undergoes log rotation individually.

For managed deployments on Ops Manager or Cloud Manager, you can configure automated log rotation for any cluster managed by a MongoDB agent. To do so, navigate to your deployment's **MongoDB Log Settings** page and toggle **System Log Rotation** to on, then configure the log rotation settings. You can set both the file size and time thresholds beyond which your logs are automatically rotated. Atlas rotates logs automatically by default.

Case study: Auditing for compliance

Consider auditing in the context of a healthcare information management system. The system provides appointment scheduling, patient record management, prescription management, and more. Healthcare information is among the most sensitive personal information that exists and must be handled with care to ensure the highest standards of data security, integrity, and privacy. Regulations such as the **Health Insurance Portability and Accountability Act (HIPAA)** codify this need. Auditing for such a system must do the following:

- Track access and modifications to patient records
- Monitor the actions of all admin users
- Ensure compliance with data privacy regulations and standards
- Enable quick investigation and response to suspicious activity

Given the preceding requirements, a sound auditing strategy might include the following features:

- **Configuration and filtering:**

    - Filters to audit CRUD operations on key collections, for example, medical records, prescriptions, and schedules

    - Filters to monitor the behavior of admin users and others with access to sensitive data

- **Attribution and identification:**

    - Secure authentication, **Unique User Identification** (UUID)

    - Logs of detailed user information, such as ID, IP address, and actions taken

- **Periodic review and analysis:**

    - Routine review of audit logs for anomalous patterns and suspicious activity

    - Log analysis tools to highlight acute anomalies or chronic patterns

- **Retention and backup:**

    - Audit log retention policies in conformance with relevant regulations (e.g., a six-year retention term under HIPAA)

    - Regular backup of audit logs to ensure data integrity via redundancy

- **Incident response:**

    - Response plan leveraging audit logs as primary sources in investigations

    - Audit-log-based incident analysis procedure

While this is not meant to be a comprehensive list or policy recommendation, this list illustrates the many ways a robust auditing practice can bolster the health and security of a health information system.

Troubleshooting auditing

Auditing is an essential component of a robust system architecture, but it is only as effective as your strategy surrounding it; simply having audit logs does not guarantee "robust auditing." It is therefore important to periodically review your auditing practice itself, much as you periodically review the audit logs, to ensure you are making the most of the data you have collected. Some factors you should consider during these strategic reevaluations include the following:

- **Frequency of audit review:** Is the frequency with which you review your audit logs appropriate to the activity load of your system? Too infrequent and it becomes harder to find the information you're looking for, the more incidents may accumulate between reviews to split attention, and the more likely you are to forget older incidents.

- **Review prioritization:** When you use analysis tools, how clear are your search priorities? Patterns are easiest to spot when you know what you're looking for and can narrow the scope of the information to investigate early in the process. If your review sessions are too wide-ranging, consider examining your priorities.

- **Alerts and real-time response:** While audit logs are meant to be long-term artifacts, this does not preclude their usefulness in remediating current issues. Make sure you have real-time response plans in place for specific anomalies.

- **Conduct internal compliance reviews:** Regularly assess how your auditing regimen aligns with or deviates from the relevant regulations in your jurisdiction.

- **Monitor performance:** Auditing can impact your system's performance if overused. If you experience bottlenecks, consider rewriting your audit filters to be more specific and reduce the overall volume of audit activity.

- **Stay informed:** Stay updated on best practices and updates related to auditing in MongoDB to avoid known issues.

Tools for audit analysis

With a robust auditing regimen and regular review process in place, the final piece of the puzzle is the tooling you'll use to analyze your audit logs. Your options can be divided into three categories:

- **First-party tools:** MongoDB provides Compass, a graphical tool for intuitively viewing and querying document-model data. If you configured your deployment to write audit logs as JSON or BSON, you can import your audit logs directly into a MongoDB collection and use Compass to view them just as you would view any other data in a collection.

- **Third-party tools:** Any third-party tool that can ingest JSON, BSON, or syslog data can integrate with your MongoDB deployment. For example, you could use Splunk, a popular data analysis platform for indexing and analyzing audit logs.

- **System tools and custom scripts:** Finally, you can use command-line utilities common to most systems, such as grep, or write your own scripts in a language of your choice to read, filter, and analyze your audit data.

Summary

In this chapter, you explored monitoring, backups, auditing, and security configuration in MongoDB and how each of these is a crucial piece of the overall puzzle that is operational design, analysis, and refinement. You learned about the various challenges, opportunities, and tools available in each facet, and how to develop and implement strategies that ensure your database system meets and anticipates your users' needs.

MongoDB affords a high degree of granular control over these facets of your system, requiring and rewarding a thoughtful approach by system architects. Armed with the knowledge in this chapter, you can design a system that is fast, reliable, and safe for users, and easy to administer and scale for developers.

In the next chapter, you will learn about MongoDB Atlas in detail, exploring its many conveniences for MongoDB development and deployment, as well as powerful extensions to the database's core functionality.

Get This Book's PDF Version and Exclusive Extras

UNLOCK NOW

Scan the QR code (or go to `packtpub.com/unlock`). Search for this book by name, confirm the edition, and then follow the steps on the page.

Note: Keep your invoice handy. Purchases made directly from Packt don't require an invoice.

7

Security

In today's technology-driven world, data security is paramount. With the increasing volume of sensitive information being stored and transmitted, ensuring its protection is crucial to avoid potential risks and consequences.

Security is an ongoing process that requires continuous monitoring and improvement. As administrators, it's essential to stay informed about the latest security practices, respond to incidents when they occur, and proactively address potential vulnerabilities before they lead to problems.

MongoDB offers a variety of security measures to protect your data, whether it's at rest, in transit, or in use. Security involves two key components: authentication, which controls who can access the data, and authorization, which defines the level of access. Additionally, protecting data requires encryption, such as **Transport Layer Security (TLS)** and MongoDB's Queryable Encryption.

This chapter will cover the following topics:

- Application security
- Data security
- Security mechanisms for self-managed deployments

Technical requirements

To follow along with the tutorials in this chapter, you need access to the following:

- MongoDB installed locally
- MongoDB Node.js driver

Application security

Application security refers to the measures and practices used to protect applications from security threats and vulnerabilities. This includes safeguarding data, ensuring proper access controls, and preventing unauthorized actions within the application.

It involves two pillars: authentication, or who can access your database and data, and authorization, which determines the user's level of allowed access in the database.

Security requires constant monitoring and reevaluation. As a MongoDB administrator, you must remain aware of what methods you're using for application and data protection, best practices for these methods, and changes to them. The best security strategy both responds to incidents and proactively tries to prevent them.

To protect your data's authentication, MongoDB offers support for multiple authentication methods, such as SCRAM and X.509 certification.

SCRAM

MongoDB's default method for authentication is **SCRAM**, or **Salted Challenge Response Authentication Mechanism**, created by the **Internet Engineering Task Force (IETF)**. When a user authenticates themselves, MongoDB uses SCRAM to verify the supplied user credentials against the user's name, password, and authentication database. SCRAM enables user authentication without sending a plaintext password over a network, where it can be intercepted by malicious attackers.

SCRAM authentication in MongoDB uses the following components:

- **Salted password**: A salt is a random sequence generated for each user. The salt is combined with each user's password to make passwords more secure by making them more unique and preventing brute-force attacks.

- **Secure password storage**: Salted passwords and authentication data are stored in MongoDB using methods to improve security, such as password encryption.

- **Challenge-response**: SCRAM uses a method for authentication called challenge-response. Essentially, the client first sends a challenge to the server (in your case, to MongoDB), including its username and a unique random value, known as a *nonce*. The server responds with its own nonce concatenated with the client's nonce, as well as a salt. The client responds with a "proof," which is computed using a hash function that takes the data sent by the server and the client's original password. Finally, the server checks the client's proof, and if it matches its own proof based on information stored in its database, the server sends a message confirming that authentication was successful.

- **Number of iterations**: You can configure the number of iterations between the client and server allowed in SCRAM authentication. More iterations means that more time is required to compute the response, which makes brute-force attacks challenging to execute.

- **Secure communication channel**: For the most secure authentication, communication between the client and server must be encrypted, typically by using TLS.

The main idea behind SCRAM is that the user's password is never transmitted over the network. Thus, even if an attacker could intercept this communication, they would not be able to discover the user's password because they don't know the hash function used, nor the salt.

SCRAM is secure, simple, and easy to understand. However, it requires some work to manage. Since authorization occurs locally, additional responsibilities are added to the administrator. You must also have a plan if a credential becomes exposed.

X.509 certification

In addition to traditional authentication options, such as passwords, you can use authentication based on X.509 certificates in MongoDB. X.509 is an **International Telecommunication Union (ITU)** standard that defines the format of public key certificates. Digital certificates that follow the X.509 standard are used to authenticate clients and servers over secure connections. These certificates contain information such as the user's or server's identity or public key, as well as a **Certificate Authority (CA)**'s signature.

MongoDB supports X.509 certificate authentication for clients as well as for internal authentication of individual replica set members. For production use, your MongoDB deployment should use valid certificates generated and signed by a CA. You or your organization can generate and maintain an independent CA or use certificates generated by third-party TLS vendors.

To authenticate to servers, clients can use X.509 certificates instead of usernames and passwords. For internal authentication between members of sharded clusters and replica sets, you can use X.509 certificates instead of keyfiles.

X.509 is a powerful authentication mechanism but requires careful certificate management. Best practices include repeated certificate renewal, restricting access to keys for client and server certificates, and monitoring connections to your database.

X.509 certification requires the following fundamentals:

- **X.509 certificates**: Digital certificates that follow the X.509 standard. These contain information such as the user's or server's identity and public key, as well as a CA's signature. They are used during authentication.

- **CA:** This is a trusted entity responsible for issuing and signing digital certificates. The CA guarantees the authenticity of the certificates and, therefore, the identity of the users and servers involved in the communication.

- **Client certificate:** This is the digital certificate used by the client (application or user) to authenticate with MongoDB. This certificate is CA-signed and contains customer-specific information.

- **Server certificate:** This is the digital certificate used by the MongoDB server to authenticate with clients, which is signed by the CA as well.

These are the essential steps for implementing X.509 certificate authentication in MongoDB:

- **Choosing a CA:** Selecting or creating a trusted CA is the first step. In corporate environments, there is usually an internal CA, but you can also use recognized public CAs, such as AWS or Google Cloud.

- **Certificate generation:** The CA is responsible for generating server and client certificates. For this, you must create a pair of keys (public and private) for each entity, sign the keys with the CA, and store them correctly.

- **Certificate distribution:** All machines that will access MongoDB should have a client certificate. Additionally, make sure that you configure the server certificate in MongoDB.

So far, we have discussed two different methods for user authentication, or who can access your database. The next section describes how you can control authentication and authorization, or what data a user can access, by using **Role-Based Access Control (RBAC)**.

Authorization and role-based access control

While authentication is about controlling who can access your database, authorization is about defining how a user can interact with your database and its data. MongoDB controls user authorization through RBAC, which is used to efficiently define permissions for users.

In MongoDB, you can efficiently manage user permissions with RBAC. A **role** in MongoDB is a designation assigned to a user that defines certain permissions. Roles allow database-level granularity in access; in other words, roles are attached to databases, and by granting a user a role for a specific database, you define their permissions for how they interact with that database.

For example, a user with a read access role on a certain database can read data on that database but cannot change or delete it. This role does not affect how the user can interact with other databases. There are a few exceptions to this definition, including when roles are assigned on the admin database.

In MongoDB, roles can be built-in or user-defined. Built-in roles are already defined by MongoDB. User-defined roles can be created and defined by the user as needed. Assigning roles to users, rather than granting individual permissions for each user, simplifies the access management process, especially in large and complex environments.

Using RBAC has several advantages:

- It provides granular control over permissions. Organizations can define a wide range of roles to reflect the different responsibilities and access needs of users.

- It helps enforce the principle of least privilege, a security practice that involves granting users only the permissions they absolutely need to perform their tasks.

- It can help simplify the audit process by making it easier to verify who has access to what.

To understand RBAC, it's important to understand the three aspects of database access:

- **Resources:** The entities involved in database authorization, including databases, collections, clusters, and users themselves.

- **Database actions**: The possible actions that can be performed within or on a database, collection, or cluster. These include actions such as **create/read/update/delete (CRUD)**, replication actions, sharding actions, and database deployment.

- **Database built-in roles**: The pre-existing roles defined by MongoDB. Roles are attached to specific databases. Each role contains different permissions, and some roles supersede others. For example, a user with only a read role can only read data on a certain database, but a user with a readWrite role can read data and write to collections in a certain database. Built-in roles follow this hierarchy:

  a. **Level 0 – database user:** This level includes basic roles that every database can provide. Level 0 includes the following roles:

     - read
     - readWrite

  b. **Level 1 – database administrator:** This level includes roles that allow database management. These roles can be attached to any database. Level 1 includes the following roles:

     - dbAdmin
     - dbOwner
     - userAdmin

c. **Level 2 – cluster administrator:** This level includes roles that allow basic and management roles on multiple databases. These roles can only be attached to the admin database in a cluster. Level 2 includes the following roles:

- dbAdminAnyDatabase
- clusterAdmin
- clusterManager
- directShardOperations
- enableSharding
- hostManager
- userAdminAnyDatabase
- readAnyDatabase
- readWriteAnyDatabase
- clusterMonitor
- backup
- restore
- root

Higher-level roles can inherit permissions from lower-level roles, meaning that you can grant roles to specific users, which simplifies permission management because you don't need to grant multiple different permissions to multiple users. For example, if you grant the readAnyDatabase role to a user, you do not need to additionally grant the read role to a user since readAnyDatabase already includes the permissions that read includes.

User-defined roles

If MongoDB's built-in roles do not fully describe the privileges you want for a user, you can create custom user-defined roles using MongoDB's db.createRole() method in mongosh. Similar to built-in roles, user-created roles are defined on a specific database and are only applicable to that database, with the exception of roles created on the admin database, which can apply to and inherit from roles defined on other databases.

You can use the db.createRole() method in the MongoDB Shell to create a new role. For example, say you want to define a very stripped-down user role in which an application can only read collection metadata or perform queries on data. The built-in read role offers more permissions than these, so we need to create a barebones role:

```
db.createRole( {
    role: "my-role",
```

```
    privileges: [
      {
        resource: {
          db: "my-db",
          collection: ""
        },
        actions: [ "find" ]
      }
    ],
    roles: [ ]
} )
```

By calling this method, we have created a role called my-role that operates on all collections in the database called my-db. This role only contains the find privilege action, which allows it to perform queries, list collections, and more read-only tasks.

db.createRole() allows you to customize the roles that you create. This is important for limiting access to data based on users. As with built-in roles, you want to ensure that you're following the **principle of least privilege** when creating a role; that is, grant a user or application the minimum possible role that they need to perform their task.

If necessary, you can use this in conjunction with the external authentication mechanisms described throughout this chapter. However, to ensure the maximum level of control over your roles, it is best practice to create authorization roles within your MongoDB deployment while using an **External Identity Provider** (EIP) for authentication only.

Another use case of user-defined roles is that you can define access privileges by restricting based on a client's IP address. To do this, you define the clientSource and serverAddress parameters when creating a user-defined role. The clientSource parameter is the IP address of the client trying to connect to the MongoDB server, and serverAddress is the IP address of the MongoDB server being connected to. If either of these parameters is set, the user will only be able to connect to the MongoDB server if the corresponding IP address is within the restrictions.

For example, if you set clientSource to 194.154.1.1, only users with the IP address 192.168.1.1 will be able to connect to the MongoDB server. If you set serverAddress to 192.154.1.1, only users who are connecting to the MongoDB server with the IP address 192.154.1.1 will be able to connect. These two parameters can also be used in conjunction to further restrict access: for example, setting both clientSource and serverAddress to ensure that only users with the IP address 192.168.1.1 can connect to a MongoDB server that uses the IP address 192.154.1.1.

Now that you've learned how to use security mechanisms to configure who is able to access your database and what they're able to access, continue reading to learn about how to protect your data at all points of its life cycle through encryption and aggregation pipeline methods.

Data security

With an increase in the need to protect sensitive information and data privacy regulations becoming more stringent, organizations are placing greater emphasis on data security. Regulations such as the European Union's **General Data Protection Regulation**, which aims to protect the privacy of European citizens; the **Health Insurance Portability and Accountability Act (HIPAA)** in the United States, which governs data security in the healthcare sector; and the **Payment Card Industry Data Security Standard (PCI DSS)**, a compliance framework for credit cardholder data and security, all dictate that organizations prioritize the safety and security of personal data.

Data must be protected at all points in its life cycle: at rest on the physical disk, in transit between the client and server, and in use within a client. MongoDB provides security features such as key management, TLS support, Queryable Encryption, and Client-Side Field Level Encryption to ensure that your data is protected at all times. If you are using a self-managed deployment, you can also use some of these methods in conjunction with those described in the next section, which covers security for self-managed MongoDB deployments.

Encryption at rest with key management

Encryption at rest protects data stored on a physical disk. Data is automatically encrypted at the file level, ensuring that even if someone gains physical access to the disk, your data remains secure.

MongoDB Enterprise Advanced offers support for encryption at rest. MongoDB uses the AES-256 encryption algorithm to encrypt data. AES-256 is a strong encryption algorithm and is used in a wide variety of compliance standards. This algorithm uses a symmetric key, meaning that it uses the same key to encrypt and decrypt data.

Encryption at rest uses multiple levels of keys to provide a combination of security and performance. It involves a **master key**, which is a highly secret and protected encryption key that is used to encrypt other keys, known as **data keys**. Data keys, or database keys, are used to encrypt the data within a specific database, or even specific sets of data within a database.

Encryption at rest generally involves the following steps:

1. Generate the master key using a **Cryptographically Secure Random Number Generator (CSRNG)**. This key must be stored securely, preferably by using an external **Key Management Service (KMS)**. If the master key is compromised, then all database/data keys are compromised as well. Typically, keys are 256 bits.

2. Generate keys for each database, or (optionally) for each set of data, also with a CSRNG. These keys are directly used to encrypt data, so they must be readable by the database.

3. Encrypt data with the data keys. When data is written to the database, the system uses the key corresponding to the database (or set of data) to encrypt the data before writing it to disk. Similarly, when the data is read, the process is reversed: the encrypted data is read from the disk and then decrypted using the database key.

4. Encrypt the data keys with the master key. To increase security, data keys are encrypted with the master key. Even if the data keys are compromised, they are useless without the master key. Data keys should be stored in a secure location, but readable by the database.

The advantage of this multi-level system is that the most critical master key can be securely stored and rarely accessed. Database keys, which are accessed more frequently, are less critical in terms of exposure because they are always encrypted when stored.

The following best practices should be kept in mind when using encryption at rest:

- **Secure storage:** You must use a secure filesystem or storage device that supports data encryption.

- **Performance:** Encryption can impact performance for intensive read or write operations. Ensure that you keep performance impact in mind when choosing encryption algorithms.

- **Key management:** Ensure that you securely store your encryption keys.

- **Backup and recovery:** When creating backups of encrypted data, it's important to ensure that the backups are also encrypted.

- **Version compatibility:** Check the MongoDB version compatibility with encryption at rest since this feature may vary between versions.

- **Lost key recovery:** Ensure that you have mechanisms in place in case you lose an encryption key. Recovering data without an encryption key can be impossible.

Key management is important for protecting data at rest via encryption. The concept of key management is also important for protecting data when it's in use, particularly in CSFLE and Queryable Encryption, which you will read about later in this section.

Encryption in transit with TLS

Encryption in transit protects data during transmission between MongoDB clients and servers. This is achieved by using the TLS protocol, which encrypts data before it's sent over the network.

Transport encryption protects MongoDB by encrypting all network traffic, meaning that a packet transmitted using TLS/SSL can only be read by the end client. Network encryption should be used whenever possible. TLS provides the following security benefits:

- **Authentication**: Servers and clients authenticate each other using certificates
- **Confidentiality**: Ensures that data in transit cannot be read or decoded by malicious actors who may be monitoring the network
- **Integrity**: Ensures that data remains intact during transmission over the network

In MongoDB Atlas, network encryption is enabled by default and cannot be disabled. For on-premises clusters, you may choose to implement TLS by setting the `net.tls.mode` parameter in the configuration file to one of the following values:

- `requireTLS`: The client must use TLS
- `preferTLS`: The client can use TLS, and replication will be used whenever possible
- `allowTLS`: The client can use TLS
- `disable`: The server does not support TLS

To use TLS/SSL with MongoDB, you must have TLS/SSL certificates as **Privacy-Enhanced Mail (PEM)** files, which are concatenated certificate containers. These files can be issued by a CA, or they can be self-signed. You or your organization can generate and maintain an independent CA, or use certificates generated by third-party TLS vendors such as AWS or Google Cloud.

These are some considerations for enabling encryption in transit for MongoDB:

- **System requirements**: You must configure a TLS/SSL certificate from a trusted CA.
- **Resource consumption**: Encryption in transit can have a performance impact on large read or write operations. Keep performance in mind to ensure that your system can handle additional overhead.
- **Driver compatibility**: Ensure that MongoDB drivers used in your application support encryption in transit. Some drivers may require a specific configuration to use it.
- **Latency**: Encryption introduces some latency due to the encryption and decryption of data. This may be negligible in most cases but is something to consider in latency-sensitive applications.

- **Proper configuration:** You must configure MongoDB to use TLS/SSL connections, and ensure that all connections are secure.

- **File safety:** Keep the .pem (certificate) file in a secure directory, and be aware of the permissions of the directory containing the file. Ensure that the directory is only accessible by the MongoDB user and that other users do not have read, write, or execute permissions.

Client-Side Field Level Encryption

In-use encryption secures data that is being transmitted, stored, and processed, and supports queries on that encrypted data. MongoDB provides CSFLE and Queryable Encryption to facilitate in-use encryption, which works alongside in-transit and at-rest encryption to protect data throughout its complete life cycle. Both of these methods use the key management method of encryption described earlier, which involves data keys to encrypt the data and a master key to encrypt the data keys. You cannot use Queryable Encryption on a collection that you are using CSFLE on, and vice versa.

CSFLE allows applications to encrypt specific document fields in a collection before sending that data to MongoDB. With this technique, the encryption and decryption processes take place exclusively on the client side, ensuring that the database server never has access to unencrypted data. Sensitive data is stored and processed securely via key management, ensuring that even though an attacker could obtain encrypted data from sensitive fields, they would not have the keys or the necessary context to decrypt them.

CSFLE is an excellent option for organizations that want to encrypt one field, but not every field in their database. By protecting data at the field or document level, CSFLE can be used in situations where certain data, such as **Personally Identifiable Information** (PII), requires extra protection due to regulations or privacy requirements.

MongoDB offers flexibility when you adopt CSFLE. To perform CSFLE, MongoDB can use two types of encryption algorithms. The first is the deterministic encryption algorithm, which ensures that a specific input value will always result in the same encrypted value each time the algorithm is executed. However, if the unencrypted data has low cardinality, or a small number of distinct values, deterministic encryption can make it easier to perform frequency analysis on the encrypted data, essentially, to reverse-engineer it back to its unencrypted form. Additionally, deterministic encryption does not support encrypting entire objects and arrays. If you need to make queries to your encrypted data, it is possible to do so when using the deterministic algorithm. However, it is better to use Queryable Encryption if you need to make queries.

The second type of encryption algorithm is randomized encryption, which ensures that a given input value always encrypts to a different output value each time the algorithm is executed. While randomized encryption provides stronger guarantees of data confidentiality than deterministic encryption, it also prevents support for any read operations, which must operate on the encrypted field to evaluate the query. Randomized encryption supports encryption on entire objects and arrays.

MongoDB allows you to automatically encrypt your data before writing it to the database. For read operations, the driver encrypts field values in the query prior to issuing the read operation. For read operations that return encrypted fields, the driver automatically decrypts the encrypted values only if the driver was configured with access to the data keys and master key used to encrypt those values.

MongoDB uses schema validation to enforce encryption of specific fields in a collection. Without a client-side schema, the client downloads the server-side schema for the collection to determine which fields to encrypt. Because CSFLE and Queryable Encryption do not provide a mechanism to verify the integrity of a schema, relying on a server-side schema means trusting that the server's schema has not been tampered with. If an adversary compromises the server, they can modify the schema so that a previously encrypted field is no longer labeled for encryption. This causes the client to send plaintext values for that field. To avoid this issue, use client-side schema validation.

You also have the option to explicitly encrypt fields when using CSFLE. While this allows more fine-grained control over security than automatic encryption, it can result in increased complexity when configuring collections or writing client-side code. You must explicitly specify when to encrypt data during read and write operations. Even if you are explicitly encrypting your fields, you have the option to automatically or explicitly decrypt your encrypted fields.

While MongoDB abstracts much of the complexity associated with key management, you must properly manage and protect the encryption keys, especially the master key. When you set up CSFLE, you must define which fields in your collections should be encrypted and with which algorithm. The client automatically generates data encryption keys for each encrypted field. Each client has its own data encryption keys. When a client wants to access encrypted data, MongoDB automatically provides the appropriate decryption keys to decrypt the protected fields. This process is transparent to the client, meaning that the client does not need to manage decryption keys or perform manual decryption operations. MongoDB takes care of this automatically; even if you are explicitly encrypting and decrypting your fields, you can simply call an encrypt or decrypt method to perform the operation.

If you implement CSFLE, keep the following considerations in mind:

- **Performance**: Client-side encryption and decryption can impact performance, especially for intensive read or write operations. Keep this in mind when choosing your encryption algorithm.

- **Encrypted data querying**: Querying for encrypted fields can add some overhead, especially if the field is encrypted using random encryption. In this case, you may need to query a randomly encrypted field by using a proxy. See the MongoDB documentation to learn more.

- **Master key**: Keep secure backups of your master key. Losing or compromising the master key means losing access to data

- **Driver compatibility**: Not all programming language drivers support CSFLE, or to the same extent.

- **Data regulations**: You can use CSFLE to comply with data protection regulations such as GDPR, as MongoDB never sees unencrypted data. If you need to comply with a certain regulation, ensure that you keep all the requirements of the regulation in mind.

- **External KMS**: You can use an external KMS such as AWS KMS or Google Cloud KMS to manage your encryption keys.

For more information on implementing CSFLE, refer to the MongoDB documentation: `https://www.mongodb.com/docs/manual/core/csfle/`.

Queryable Encryption

Queryable Encryption enables a client application to encrypt data and send it over the network while maintaining queryability. Like in CSFLE, sensitive data is transparently encrypted and decrypted by the client and only communicated to and from the server in encrypted form. Unlike CSFLE, however, Queryable Encryption uses **searchable encryption** schemes based on **structured encryption**, meaning that the data is encrypted in such a way that queries can be executed over the encrypted data. It uses a master key and data key as described previously in the Key Management section.

Queryable Encryption works in the following way:

1. When a query is submitted, the MongoDB driver analyzes the query. If the driver recognizes the query is against an encrypted field, it requests the encryption keys from a customer-provisioned key provider such as AWS KMS. It then submits the query to the MongoDB server with the fields encrypted.

2. Queryable Encryption implements a fast, searchable scheme that allows the server to process queries on fully encrypted data, without knowing anything about the data. The data and the query itself remain encrypted at all times on the server.

3. The MongoDB server returns the encrypted results of the query to the driver.

4. The query results are decrypted with the keys held by the driver and returned to the client, shown as plaintext.

In order to enable Queryable Encryption on your application's data, you must create an encryption scheme. When you create this scheme, when you choose fields to be encrypted, you can determine how you want to query these fields. You can either use equality queries, which test for equality, or range queries, which test for values within a specific range.

The following tutorial offers an overview of how to use Queryable Encryption with MongoDB. This tutorial uses automatic encryption. For more information, including details and the most up-to-date instructions, see the Queryable Encryption Quick Start in the MongoDB documentation:

`https://www.mongodb.com/docs/manual/core/queryable-encryption/quick-start/`. This tutorial uses the MongoDB Node.js driver. For the code used in this tutorial, you can refer to `https://github.com/mongodb/docs/tree/master/source/includes/qe-tutorials/node`, which contains all the code for the Queryable Encryption Quick Start sample application.

To get started with Queryable Encryption using MongoDB and the Node.js driver, follow these essential steps:

1. **Use the correct driver**: Queryable Encryption is not supported on all versions of all MongoDB drivers. For updated information on which drivers and which versions support Queryable Encryption, see the MongoDB documentation.

2. **Download the libmongocrypt library**: This library performs encryption and decryption and manages communication between the driver and the KMS. Depending on which driver you use, you may need to download `libmongocrypt` if it is a dependency for that driver.

3. **Download the Automatic Shared Encryption Library**: The Automatic Encryption Shared Library is a dynamic library (meaning its functionality is accessed at runtime) that enables your application to perform automatic encryption. The Automatic Shared Encryption Library reads the encryption schema, which you will create later, to determine which fields to encrypt or decrypt. It does not perform any actual encryption or decryption.

4. **Generate your master and data keys:** The following snippet of code generates a master key and stores it in a file called ./customer-master-key.txt. If you are using Queryable Encryption in production, you want to ensure that you securely store your master and data keys in a KMS.

The following code snippet generates a random 96-byte master key:

```
if (!existsSync("./customer-master-key.txt")) {
  try {
    writeFileSync("customer-master-key.txt", randomBytes(96));
  } catch (err) {
    throw new Error(
       `Unable to write Customer Master Key to file due to the
following error: ${err}`
    );
  }
}
```

5. **Create your encryption schema:** To encrypt a field, add it to your encryption schema. If you want to perform queries on this field, you must specify whether you want to perform equality queries or range queries on the field.

For example, suppose we have a bunch of medical records that we want to encrypt. The following code snippet defines three fields to be encrypted using the encryption schema. One field, name, can be queried for equality, the bill field can be queried for inequality (range query), and the final one cannot be queried, because we have not defined a query type for the field:

```
const encryptedFieldsMap = {
  encryptedFields: {
    fields: [
      {
        path: "name",
        bsonType: "string",
        queries: { queryType: "equality" },
      },
      {
        path: "bill",
        bsonType: "int",
        queries: { queryType: "range" },
      },
```

```
      {
        path: "procedure",
        bsonType: "object",
      },
    ],
  },
};
```

6. **Create the encrypted collection**: You must provide encryptedFieldsMap as an option when creating this collection, as well as the information for the master key. This will create your encrypted database and collection, and automatically generate data keys for your collection that can be used to decrypt the data:

```
await clientEncryption.createEncryptedCollection(
  encryptedDatabase,
  encryptedCollectionName,
  {
    provider: kmsProviderName,
    createCollectionOptions: encryptedFieldsMap,
    masterKey: customerMasterKeyCredentials,
  }
);
```

7. **Insert your documents**: You can observe your data and see how your fields get encrypted. Like with unencrypted data, you can use the insertOne() or insertMany() method. The driver will handle encrypting the data and securely uploading it to the server.

For example, we can insert the following three documents:

```
const patient1 = {
  name: "Jon Doe",
  bill: 1500,
  procedure: {
    code: 174839,
    recoveryTime: 30,
    name: "appendectomy"
  },
};
const patient2 = {
  name: "Jane Doe",
  bill: 1800,
```

```
      procedure: {
        code: 149174,
        recoveryTime: 60,
        name: "ankle surgery"
    },
  };
  const patient3 = {
    name: "Jake S",
    bill: 700,
    procedure: {
        code: 198347,
        recoveryTime: 90,
        name: "LASIK"
      },
  };
  await myColl.insertMany([ patient1, patient2, patient3 ]);
```

After the preceding documents are inserted, you can view them in your database and see that the name, bill, and procedure fields are all encrypted.

8. **Perform range queries on your data**: Suppose we want to find all patients whose medical bills were more than $1,000, meaning that the value for the bill field in their record is greater than 1000 and less than 2000. We can do so by performing the following range query:

```
  const findResult = await encryptedCollection.find({
    "bill": { $gt: 1000, $lt: 2000 },
  });
  for await (const doc of findResult) {
    console.log(doc);
  }
```

The query results will contain the following two documents, which have been decrypted by the server:

```
  {
    name: "Jon Doe",
    bill: 1500,
    procedure: {
        code: 174839,
```

```
      recoveryTime: 30,
      name: "appendectomy"
    },
  },
  {
    name: "Jane Doe",
    bill: 1800,
    procedure: {
      code: 149174,
      recoveryTime: 60,
      name: "ankle surgery"
    },
  }
}
```

Now, you have created an application that uses Queryable Encryption. You can perform queries for equality and a range of values on the data in your database while ensuring that the data remains encrypted until it gets to your application. You can expand this by adding more data and trying out different encryption algorithms to see how they improve or impact the performance of your application.

Now that you have learned about both CSFLE and Queryable Encryption, see the next section to learn how these methods compare when it comes to protecting your application's data.

Comparing CSFLE and Queryable Encryption

CSFLE and Queryable Encryption are both robust data security mechanisms provided by MongoDB. Both of these methods encrypt data on the client side before sending it over the network. They can be used in the same application; however, they cannot be used on the same collection. Therefore, you need to make decisions on which encryption mechanism to use based on your application's needs.

Queryable Encryption is best used in the following scenarios:

- You are developing a new application
- You expect users to run queries, including ranged, prefix, suffix, or substring queries, against encrypted data
- Your application can use a single key for a given field

CSFLE can be used in the following scenarios:

- Your application already uses CSFLE.

- You need to use different keys for the same field. This can be encountered when separating tenants or using user-specific keys.

- You need to be flexible with your data schema and potentially add more encrypted fields. Adding encrypted fields for Queryable Encryption requires rebuilding metadata collections and indexes.

$redact pipeline operator

One more method of data security that doesn't involve encryption is the $redact pipeline operator. When you construct an aggregation pipeline, you can use the $redact aggregation pipeline stage to restrict the content of information stored in the documents themselves.

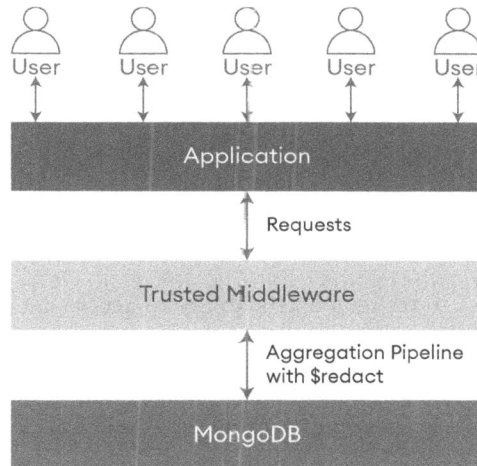

Figure 7.1: $redact pipeline operator workflow

$redact restricts access to the content in a document based on access criteria stored in the document itself. This is a useful, easily implementable way to restrict user access to data; however, because the data is still being stored in MongoDB and is unencrypted, there is a potential for a malicious actor to compromise the data. When using $redact, ensure that you are also employing other security mechanisms to secure your data.

For example, we can control user access to data based on a tags field. Imagine a collection that holds data of the following form:

```
{
  _id: 1,
  title: "123 Department Report",
  tags: [ [ "bar" ], [ "foo" ] ],
  year: 2014,
  subsections: [
      {
          subtitle: "Section 1: Overview",
          tags: [ [ "bar", "baz" ], [ "foo" ] ],
          content:  "Section 1: This is the content of section 1."
      },
      {
          subtitle: "Section 2: Analysis",
          tags: [ [ "bar" ] ],
          content: "Section 2: This is the content of section 2."
      },
  ]
}
```

We want the tags field to determine a user's ability to access data. Tags need to match the innermost array. For the previous example, if a user has the access tag of bar, then they can access the high-level document and the embedded-level document with the subtitle field Section 2: Analysis. They cannot access Subsection 1 because they don't have either the foo tag or the bar and baz tags. If they have the access tags of bar and foo, then they can access the entire document.

Now, imagine a user with the bar access tag. To run a pipeline query for this user, we use the db.collection.aggregate() function with the $redact pipeline stage:

```
var userAccess = [ "bar" ];
db.collection.aggregate(
    [
      { $redact: {
          $cond: {
              if: { $gt: [ { $size: { $setIntersection: [ "$tags", userAccess
] } }, 0 ] },
              then: "$$DESCEND",
```

```
            else: "$$PRUNE"
          }
        }
      }
    ]
);
```

The aggregation operation returns the following "redacted" document for the user:

```
{
    _id: 1,
    title: "123 Department Report",
    tags: [ [ "bar" ], [ "foo" ] ],
    year: 2014,
    subsections: [
        {
            subtitle: "Section 2: Analysis",
            tags: [ [ "bar" ] ],
            content: "Section 2: This is the content of section 2."
        },
    ]
}
```

This way, you can control the information in a document that the user gets to see. This is different from field-level encryption, which encrypts specific fields and requires multiple keys to decrypt; rather, the user will never see the data that they do not have access to.

By using $redact along with CSFLE or Queryable Encryption, you can ensure the utmost safety and security of your data. Continue reading to learn about methods you can use on a self-managed deployment.

Security in MongoDB deployments

Security in MongoDB deployments is essential for ensuring the integrity and confidentiality of your data. By securing your application, data, and deployment, you can safeguard your entire system against potential threats.

This section explores various security methods available for protecting your self-managed MongoDB deployment. We'll cover MongoDB 8.0's deprecation of **Lightweight Directory Access Protocol (LDAP)** support and how to transition to Microsoft **OpenID Connect (OIDC)** for more modern, efficient external authentication.

Additionally, we'll discuss Kerberos authentication, creating custom user roles, and strengthening your deployment with network hardening. These methods can be used together to enhance the security of your database from multiple angles.

LDAP deprecation

MongoDB Enterprise Advanced provided support for both authentication and authorization using LDAP. As mentioned earlier in this chapter, authentication refers to who can access your database, while authorization refers to what a user can access. Starting in MongoDB 8.0, support for both LDAP authentication and authorization is deprecated. It is still available to use but will be removed in a future release. Users should consider using Microsoft's OIDC authentication instead.

To learn more about LDAP, see the MongoDB documentation: `https://www.mongodb.com/docs/manual/core/security-ldap-external/`.

Why deprecation?

In MongoDB 8.0, support for LDAP authentication and authorization was deprecated in both MongoDB Enterprise Advanced and MongoDB Atlas. Developers can still use it; however, support for LDAP is not going to be updated going forward, and will be removed in a future release, so it is encouraged to start migrating your applications to use OIDC authentication and authorization. Although LDAP is used extensively, it's not inherently designed for cloud environments, resulting in the potential for credentials to be exposed when using LDAP authorization with MongoDB Atlas. In addition, accessing an LDAP server over the internet results in a complex network setup that can lead to connectivity issues and increase the risk of production problems.

MongoDB 7.0 introduced support for Workforce/Workplace Identity Federation using OIDC, which offers a modern and streamlined alternative to LDAP. In this section, you can learn about OIDC as well as how to migrate your application to use it.

OIDC overview

Support for OIDC was introduced in MongoDB 7.0. Similar to LDAP, OIDC verifies users on an authorization server, following OAuth 2.0 authorization specifications. OIDC allows **Single Sign-On (SSO)** access to your MongoDB database using any identity provider that supports OIDC, such as Microsoft **Active Directory Federation Services (ADFS)**, Microsoft Entra ID, Okta, and Ping Identity.

At a high level, the OIDC authentication process follows this workflow:

1. Your client application, or user, sends authentication credentials to MongoDB.

2. MongoDB sends a request to an OpenID provider that has been implemented following OIDC and the OAuth 2.0 protocol such as ADFS, Microsoft Entra ID, or Okta.

3. The OpenID provider authenticates and authorizes the user. If successful, the provider responds to MongoDB with an identity token and sometimes an access token. These tokens identify the user, and can also include information about when and how the user authenticated.

4. MongoDB sends a request to the user with the access token.

5. The user obtains access to MongoDB using the information given in the access token.

MongoDB offers two forms of OIDC: Workforce Identity Federation, which enables human users to authenticate using an EIP, and Workload Identity Federation, which enables applications to authenticate using external programmatic identities such as Google service accounts. Some of the advantages of Workforce and Workload Identity Federation are as follows:

- **No credentials are stored in MongoDB**: With LDAP, user credentials are stored in MongoDB, which means that they can be compromised by a malicious actor.

- **Reduced cross-application risk**: In an LDAP connection, the user's LDAP credentials are sent to MongoDB within the connection string, which can expose credentials over a network. However, with Workforce and Workload Identity Federation, MongoDB never receives a secret. Instead, OIDC and OAuth 2.0 grant access tokens for specific resources. If a token is compromised, the token cannot be used to access other applications.

- **Improved security**: Identity Federation grants access through access tokens, which are typically only valid for one hour.

- **Authenticate without passwords**: If your applications are running on specific cloud resources such as GCP or Azure, you can authenticate without passwords, which means that you do not have to periodically renew credentials.

Using OIDC with MongoDB

MongoDB and OIDC offer two types of identity authentication: Workload Identity Federation, which authenticates applications, and Workforce Identity Federation, which authenticates users. This tutorial focuses on Workload Identity Federation, which uses the OAuth 2.0 protocol. As always, for the most detailed and up-to-date information, see the official MongoDB documentation. Support for OIDC is only available when running a MongoDB Enterprise deployment on Linux.

To set up OIDC with MongoDB for application authentication, follow these steps:

1. Ensure that your MongoDB Enterprise deployment is running MongoDB 7.0 or later.

2. Configure an EIP, such as Microsoft Azure or Google Cloud. This EIP issues OAuth 2.0-compliant identity and access tokens. When you configure your EIP, you can create groups of users, if you want to define different permissions for different groups. However, best practices dictate that you define user permissions within MongoDB instead of your EIP. For step-by-step instructions on how to configure an EIP, see the MongoDB documentation.

3. Configure your server to use OIDC using your configuration file. Under the `setParameter` option, set the `authenticationMechanisms` parameter to `MONGODB-OIDC`, and set the `oidcIdentityProviders` parameter to specify the configuration for your EIP. For Workload Identity Federation, set the `supportsHumanFlows` field to `false`:

    ```
    setParameter:
       authenticationMechanisms: MONGODB-OIDC
       oidcIdentityProviders: [ {
             "issuer": "https://okta-test.okta.com",
             "audience": "example@kernel.mongodb.com",
             "authNamePrefix": "okta-issuer",
             "matchPattern": "@mongodb.com$",
             "JWKSPollSecs": 86400,
             "supportsHumanFlows": false
       } ]
    ```

    If you want to configure multiple identity providers, you can include the configuration information as additional documents in the array passed to `oidcIdentityProviders`. The priority of each EIP is determined by array order, with the first EIP in the array being the first selected.

4. Authorize users by creating roles. On the admin database, use the `db.createRole()` command to create roles that map the EIP group (see step 2) to a MongoDB role.

    You can specify an EIP role by using the following format:

    ```
    <authNamePrefix>/<authorizationClaim>
    ```

For example, if we are using Okta as our EIP, we can create roles based on the Everyone group in the EIP that are able to read and write to any database, by running the following command:

```
db.createRole( {
    role: "okta/Everyone",
    privileges: [ ],
    roles: [ "readWriteAnyDatabase" ]
} )
```

This is how you can enable OIDC for your MongoDB deployment for fast, secure, and efficient token-based authentication.

Kerberos

MongoDB Enterprise Advanced offers the Kerberos method for authentication. Originating from MIT's Project Athena, Kerberos provides strong authentication for client-server applications through a cryptography-based approach to issuing access tickets. Tickets are sets of encrypted data, such as client information. Kerberos has become an essential tool for securely managing identities in distributed environments.

The integration of Kerberos into MongoDB's authentication mechanisms ensures that only authenticated users can access and interact with MongoDB's stored data. However, MongoDB itself must perform authorization. You can use Kerberos authentication with a different form of authorization, such as OIDC.

To use Kerberos to authenticate against MongoDB, you first need to understand and configure a few components, both on Kerberos and MongoDB:

The MongoDB components are as follows:

- **Configuration file**: Use the MongoDB configuration file to choose Kerberos security options.

The Kerberos components are as follows:

- **Key distribution center**: This system manages keys and distributes tickets. It includes two parts:

  - **Authentication server**: This server authenticates users and issues them **ticket-granting tickets**, or **TGTs**.
  - **Ticket-granting service**: After a user has a TGT, they can request service tickets. A MongoDB user can request a ticket for the MongoDB service.

- **Principal**: Principals include users, services, and hosts, any entity that is present during the authentication process. Every principal requires a unique name.
- **Ticket**: Encrypted data that is used to prove a client's identity to a server. A ticket contains data such as client information and a session key. Because this data is encrypted using the server's key, it can be unencrypted by the server.
- **Realm**: A domain in Kerberos that manages the principal entities.

You can set up Kerberos by using the following steps:

1. Configure the key distribution center and define all the principals for users and services that will be involved in the operation.
2. Configure MongoDB to use Kerberos authentication by specifying the option in the configuration file and restarting your server.
3. Create users in MongoDB if you haven't already.
4. Users get a TGT from the authentication server.
5. By using the TGT, the customer can request a service ticket from the ticket-granting service for MongoDB.
6. The MongoDB driver authenticates with MongoDB using this service ticket.
7. By using the service's encryption key, MongoDB decrypts the ticket information, validates the ticket, and establishes an authenticated session.

Integration of MongoDB with Kerberos provides a strong and secure authentication method for environments that already use Kerberos. If you are using a **Local Area Network** (**LAN**) or a non-Linux environment, you can use Kerberos to authenticate on your self-managed deployment over OIDC.

Here's a documentation page for further reading: `https://www.kantega-sso.com/articles/the-difference-between-kerberos-saml-og-openid-connect-oidc`.

Network hardening

Network hardening involves different techniques to minimize vulnerabilities in your deployment. With a self-managed MongoDB deployment, you can use the following:

- Firewalls allow you to filter access to your network at a granular level. An administrator can limit which users get access to a network, which increases your network's protection against malicious attackers.

- A **Virtual Private Network (VPN)** hides your IP address and forwards traffic to a new one. This way, malicious attackers cannot get access to your IP address.

- IP forwarding allows servers to forward packets to other systems from source to destination. However, it is susceptible to malicious attacks and can allow bad actors to gain unauthorized access to your network or bypass firewalls. To prevent risks from IP forwarding, you can disable it on the machine that hosts your deployment.

Generally, you can use firewalls along with a VPN, or firewalls along with disabling IP forwarding. You can also use a VPN along with disabling IP forwarding, but this has some exceptions and limitations depending on where your VPN is routing traffic, since this can involve IP forwarding. If traffic is routing beyond your server, then you might need to keep IP forwarding enabled.

Summary

In this chapter, you learned about the various security mechanisms that MongoDB offers. This includes application security, which protects access to your application; data security, which protects the data itself throughout its life cycle; and other additional security mechanisms that can be applied to a self-managed MongoDB deployment. With the knowledge of all these mechanisms, you can choose the proper combination of security measures to ensure that your application has the protection that it needs.

In the next chapter, we dive into MongoDB Atlas, the cloud platform for modern database management. You'll learn how to set up organizations, projects, and clusters, interact with Atlas using UI, CLI, and APIs, and implement secure access controls. The chapter also explores scaling strategies, automation tools, and data visualization with Charts and Power BI.

8

MongoDB Atlas

MongoDB Atlas is a comprehensive solution designed to streamline and enhance data management for developers. This platform is tailored to meet the needs of modern applications, which often involve handling large data volumes, require automation, and demand rapid scalability and adaptability to change.

MongoDB Atlas provides a straightforward, user-friendly interface for maintaining databases, along with automated backups and point-in-time data snapshots. Atlas incorporates a wide array of features, including automated scaling, robust monitoring and alerting, Vector Search and full-text search, triggers, embedding models, and performance optimization tools to diagnose and improve poorly constructed queries.

The goal of these features is to create a single platform that unites different workloads and caters to developers throughout the organization. MongoDB Atlas accommodates both start-ups and well-established enterprises, ensuring all cloud-based database needs are met.

As we examine the new features released with MongoDB 8.0, you'll gain a clear understanding of how MongoDB Atlas is not just a database service but a versatile and powerful asset designed to meet the modern developer's demands.

This chapter will cover the following topics:

- Setting up your organization
- Exploring tools for interacting with your Atlas deployments
- Sizing an Atlas cluster
- Scaling in Atlas
- Configuring authentication and authorization
- Securing your Atlas deployment
- Deprecated services in Atlas

This overview won't cover every single MongoDB Atlas feature, as that would be extensive. Instead, it blends recently introduced functionalities with foundational concepts. The aim is to provide you with the necessary knowledge to quickly start using Atlas and accelerate your innovation.

Technical requirements

In order to follow along, you'll need to have the following:

- MongoDB Atlas account
- Python 3.7+
- Atlas CLI

You can find the coding examples used on GitHub: `https://github.com/PacktPublishing/The-Official-MongoDB-Guide`.

Setting up your organization

In MongoDB Atlas, understanding organizations, projects, and clusters is key, as these elements form the basic framework for managing your databases. Organizations are the top-level containers that encompass projects, while projects can host multiple clusters. Each level, that is, the organization, project, and cluster levels, has a distinct role in managing resources, access, and data within Atlas.

Let's explore these key elements.

Managing organizations in MongoDB Atlas

At the organization level, MongoDB Atlas equips you with tools to manage the overarching structure that governs all projects. This involves setting global policies, establishing operational rules, and maintaining security parameters that apply uniformly across projects. The following are key capabilities provided by Atlas to facilitate efficient organization-level management:

- **Centralized billing and access management**: Atlas provides centralized billing, offering a comprehensive view of expenses across projects, which streamlines financial management. Access management is paramount in assigning user roles and permissions, ensuring both security and operational efficiency.
- **Establishing resource policies**: As an organization owner, you carry the responsibility of creating resource policies. These dictate how projects and clusters use their resources, such as setting limits on cluster configurations, choosing cloud regions, and determining standards for scaling and performance. These measures ensure effective governance aligned with broader operational and financial strategies.

- **Flexibility**: Users can participate in multiple organizations simultaneously. This fosters collaboration across teams and projects, supporting seamless interactions while maintaining clear boundaries and robust security controls for each distinct organization.

- **Enhancing efficiency with resource tags**: MongoDB Atlas has introduced resource tags for organizations and billing, a new feature that allows you to categorize your projects and clusters. With tags, you can systematically filter and organize resources based on specific criteria, such as department, environment, or cost center. This addition simplifies management, improves visibility, and connects tags directly to billing, facilitating better financial tracking and accountability.

Project-level configuration

Focusing on the project level, the emphasis shifts to configuring and managing individual components and applications related to specific initiatives or teams. Within an organization, you can have up to 250 projects, offering ample room to grow and segment different workloads. This structure enhances team and environment isolation, ensuring that each project operates independently without interference from others.

The separation of organizations and projects offers significant benefits, such as segregation of duties, enhanced isolation, streamlined management, and improved scalability. This structured approach is scalable, accommodating additional projects and infrastructure as your organization's needs evolve.

Understanding clusters

In Atlas, a cluster serves as your database deployment, consisting of replica sets that run the MongoDB database to store and manage your data. Clusters provide high availability and scalability, which is great for supporting varying application needs.

Atlas allows you to deploy clusters across multiple geographic regions and cloud providers, including **Amazon Web Services (AWS)**, Microsoft Azure, and **Google Cloud Platform (GCP)**. This multi-cloud capability helps avoid vendor lock-in, enhancing resilience and negotiating leverage. It provides redundancy and ensures continued operations even during provider outages, while accessing each cloud platform's unique strengths and offerings.

A multi-cloud strategy also strengthens disaster recovery plans by distributing data across different environments, minimizing risks, and maintaining availability. Atlas empowers organizations to align their database architecture with business continuity goals.

Atlas offers various cluster tiers tailored for specific use cases; the M0 free tier is perfect for learning and small-scale projects, whereas dedicated clusters manage production workloads and large-scale applications. Within a single project, you can establish up to 25 clusters, supporting diverse environments such as testing, development, and production. However, only one M0 free-tier cluster is allowed per project.

As we move forward in this chapter, we'll dive deeper into the specifics of clusters and guide you through setting up your own.

Exploring tools for interacting with MongoDB Atlas

After setting up your organization, projects, and clusters in MongoDB Atlas, the next step is leveraging the platform's tools to unlock the full potential of your database deployments. With a large selection of options, MongoDB Atlas equips both new users and seasoned developers with tools designed to streamline management, enhance efficiency, and optimize performance. In this section, we'll introduce key tools, ranging from the Atlas **User Interface** (UI) for intuitive navigation to programmatic access options such as the Atlas Admin API, that support everything from day-to-day operations to advanced automation workflows. Let's explore how these tools can improve your MongoDB Atlas experience.

Atlas UI

For those embarking on their MongoDB Atlas journey, the Atlas UI serves as an intuitive starting point. Recent enhancements to the UI focus on aligning with the developer workflow, resulting in increased efficiency and user-friendly navigation. This update ensures that every interaction with your data is seamless and insightful.

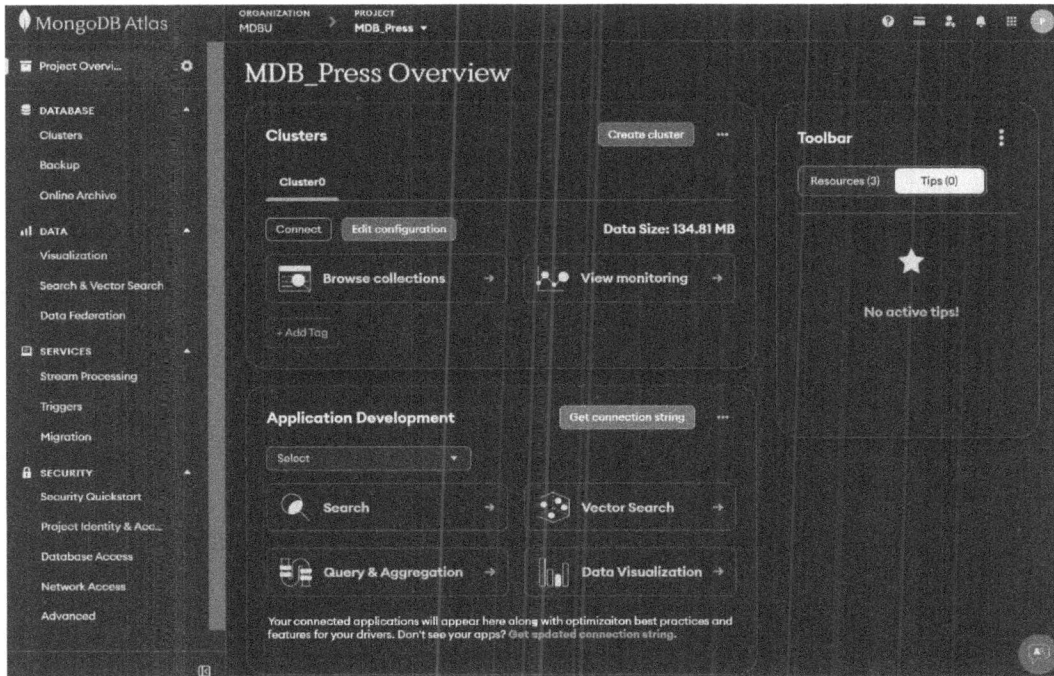

Figure 8.1: Atlas UI

With intuitive navigation, the Atlas UI grants easy access to organizations, projects, and clusters, offering a holistic overview of your resources. Notable features include the following:

- **Data Explorer**: Perfect for quick inspection and updates of data without needing to write code. It empowers organizations by making it easier to monitor, manage, and adjust data across projects and clusters.
- **Atlas Search**: Integrated search capabilities within your data.
- **Dashboards for monitoring**: Visualize cluster metrics and database health in real time.
- **Performance Advisor**: A tool designed for clusters running M10 or larger tiers. It helps organizations optimize query performance by analyzing slow-running queries and recommending efficient indexing strategies. Available within the Atlas interface, the Performance Advisor enhances project development and cluster operations by identifying and eliminating bottlenecks, reducing operational costs, and ensuring optimal resource utilization, thereby empowering teams to deliver better user experiences and improve overall system performance.

Each feature provides unique perspectives for managing and interacting with your data, making the Atlas UI a powerful tool for users at any level.

Atlas CLI

For those who prefer using the terminal, the Atlas **Command-Line Interface (CLI)** is an invaluable tool for managing MongoDB Atlas deployments directly from the command line. Recent enhancements have further elevated its capabilities, particularly with the addition of local development environment support. When used in conjunction with Docker, setting up single-node replica sets becomes a breeze, significantly reducing both setup time and complexity.

This local development support is particularly helpful as it allows developers to build, test, and refine their applications in an environment that closely mirrors production. This ensures smoother transitions when deploying to the cloud and reduces the risk of unexpected issues arising from environment discrepancies.

The best part is that it's easy to get up and running. All you need installed is the Atlas CLI and Docker. After that, run the following command in your terminal:

```
atlas deployments setup
```

This will open an interactive setup prompt that lets you configure your local Atlas deployment.

> If you're interested in learning more about Atlas local deployments, make sure to visit the Atlas documentation (https://www.mongodb.com/docs/atlas/cli/current/atlas-cli-local-cloud/), where you can find more information and tutorials related to this new feature.

In addition, the Atlas CLI offers several key functionalities that streamline your workflow:

- **Resource management**: Create, modify, and delete organizations, projects, and clusters
- **Automated processes**: Script and automate repetitive tasks to save time and reduce errors
- **Integrated security**: Configure and manage security settings, including access levels and authentication
- **Deployment customization**: Tailor cluster deployments to the changing needs of your applications
- **Monitoring and analysis**: Access real-time metrics and performance data

In summary, the Atlas CLI provides a robust way to manage MongoDB Atlas efficiently from the command line, supporting both local development and cloud deployments with ease.

Programmatic access and automation

For developers interested in programmatic control and automation, MongoDB Atlas provides tools to simplify database management:

- **Atlas Admin API**: A RESTful API offering comprehensive control over your MongoDB Atlas environment. It allows for automation and integration of operations with existing systems, enabling seamless DevOps workflows.

- **Kubernetes Operator**: Designed for cloud-native deployments, it integrates MongoDB clusters within a Kubernetes environment using declarative management and **Custom Resource Definitions (CRDs)** for consistent automation.

- **HashiCorp Terraform MongoDB Atlas Provider**: Enables managing Atlas resources as infrastructure as code using **HashiCorp Configuration Language (HCL)**. This allows you to define, deploy, and update your Atlas environment programmatically, integrating Atlas into your continuous delivery workflows.

- **Atlas AWS CloudFormation resources**: Simplifies the provisioning and management of Atlas features on AWS through YAML or JSON-based templates. This enables the quick and reliable deployment of services or applications (stacks) that can be easily updated or replicated as needed.

The Atlas Kubernetes Operator represents a significant advancement for organizations adopting cloud-native approaches to application deployment. But what exactly does it do, and how can it streamline your database operations? Let's explore this powerful tool in depth.

What is the Atlas Kubernetes Operator?

At its core, the Atlas Kubernetes Operator allows you to manage your MongoDB Atlas resources directly from within your Kubernetes environment. Think of it as a bridge that connects your Kubernetes clusters to MongoDB Atlas, enabling you to define and manage Atlas resources using the same declarative approach you use for the rest of your Kubernetes infrastructure.

How does this work in practice? When you deploy the Atlas Kubernetes Operator to your Kubernetes cluster, it introduces CRDs that represent Atlas resources, that is, projects, database deployments, users, and more. These CRDs allow you to describe your desired Atlas state in YAML files, just as you would define Kubernetes Pods, Services, or Deployments.

The power of declarative management

What makes this approach so powerful? Consider this scenario: You need to provision a new MongoDB cluster for your application. Without the Kubernetes Operator, you might do the following:

1. Log in to the Atlas UI.

2. Navigate through several screens to create a project.

3. Configure and deploy a cluster.

4. Set up database users.

5. Configure network access.

With the Atlas Kubernetes Operator, you simply define these resources in YAML:

```yaml
apiVersion: atlas.mongodb.com/v1
kind: AtlasProject
metadata:
  name: my-project
spec:
  name: "Production Application"
  projectIpAccessList:
    - ipAddress: "192.0.2.0/24"
      comment: "Production network"
---
apiVersion: atlas.mongodb.com/v1
kind: AtlasDeployment
metadata:
  name: my-cluster
spec:
  projectRef:
    name: my-project
  deploymentSpec:
    name: "Production Cluster"
    providerSettings:
      instanceSizeName: M10
      providerName: AWS
```

The preceding code is just a visual example and is not meant to be run locally. To get started with the Atlas Kubernetes Operator, check out the Atlas documentation on it (`https://www.mongodb.com/docs/atlas/operator/v2.7/ak8so-quick-start/`).

The operator continuously reconciles this definition with Atlas, ensuring your actual resources always match your desired state. This enables GitOps workflows, where your infrastructure definitions live alongside your application code in version control.

One of the greatest advantages is the ability to automate complex, multi-step workflows that would otherwise require manual intervention or custom scripts using the Atlas API.

With version 2.0, the Atlas Kubernetes Operator introduced an important safeguard: deletion protection. This feature changes how the operator handles resource deletions.

Previously, if you deleted a custom resource in Kubernetes (perhaps accidentally), the operator would dutifully delete the corresponding resource in Atlas. This could lead to unintended data loss or service disruption if someone unfamiliar with the operator's behavior removed a resource.

Now, by default, when you delete a custom resource in Kubernetes, the following occurs:

1. The resource in Atlas remains intact.
2. The operator simply stops managing that resource.
3. You can continue to manage it directly through the Atlas UI or API.

This behavior provides a safety net. For example, if someone accidentally deletes an AtlasProject resource from Kubernetes, your actual Atlas project (along with all its clusters and data) remains untouched.

Getting started with the Atlas Kubernetes Operator

Here are the steps to get started with the Atlas Kubernetes Operator:

1. Install the operator in your Kubernetes cluster using the official documentation or Helm charts.
2. Configure Atlas access by creating the necessary API keys and Kubernetes Secrets.
3. Define your resources using the CRDs provided by the operator.
4. Apply your configurations and let the operator synchronize them with Atlas.

As Kubernetes continues to be the platform of choice for modern applications, the Atlas Kubernetes Operator will play an increasingly vital role in database management. MongoDB continues to enhance the operator with new capabilities, making it a cornerstone of cloud-native MongoDB Atlas deployments.

By embracing the operator pattern and declarative management for your Atlas resources, you're not just simplifying database operations; you're aligning with industry best practices for infrastructure management and positioning your organization for more efficient, scalable, and reliable database operations.

Exploring data through the Atlas BI Connector

The MongoDB Atlas Connector for Power BI provides another way to interact with your MongoDB data. This Microsoft-certified solution bridges the gap between development and analytics teams, allowing Power BI users to natively transform, analyze, and share dashboards incorporating live MongoDB Atlas data. With this connector, you can harness MongoDB's document model while working within the familiar Power BI interfaces that analysts know and love.

DirectQuery mode is a significant enhancement to the MongoDB Atlas Power BI Connector.

DirectQuery provides a direct connection to your MongoDB Atlas database, allowing Power BI to query data in real time rather than importing and storing it within Power BI. This means your visualizations and reports always reflect the most current data in your MongoDB Atlas database.

How DirectQuery works with MongoDB Atlas

The Power BI Connector works through MongoDB's Atlas SQL interface, which is powered by Atlas Data Federation. Here's how the process works:

1. Enable **Atlas SQL Interface** from the Atlas console.
2. Use the provided SQL endpoint/URL in the **MongoDB Atlas SQL Connection** dialog within Power BI Desktop.
3. Select **DirectQuery** as your connectivity mode (instead of Import).
4. Leverage query folding with Power Query to optimize data retrieval and transformation.
5. Build, save, and publish reports to the Power BI online app.

By using DirectQuery with MongoDB Atlas, we can create reports that always display the most current data without needing to import or refresh datasets. This approach gives us direct access to our MongoDB data while taking advantage of Power BI's visualization capabilities. Next, let's take a closer look at the benefits of DirectQuery for Atlas.

Benefits of DirectQuery for MongoDB Atlas

DirectQuery was developed to address the growing need for real-time access to operational data within analytics platforms, especially as businesses increasingly rely on up-to-date insights for decision-making. Traditional methods, such as importing large datasets into analytics tools, often introduced performance challenges, storage complexities, and delays stemming from stale data. DirectQuery mitigates these issues by enabling a live connection to your database, ensuring that analytics always reflect the latest state of your data.

This solution is particularly beneficial in the following instances:

- You need to analyze large datasets where import would be impractical
- Up-to-date information is important for decision-making
- You want to avoid performance issues from repetitive data imports
- You need to simplify storage complexities for large datasets

With DirectQuery support, you can easily connect to real-time MongoDB Atlas data while retaining the flexibility to use Import mode when detailed modeling for manageable data volumes is necessary. This enhancement helps businesses to use the full capabilities of MongoDB Atlas within Microsoft Power BI, enabling a smooth integration between operational databases and analytics platforms to drive informed decisions.

Atlas Charts

Atlas Charts is MongoDB's native data visualization tool that allows you to create compelling visual representations directly from your Atlas data. Instead of exporting your data to external visualization tools, you can seamlessly transform your MongoDB collections into insightful charts and dashboards, all within the Atlas ecosystem.

Here's what makes Atlas Charts particularly valuable:

- **Seamless integration with MongoDB Atlas**: Connect Charts directly to your Atlas projects and visualize cluster data with minimal setup
- **Document data-handling**: Unlike traditional BI tools, Charts natively understands MongoDB's document model, including embedded objects and arrays
- **Built-in aggregation functionality**: Process your collection data using various metrics and calculations without writing complex queries
- **Diverse chart types**: Create visualizations ranging from bar charts and scatter plots to geospatial charts, each designed to showcase different aspects of your data

Charts organizes your visualizations through key concepts:

- **Data sources:** MongoDB collections containing the data you want to visualize
- **Charts:** Individual visualizations that map to a single data source
- **Dashboards:** Collections of one or more charts that provide a comprehensive view of your data

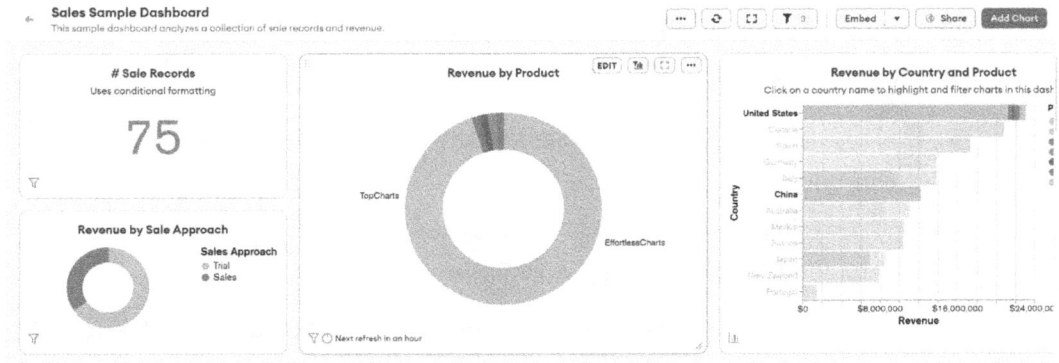

Figure 8.2: Atlas Charts dashboard showcasing sample visualizations of sales volume and revenue trends

Secure sharing with passcode-protected dashboards

How do you share valuable insights with stakeholders outside your organization while maintaining data security? Atlas Charts now offers passcode-protected dashboards as an enhanced security feature for shared dashboards.

This feature adds an extra layer of protection, ensuring only authorized users with the correct passcode can access your visual insights. Implementing this security measure is straightforward.

To implement this security measure, follow these steps:

1. Check the box to protect your public link with a passcode when sharing, as shown in the following screenshot.
2. A passcode will be automatically generated (you can regenerate this as needed).
3. Share both the dashboard link and the passcode with intended recipients.
4. Viewers will be prompted to enter the passcode before accessing your dashboard.

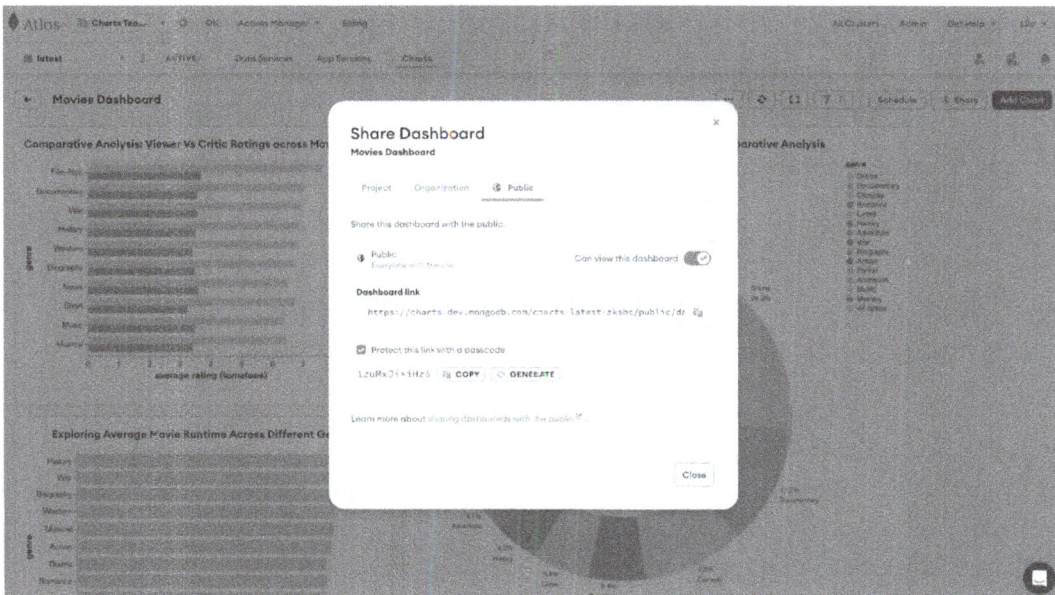

Figure 8.3: Atlas Charts dashboard featuring options to set your charts

This feature bridges the gap between accessibility and security, making it easier to share data visualizations beyond your Atlas organization while maintaining control over who sees them.

Enhancing table charts with hyperlinks

How can you make your table charts more interactive and navigable? Atlas Charts now offers hyperlink customization, one of the most requested features from users. This powerful enhancement transforms static data into actionable content, creating a more dynamic user experience.

With hyperlink customization, you can do the following:

- Format columnar data as interactive links using http, https, mailto, or tel protocols
- Build links dynamically using field values from your documents
- Create connections between your visualizations and external resources
- Provide direct access to related information without leaving your dashboard

Let's look at a practical example. Imagine you have a collection of movies in your MongoDB database. Using Atlas Charts, you can create a table showing movie titles, genres, and ratings. With hyperlink customization, you can turn each movie title into a clickable link that directs users to its corresponding IMDb page.

Creating charts with Natural Language Mode

What if you could create sophisticated data visualizations by simply asking questions in plain English? With Natural Language Mode in Atlas Charts, you now can!

Natural Language Mode reduces technical barriers by allowing you to do the following:

- Generate charts by asking questions such as *"Show me the sales performance by country and product for Q4 FY2023"*
- Create visualizations without specialized knowledge of BI tools
- Explore your data through conversation rather than complex configuration

Atlas Charts transforms how you interact with your MongoDB data by providing intuitive visualization tools that integrate seamlessly with your existing Atlas environment. Whether you're creating dashboards to monitor business metrics, sharing insights securely through passcode protection, enhancing tables with interactive hyperlinks, or exploring data through natural language queries, Charts empowers you to extract maximum value from your MongoDB data.

Familiar tools

Additionally, you can use tools you might already be familiar with if you have been managing your own MongoDB deployments, such as the following:

- **MongoDB Shell (`mongosh`)**: A familiar tool for exploratory data analysis and query testing
- **MongoDB Compass**: A GUI offering a visual interface for database management

Throughout this chapter, we'll use the Atlas CLI and `mongosh` for many examples. However, everything discussed can be adapted to the tool you prefer.

Sizing an Atlas cluster

An Atlas cluster is the fundamental deployment unit within this service. It can be configured as a replica set or a sharded cluster. These clusters operate across major cloud providers, including AWS, Azure, and Google Cloud, giving you flexibility in where your data resides while removing the burden of infrastructure management.

Atlas clusters include numerous capabilities that benefit development teams. You'll get automated backups with point-in-time recovery, built-in monitoring tools, and comprehensive security features, including network isolation, encryption, and **Role-Based Access Control** (**RBAC**). The service handles routine database maintenance tasks, such as upgrades and patches, automatically. This allows your team to concentrate on application development rather than spending time on database administration tasks.

Effectively sizing your MongoDB Atlas cluster is an important step for any project. While there's no universal "one-size-fits-all" configuration, this section will provide a starting point and guide you through the decision-making process based on your specific requirements. It's a good idea to document the rationale behind your sizing choices, as this record will be invaluable for future scaling and optimization efforts.

When planning your Atlas deployment, you'll need to select from several available cluster tiers. These tiers differ in their resource allocations, which directly affect performance, capacity, and cost. Let's examine what resources each tier provides to help you match your application needs with the appropriate configuration.

Storage, RAM, CPU, IOPS, and connections per tier

Atlas clusters come in several tiers, ranging from small development instances (M0, M2, and M5) to large enterprise-grade deployments (M300+). Each tier provides specific allocations across five key aspects:

- **Storage**: The amount of disk space available for your data and indexes
- **RAM**: Memory available for the WiredTiger cache and operations
- **CPU**: Processing power for query execution and database operations
- **IOPS**: This stands for **input/output operations per second**, which is a measure of disk performance
- **Connections**: Maximum number of simultaneous client connections

For example, an M30 cluster provides 8 GB RAM per node, while an M80 offers 64 GB RAM per node, an 8x increase that can dramatically change how your working set operates in memory.

As you progress from lower to higher tiers, these resources increase in a somewhat non-linear fashion. Some resources might increase exponentially between certain tier jumps, while others grow more gradually.

One of Atlas's features is the ability to provision storage independently from other resources. For M10+ clusters, you can select the storage capacity that matches your data volume without necessarily changing other specifications.

When selecting storage, consider not just your current data size but your projected growth. How much data do you expect to accumulate over the next 6–12 months? Building in some headroom prevents frequent adjustments while still keeping costs reasonable.

Storage requirements

Accurately predicting exactly how much storage your MongoDB deployment will require can be challenging, especially for new applications. However, we can make reasonable estimations using several key metrics that will get you close enough for initial planning.

Let's break down the specific metrics you'll need to consider when calculating your total storage requirements.

Document size calculation

The foundation of your storage estimation begins with understanding your average document size. If you already have a collection with data in it, you can use the following command in the MongoDB Shell:

```
db.collection.stats().avgObjSize  // Returns average object size in bytes
```

> If your data already exists in a MongoDB database, you can obtain most of the following information by running db.stats() and db.col.stats() in the MongoDB Shell.

For new applications, you can estimate this by creating sample documents that match your expected data model and measuring their BSON size in the MongoDB Shell:

```
let doc = {'_id': ObjectId('600e8fcf36b07f77b6bc8ecf'), 'name': 'Mina'};
print(bsonsize(doc));
```

Collection size calculation

Once you know your average document size, you can estimate a collection's size:

```
Collection Size = Average Document Size × Number of Documents
```

For example, if your average document is 2 KB and you expect 1 million documents, you'd have the following:

```
2KB × 1,000,000 = 2GB (raw data size)
```

Total collection size

Your database likely consists of multiple collections. Sum up all collection sizes to get your raw data storage needs:

```
Total Raw Data Size = Sum of All Collection Sizes
```

Index size

Indexes consume extra disk space in addition to the space used by your raw data. One approach to estimate the index size is to calculate it as a fraction or percentage of your total data size:

```
Index Size = Raw Data Size × (0.2 to 0.5)
```

For this example, estimating indexes at 30% of your data size provides a reasonable starting point:

```
Index Size = 2GB × 0.3 = 600MB
```

This can vary significantly based on the number and types of indexes you create. Some indexes take up more space than others. It's important to remember that this is a very rough estimate.

WiredTiger compression

MongoDB's WiredTiger storage engine provides substantial storage savings through compression. By default, WiredTiger applies the following:

- Collection data compression
- Index compression

The level of compression achievable with MongoDB is highly variable and depends on numerous factors, making it challenging to predict the exact amount. For a cautious estimate, a 20% reduction in size can be assumed. In optimal conditions, compression rates could potentially reach as high as 80%.

This means your actual disk usage may be significantly lower than raw data calculations suggest:

```
Compressed Data Size = Raw Data Size ÷ Compression Ratio
Compressed Index Size = Index Size ÷ Index Compression Ratio
```

For our example, this looks as follows:

```
Compressed Data Size = 2GB ÷ 4 = 500MB
Compressed Index Size = 600MB ÷ 2 = 300MB
```

Buffer size

MongoDB needs working space beyond your compressed data size. A good practice is to add a buffer:

```
Total Storage Needed = (Compressed Data Size + Compressed Index Size) ×
1.5
```

Using our example, this looks as follows:

```
Total Storage Needed = (500MB + 300MB) × 1.5 = 1.2GB
```

This 50% buffer accommodates the WiredTiger storage engine's needs and provides room for temporary operations.

Future growth projections

How will your data grow over time? Consider these approaches:

- **Linear projection**: Calculate the monthly growth rate based on historical data
- **Seasonal adjustments**: Account for busier periods if your application has cyclical usage
- **User-based projection**: Estimate storage per user and multiply by projected user growth

For example, if you're currently growing at 5 GB per month, you'd have the following:

```
Year 1 Additional Storage = 5GB × 12 = 60GB
```

If you expect user growth to accelerate this by 20% in year two, you'd have the following:

```
Year 2 Additional Storage = 60GB × 1.2 = 72GB
```

Additional considerations

While the preceding calculations provide a solid foundation, several other factors may influence your total storage needs:

- **Data retention policies**: Will you archive or delete older data? How frequently?
- **Workload variations**: Development, testing, and production environments may have different storage patterns.
- **Sharding strategy**: How you distribute data across shards affects storage distribution.

It's beneficial to document your reasoning behind your estimation choices. Don't be overly concerned with precise estimates, as Atlas offers flexible scaling options, which will be discussed later.

RAM requirements

Understanding your working set is fundamental to properly sizing your MongoDB Atlas cluster's memory requirements. The working set represents the subset of your data and indexes that your application actively accesses during regular operations. When your working set fits within available RAM, MongoDB can serve most queries from memory, resulting in significantly faster response times compared to queries that rely on disk access.

Your working set typically consists of two main components:

- **Frequently accessed documents**: These are the data that your application reads or writes regularly during normal operations
- **Indexes**: Indexes are important to keep in memory because they directly impact query execution speed

WiredTiger memory allocation

MongoDB Atlas uses the WiredTiger storage engine, which dedicates a portion of available RAM to cache and memory-intensive operations. The cache allocation depends on the cluster tier:

- **M40 or larger clusters**: WiredTiger dedicates 50% of the physical RAM for its cache by default. The remaining memory is reserved for other operations, such as sorts, aggregations, calculations, the underlying operating system, and other services running on the host.
- **Smaller clusters (M30 or below)**: WiredTiger allocates 25% of physical RAM to its cache. This difference in allocation percentage is important when estimating effective memory availability for your working set.

To calculate the RAM available for your working set, multiply the total RAM by either 0.5 (for M40+ tiers) or 0.25 (for M30 and smaller tiers), depending on your cluster tier.

If the cache cannot fully accommodate the working set, WiredTiger will evict less-frequently-used pages to free memory. This ensures queries remain functional but may rely on slower disk I/O under heavy workloads.

RAM calculation example

To calculate RAM requirements, you need to do the following:

1. Start with your total index size (15 GB in our example).
2. Add frequently accessed data (200 GB × 20% = 40 GB). Note that 20% is an assumption and can vary greatly depending on the applications.
3. Working set = 15 GB + 40 GB = 55 GB.
4. Account for WiredTiger allocation (55 GB ÷ 0.5 = 110 GB for M40+).

For a product catalog application with 200 GB total data, 15 GB of indexes, and 20% hot data, you'd need at least 110 GB of RAM across your cluster. This suggests an M80 tier (128 GB RAM) would be appropriate.

IOPS and performance analysis

IOPS represents your database's storage system capacity for read and write operations. To choose the optimal Atlas cluster configuration, it's helpful to understand your application's IOPS requirements.

Different operations consume varying amounts of IOPS. Read operations that access data already in memory consume minimal IOPS, making efficient use of your working set. Conversely, any write operation, including inserts, updates, and deletes, requires significantly more IOPS because it modifies both data and associated indexes.

A valuable approach is to profile your application by recording all database operations it performs during typical usage. This helps determine whether your workload is read-heavy, write-heavy, or balanced. For instance, an analytics platform might be read-intensive with occasional batch writes, while an event-logging system would be predominantly write-heavy.

IOPS provisioning and scaling

MongoDB Atlas automatically ties IOPS thresholds to provisioned storage capacity. More storage means higher baseline IOPS:

- Clusters configured with **1 TB or more** storage guarantee a 3:1 ratio of IOPS to storage (e.g., 3,000 IOPS at 1 TB storage or 16,000 IOPS at 16 TB)
- Smaller clusters have tier-specific baselines, starting at **3,000 IOPS** minimum for clusters M30 and higher

This automatic scaling ensures predictable performance and prevents bottlenecks. Storage capacity also impacts burst performance, as clusters with larger disks accrue more burst credits for handling temporary spikes in activity.

Provisioned IOPS for write-heavy workloads

For clusters running on **AWS**, tiers **M30 and above** offer the ability to provision additional IOPS independently of storage size. This feature is especially useful for write-heavy applications that require high IOPS performance but do not need large storage volumes.

For **Azure-hosted clusters (M40 and above)** and select regions, users can even scale IOPS independently and customize performance without overprovisioning storage. This flexibility allows clusters to be fine-tuned for specific workload requirements, whether read-intensive or write-heavy.

Using monitoring tools to scale effectively

IOPS estimation doesn't need to be perfect from the start. MongoDB Atlas provides tools to monitor actual IOPS usage and identify performance bottlenecks:

- Use the **Disk IOPS graph** in the Atlas metrics dashboard to track usage during your workload's peak and idle periods.

- Observe metrics such as **Disk Latency** and **Disk Queue Depth** to determine whether your workload is straining your current configuration. These insights help you assess whether your cluster can sustain projected workloads or requires scaling.

Atlas supports **auto-scaling** and **manual adjustment** of IOPS through storage increases or provisioned capacity (M30+ for AWS, M40+ for Azure). This enables you to start with an estimate, monitor real-world usage, and scale dynamically to maintain application performance while optimizing costs.

This approach, starting with a reasonable estimate, monitoring actual usage, and scaling as needed, allows you to fine-tune your cluster's performance characteristics based on real operational data rather than theoretical projections.

Network throughput and connections

MongoDB Atlas clusters handle two primary types of network traffic: **client-to-server communication** (how your applications connect to your database) and **intra-cluster communication** (coordination between nodes for replication and operational consistency). Both impact performance, with multi-region clusters requiring special attention due to higher latency and increased bandwidth consumption.

Network capacity directly affects your database performance. Sufficient bandwidth ensures efficient delivery of large result sets and reduces operation latency. During traffic spikes, limited capacity can lead to dropped connections. Inadequate bandwidth may cause replication lag, particularly in geographically distributed clusters.

Bandwidth calculation

Estimate your bandwidth requirements using this simple formula:

```
Bandwidth = Average Document Size × Peak Documents Per Second
```

For example, if your average document is 10 KB and you process 100,000 documents per second, you'll need approximately 1 GB/sec of bandwidth.

Actual usage varies based on read preference configuration, replication settings, and partitioning strategy. Distributing read operations across secondary nodes can optimize bandwidth usage and reduce primary node load.

Connection management

MongoDB Atlas enforces connection limits based on your cluster tier, applied *per node* rather than per cluster. Free and shared tiers (M0, M2, and M5) support 500 to 3,000 connections per node. Dedicated tiers scale from 6,000 connections (M10) up to 128,000 connections (M200+). Select a tier that accommodates your peak requirements with room for growth.

Connection pooling

Connection pooling involves maintaining reusable connections that applications can borrow and return, rather than repeatedly establishing new connections. This strategy reduces overhead, optimizes resource usage, lowers latency, and decreases server load. For effective connection pooling, it's important to size the pool appropriately, configure timeouts to prevent stalled connections, and implement monitoring to detect any connection issues. Most MongoDB drivers offer built-in support for connection pooling with configurable options.

By estimating bandwidth needs, understanding connection limits, implementing efficient connection pooling, and strategically distributing traffic, you can optimize your MongoDB Atlas network performance. These practices are important for building a responsive database foundation that can scale effectively with your application's growth while proactively preventing performance bottlenecks.

Region selection

Selecting the right geographical region for your Atlas cluster involves more than just technical considerations. Data sovereignty requirements may legally mandate where your data can be stored and processed. Different countries and regions have specific regulations governing data storage, particularly for personal or sensitive information.

When evaluating your regulatory landscape, consider frameworks such as GDPR (Europe), HIPAA (US healthcare), or CCPA (California). These regulations may require data to remain within specific geographical boundaries. Atlas offers regions across major cloud providers and continents to help you satisfy these requirements while maintaining performance.

For multinational applications, you may need to implement a data segregation strategy, where different clusters in different regions handle data according to the applicable regulations. Atlas's project and organization structure can help manage this complexity effectively.

Latency optimization

Beyond compliance, physical proximity between your application servers and database impacts performance. Network latency increases with distance, and even milliseconds matter for responsive applications. As a general rule, position your Atlas cluster in the same region as your application servers whenever possible.

For globally distributed applications, consider these approaches:

- **Primary region selection**: Place your cluster in the region with the highest user concentration or most critical operations

- **Multi-region strategies**: For advanced deployments, Atlas Global Clusters provide location-aware sharding, automatically routing data to the appropriate geographical zone. This allows writes to occur in the region closest to your users, minimizing latency.

- **Read-local patterns**: Configure your application to read from geographically nearby secondaries while sending writes to the primary in another region. This approach balances data consistency with read performance.

When implementing a multi-region strategy, be aware of the additional costs and complexity involved. Test thoroughly to ensure your application handles region failures and network partitions appropriately.

For most applications, a good starting point is selecting a single region with the best balance of regulatory compliance and proximity to your user base. You can later evolve toward a more distributed architecture as your application's needs grow and your understanding of actual usage patterns matures.

Final cluster selection

After analyzing your various requirements, create a consolidated view of your findings. The key here is not just gathering the numbers but documenting every decision and assumption made along the way:

- **Storage needs:** Document both current size and growth rate assumptions

- **RAM requirements**: Record working set estimates and access pattern assumptions

- **IOPS projections**: Note the read/write ratio used in calculations

- **Network needs**: Document peak throughput assumptions and concurrency estimates

- **Regional constraints**: List any compliance requirements influencing location decisions

Maintaining this record serves multiple purposes: it helps justify your choices to stakeholders, provides context for future scaling decisions, and creates institutional knowledge for team members who may inherit the system.

When selecting your initial cluster configuration, remember that Atlas offers remarkable flexibility; nothing is set in stone. This should influence your decision-making approach:

- **Start practical, not perfect**: Since Atlas can easily scale up or down, you don't need to find the perfect tier immediately. Document your reasoning for each choice.

- **Balance current needs with flexibility**: Rather than over-provisioning for projected needs months away, choose a reasonable starting point with a clear path to scaling.

- **Record cost-performance trade-offs**: Note which compromises were made and the business reasoning behind them, creating accountability for the decisions.

Atlas allows you to adjust nearly all cluster parameters, that is, tier, storage, IOPS, and even region, with minimal disruption. This flexibility means your initial selection is a starting point, not a permanent commitment.

Before finalizing your production deployment, do the following:

- **Document test scenarios**: Create a clear record of the workloads used in testing and their relationship to expected production loads

- **Record baseline metrics**: Establish performance benchmarks that will serve as comparison points after future scaling operations

- **Test scaling operations**: Practice actually scaling your cluster up and down to understand the process and impact on your application

During validation, document any discrepancies between expected and actual performance. These observations provide valuable insights for future optimization.

The true advantage of Atlas is that it lets you adapt as you learn. Your initial cluster selection doesn't need to be perfect; it just needs to be a reasonable starting point. As you gather real-world usage data, you can easily adjust your configuration to match actual requirements rather than theoretical projections. This approach often results in better performance, lower costs, and less stress than trying to perfectly predict all your needs upfront.

Scaling in Atlas

Have you ever experienced that moment of excitement mixed with anxiety when your application suddenly gains traction? While user growth is the goal of most applications, it often brings with it a challenge: scaling your database to handle increased load without sacrificing performance or reliability.

As your application's user base expands, you'll likely notice several indicators that signal the need for scaling:

- Slower query response times during peak usage periods
- Increasing CPU and memory utilization across your database nodes
- Storage requirements growing faster than anticipated
- Geographic expansion of your user base, creating latency concerns

MongoDB Atlas addresses these scaling challenges through a flexible, comprehensive approach that combines both vertical and horizontal scaling strategies. But what exactly does this mean for your application?

Vertical scaling involves increasing the resources available to your existing database nodes, giving your current infrastructure more power to handle workloads. Think of it as upgrading from a compact car to a sports car without changing your route.

Horizontal scaling, on the other hand, distributes your data across multiple machines, allowing your database to handle larger datasets and higher throughput by adding more nodes rather than making existing ones more powerful. This is like adding more lanes to a highway rather than trying to make cars go faster.

Atlas provides tools and capabilities for both approaches, giving you the flexibility to choose the right strategy, or combination of strategies, for your specific needs.

Why is choosing the right scaling strategy so important?

The scaling path you select directly impacts several aspects of your application:

- **Cost efficiency**: Different scaling approaches have different cost structures. Choosing wisely prevents overpaying for unused resources
- **Performance characteristics**: Some workloads benefit more from vertical scaling, while others see greater improvements with horizontal approaches
- **Operational complexity**: Horizontal scaling introduces additional complexity that might require more management overhead
- **Future growth potential**: Initial scaling decisions can either facilitate or constrain future options as the application continues to grow

Throughout this section, we'll explore Atlas's scaling capabilities, providing you with the knowledge needed to make informed decisions about scaling your MongoDB deployments. We'll start by examining vertical scaling options, including Atlas's powerful auto-scaling features, before moving on to horizontal approaches such as sharding and Global Clusters.

By understanding the full range of scaling options available in Atlas, you'll be equipped to create a tailored strategy that aligns with your application's unique requirements and growth trajectory.

Vertical scaling in Atlas

Vertical scaling, often called "scaling up," is the process of adding more resources to your existing database nodes. In Atlas, this translates to increasing the CPU, memory, and storage capacity of your cluster without changing its basic architecture.

Think of vertical scaling like upgrading your computer rather than buying additional computers. You're making what you already have more powerful, allowing it to handle increased workloads without architectural changes.

Vertical scaling shines in several common scenarios:

- **Growing but moderate workloads**: When your application experiences steady growth that doesn't yet justify the complexity of sharding
- **Memory-intensive operations**: Applications performing complex aggregations or maintaining large working sets in memory
- **Simplicity requirements**: When operational simplicity is a priority over absolute scale
- **Development or testing environments**: Where you need to quickly adjust resources without redesigning your data model

For example, an e-commerce platform experiencing 30% monthly growth might start with an M30 cluster, then vertically scale to M40 and M50 as transaction volumes increase, before eventually considering sharding.

Trade-offs and limitations

While vertical scaling offers simplicity, it comes with important considerations:

- **Upper limits**: Cloud providers have maximum instance sizes, eventually limiting vertical scaling
- **Cost efficiency curve**: Higher tiers have a less favorable price-to-performance ratio; doubling resources can more than double costs in some cases

Vertical scaling works best as part of a comprehensive strategy. While it offers quick wins for growing applications, most successful systems eventually combine vertical scaling with horizontal distribution as they reach a larger scale.

Vertical scaling implementation options

When you're ready to vertically scale your Atlas cluster, you have several implementation options that can be tailored to your specific workload requirements. Let's explore some of the approaches we could take.

Provisioning stronger hardware

The most straightforward vertical scaling approach is upgrading your cluster tier to more powerful instances.

When upgrading your cluster tier, Atlas performs a rolling upgrade process that maintains availability throughout the transition. Your primary node remains accessible while secondary nodes are upgraded one by one.

Deploying additional nodes to existing replica sets

Another vertical scaling strategy is adding more nodes to your existing replica set. This approach enhances the following:

- **Read scalability**: More secondary nodes distribute read operations
- **Fault tolerance**: Enhanced resilience against node failures
- **Geographic distribution**: Nodes in different regions reduce latency

Adding nodes doesn't increase your primary's capacity, but it does offload read operations and improve availability. For instance, a financial services application might add read-only nodes in multiple regions to support local reporting needs while maintaining centralized write operations.

Offloading read operations and analytics workloads

For workloads with heavy read operations and analytical requirements, Atlas offers specialized node types:

- **Analytics nodes:** Secondary nodes optimized for analytical queries
- **Read-only nodes:** Non-electable secondary nodes dedicated to serving read operations

These specialized nodes allow you to vertically scale different aspects of your database independently. Your operational transactions can use standard nodes, while resource-intensive analytics run on dedicated hardware optimized for those workloads.

Consider an e-commerce platform that needs to maintain fast checkout performance while running complex inventory analytics. By adding analytics nodes, they can run heavy reporting queries without impacting the customer experience.

Each of these vertical scaling options can be implemented separately or in combination, giving you flexible ways to address performance bottlenecks before considering the complexity of horizontal scaling.

Auto-scaling capabilities

One of Atlas's most powerful features is its ability to automatically scale your resources in response to changing workloads, reducing the need for constant manual intervention.

Storage auto-scaling

Atlas's storage auto-scaling helps prevent disk space emergencies by proactively increasing storage capacity when needed.

How it works

1. Atlas monitors disk utilization across all nodes in your cluster.
2. When any node reaches 90% disk utilization, Atlas automatically increases storage.
3. After scaling, the target is to reduce utilization to approximately 70%.
4. This feature is enabled by default for new clusters.

When storage auto-scaling won't happen

- During high-speed write activity (such as bulk inserts) where Atlas doesn't have sufficient time to prepare and copy data
- When you specify different cluster tier classes for base nodes and analytics nodes (e.g., General for operational nodes and Low-CPU for analytics)
- When base tier and analytics tier nodes are deployed in different cloud provider regions

> Plan to manually scale up storage before bulk data operations to avoid hitting capacity limits during intensive write activities.

Cluster tier auto-scaling

Atlas can automatically adjust your entire cluster tier based on CPU and memory utilization patterns.

Scaling triggers

For scaling up (M30+ clusters):

- CPU utilization exceeding 75% for an hour or 90% for 10 minutes
- Memory utilization exceeding 75% for an hour or 90% for 10 minutes

For scaling down:

- CPU utilization below 45% for at least 4 hours
- No scaling activity in the previous 24 hours
- Projected memory usage at the lower tier would remain below 60%

Setting appropriate tier boundaries

Within the Atlas UI, you can set minimum and maximum cluster tiers to control auto-scaling behavior and prevent unexpected costs.

Auto-scaling considerations

Let's take a moment to look at some of the considerations we should take when using auto-scaling for our Atlas deployments:

- **Conservative design philosophy**: Auto-scaling is intentionally conservative to prevent oscillation between tiers or reactions to temporary spikes. For product launches or planned traffic increases, consider manual pre-scaling.
- **Storage and tier relationship**: If storage auto-scaling increases beyond what your current tier supports, Atlas will automatically adjust your minimum tier upward, potentially disabling downward scaling.
- **Monitoring:** Atlas logs all auto-scaling events in your Activity Feed and provides configurable alerts for auto-scaling activities, replacing the legacy email notifications.

By understanding these auto-scaling capabilities and limitations, you can achieve an optimal balance of performance, cost efficiency, and operational simplicity while avoiding potential scaling failures during operations.

Horizontal scaling in MongoDB Atlas

Horizontal scaling, often called "scaling out," allows databases to expand their capacity by distributing data and workloads across multiple nodes. This approach is ideal for accommodating high traffic loads, massive datasets, and fluctuating workload demands in modern applications. MongoDB Atlas makes horizontal scaling seamless through automated management and robust sharding capabilities.

MongoDB achieves horizontal scaling through sharding, where data is partitioned across multiple replica sets, called shards. Each shard stores a subset of the total data, making it possible to scale horizontally as capacity needs grow.

Key advantages of sharding in Atlas are as follows:

- Distributes read/write operations across multiple shards, enabling scalability for high-throughput applications
- Overcomes the limitations of individual machines by distributing workloads
- Achieves better load balancing and efficiency compared to relying solely on vertical scaling

Components of a sharded cluster

A MongoDB sharded cluster includes the following:

- **Shards**: Replica sets containing partitioned subsets of data.
- **Config servers**: Store metadata about data distribution and sharding.
- **mongos routers**: Route query requests to the correct shard(s).

Starting with version 8.0, Atlas provides **config shards**, which reduce costs for deployments with up to three shards while maintaining a fully functional sharded architecture.

Shard key selection

Choosing the right **shard key** is important for effective horizontal scaling:

- **High cardinality**: Ensure many possible unique values
- **Write distribution**: Prevent hotspots by evenly distributing writes
- **Query efficiency**: Design keys to support common access patterns, enabling queries to target specific shards

Atlas also supports three sharding strategies:

- **Ranged sharding**: Partitions data into contiguous ranges based on shard key values
- **Hashed sharding**: Employs hashed shard key values to achieve an even distribution of data and workloads
- **Zoned sharding**: Connects specific range values to designated geographic regions

Global Clusters for geographic distribution

Global Clusters extend sharding principles by combining geographic and workload distribution. This capability allows Atlas to provide **low latency** for users located across different regions.

Benefits of Global Clusters

- **Low-latency reads and writes**: Improves performance by routing requests to the nearest geographic zone
- **Data sovereignty**: Ensures regional compliance with data storage regulations
- **Enhanced availability**: Isolates regional outages, minimizing failure impact
- **Seamless user experience**: Optimizes response times for globally distributed workloads

For instance, a global e-commerce platform can use zoned sharding to serve European customers from EU-hosted shards for regulatory compliance while maintaining high-speed inventory queries across other regions.

The following are key requirements for implementing Global Clusters:

- **Sharded collections**: Collections must be sharded to leverage global data distribution
- **Zone definition**: Assign up to nine geographic zones for data placement
- **Priority mapping**: Define regions for primary, secondary, read-only, and analytics nodes

Administrative considerations

Horizontal scaling with MongoDB Atlas introduces several administrative choices for planning and maintenance.

Unlike vertical scaling (which can leverage auto-scaling), horizontal scaling involves deliberate design choices:

- **Shard key selection**: Choose keys based on access patterns
- **Sharding strategy**: Select between hashed, ranged, or zoned approaches
- **Cluster timing**: Introduce sharding once resource utilization peaks at ~70%

Cost and operational trade-offs

Horizontal scaling offers scalability at lower costs but increases administrative overhead:

- **Config server costs**: Although Atlas reduces these with config shards, they remain a consideration
- **Multi-region transfers**: Global Clusters may incur inter-region data transfer costs
- **Uneven utilization risks**: Poor shard key selection can lead to hotspots

Horizontal versus vertical scaling

Aspect	Vertical Scaling	Horizontal Scaling
Complexity	Low (auto-scaling handles upgrades)	Higher (requires shard key selection)
Cost dynamics	Expensive at larger tiers	Often more cost-effective for large workloads
Maximum capacity	Limited by the largest machine size	Add shards as needed
Data modeling impact	Minimal	Requires shard key and sharding strategy
Query efficiency	Suitable for most query patterns	Best for shard-specific queries

Table 8.1: Comparison of vertical and horizontal scaling

MongoDB Atlas integrates both approaches, enabling fine-grained auto-scaling alongside horizontal scaling for comprehensive elasticity. This allows us to easily leverage **both horizontal and vertical scaling** as workloads evolve.

For example, during holiday traffic spikes or viral events, Atlas can temporarily scale clusters up while also distributing workloads horizontally to optimize cost and performance.

Creating a comprehensive scaling strategy

The most effective scaling approaches typically combine both vertical and horizontal techniques, adapting as your application evolves.

Successful scaling strategies often layer different approaches rather than choosing between them:

- Vertical scaling provides simplicity and immediate resource adjustments
- Read-only nodes offer an intermediate step before full sharding

- Sharding specific collections allows targeted horizontal scaling
- Global distribution addresses geographic performance needs

Many applications begin with vertical auto-scaling for flexibility, then introduce horizontal elements as specific bottlenecks emerge. This hybrid approach balances simplicity with scalability.

Atlas provides tools to assess your scaling strategy through the following:

- Real-time performance dashboards
- Historical metric analysis
- Query performance statistics
- Resource usage tracking

Effective evaluation requires establishing clear baselines and objectives for your scaling initiatives. Regular review of these metrics helps identify when to adjust your approach.

A flexible scaling strategy accommodates both expected growth and changing access patterns:

- Consider data model implications for future scaling needs
- Balance immediate requirements with long-term flexibility
- Establish clear thresholds for escalating your scaling approach
- Account for potential changes in application functionality

The most resilient strategies maintain options for both vertical and horizontal expansion, allowing your infrastructure to adapt alongside your application's natural evolution.

By thoughtfully combining scaling techniques, monitoring performance metrics, and maintaining flexibility in your approach, you can build a scaling strategy that grows with your application while optimizing both performance and cost.

Configuring authentication and authorization

In the world of cloud databases, security is a paramount concern, and MongoDB Atlas is no exception. Securing your Atlas deployment involves understanding and effectively implementing two key concepts: authentication and authorization. These mechanisms are vital in creating a robust security architecture that protects your data and limits access to only those who need it.

Understanding authentication and authorization

Authentication is about verifying identities, answering the question, "Who are you?" It ensures that only legitimate users and services can access your system, serving as the initial barrier against unauthorized entry.

Once a user is authenticated, **authorization** takes over, answering the question, "What are you allowed to do?" Authorization governs user permissions within the system, granting access to specific resources and actions based on defined roles or policies. Together, these processes form the backbone of a secure MongoDB Atlas environment.

The control plane and data plane

To fully understand how authentication and authorization work in Atlas, we first need to zoom out and grasp the roles of the control plane and data plane. By distinguishing between these two planes, you'll gain clarity on responsibilities within your Atlas deployments.

The **control plane** acts as the administrative heart of your MongoDB Atlas environment. This is the domain of **Atlas users**: those who are responsible for managing the overarching infrastructure. They set up clusters, configure security settings, and handle billing operations. Think of Atlas users as the strategists who define how resources are organized and maintained.

Conversely, the **data plane** is where the hands-on management of database resources takes place. This is the realm of **database users**, individuals who interact directly with the collections and documents within your Atlas clusters. These users are tasked with the day-to-day operations, ensuring the databases are accessed and used effectively, whether in development phases or high-demand production environments.

By clearly defining the roles of Atlas users and database users within the control and data planes, you'll have a better understanding of how responsibilities are distributed, enabling smoother and more secure management of your Atlas deployments.

Workforce versus workload

One more important distinction to make before setting up your authentication and authorization is the difference between workforce and workload users. Knowing this will inform your decision on which authentication method to go with.

Workforce users are people who interact with a system. This includes roles such as administrators, developers, or analysts who use tools and interfaces designed for human use.

On the other hand, **workload** users refer to automated entities, such as programs or scripts, that perform tasks within a system without direct human involvement. These might include applications or background processes. Typically, workload users use the Atlas Admin API to efficiently manage and interact with MongoDB Atlas resources, automate routine operations, and streamline workflows.

If you are interested in using the Atlas Admin API, make sure to check out the documentation on it (`https://www.mongodb.com/docs/atlas/api/atlas-admin-api/`).

Making the distinction between workforce users and workload users is important because it helps tailor security, authentication, and access strategies to the unique needs of each group. Workforce users, being individuals, typically require authentication mechanisms that prioritize user-friendliness and integration with the organization's identity management systems, such as **Single Sign-On (SSO)**. In contrast, workload users, such as applications or automated scripts, need robust security measures that ensure seamless and secure access, often using methods such as API keys or service accounts.

Let's shift our focus to authentication.

Authentication

We could fill an entire book with hands-on material about building a robust authentication system. Instead, this section will offer a high-level overview of the authentication landscape, enabling informed decision-making for your individual use case. Once you identify a suitable approach that meets your needs, MongoDB's documentation includes tutorials to guide the implementation process.

There are two types of users in MongoDB Atlas: Atlas users and database users, each with distinct authentication methods. To start, we will focus on Atlas users, who manage the control plane and play a key role in authentication workflows.

Atlas workforce user authentication

For Atlas users, authentication can be achieved using a username and password, supplemented by multi-factor authentication for enhanced security. Alternatively, you can use SSO to integrate with popular platforms such as GitHub or Google.

In many cases, organizations require a more integrated authentication approach. To address this need, you can set up federated authentication. This enables you to connect with your chosen identity provider, such as Okta or Microsoft Entra ID, ensuring seamless access for your team. For a comprehensive list of supported identity providers, be sure to consult the Atlas documentation.

These authentication methods are great for workforce users, but what about workload users?

Atlas workload user authentication

Until recently, the only option for workload user authentication in Atlas was to use Atlas API keys, which can still be generated and used today. But the introduction of service accounts provides an improved solution.

Service accounts in MongoDB Atlas offer a modern way for applications to authenticate with the MongoDB Atlas Administration API. Unlike the traditional **Programmatic API Keys (PAKs)** you might have used to provide user access, service accounts use the OAuth 2.0 standard, streamlining and automating authentication processes. This means your applications, rather than individual users, can securely and efficiently interact with MongoDB Atlas resources, letting development teams choose the authentication workflows that best suit their needs.

One of the improvements service accounts provide over API keys is in the realm of security and automation. Where PAKs require diligent management and rotation to maintain security, service accounts automate much of this through the OAuth 2.0 client credentials flow. This means less manual work for you, as you can simply regenerate client secrets without having to change the service account's other settings. The OAuth 2.0 approach is also broadly compatible, making it easier to integrate various services and components across your technology stack.

The ability of service accounts to sync up with your existing identity provider is a game-changer. This allows your organization to manage authentication using familiar cloud-native identity systems, fitting seamlessly into your current setup. By allowing you to use established identity and access control measures, MongoDB Atlas makes it easy to incorporate service accounts into the authentication strategies you already have, all while lightening the load on your IT and security teams.

Database user authentication

Having covered authentication methods for Atlas users, let's dive into the authentication mechanisms available for database users in MongoDB Atlas.

Salted Challenge Response Authentication Mechanism (SCRAM) provides a simple username and password setup. This method is ideal for development environments prioritizing speed, but it may not be suitable for production applications due to its simplicity. Even in development, robust security practices are important. Use strong passwords and consider tools such as HashiCorp Vault for secure credential management.

For a more integrated authentication experience, identity federation connects with your organization's existing identity providers, similar to federated authentication for Atlas users. It supports two main types of database users.

First, we have workforce users: these are human users accessing and managing MongoDB Atlas through interfaces such as the web UI or command-line tools. Identity federation allows them to authenticate using credentials managed by your organization's identity provider, such as Okta or Microsoft Entra ID, streamlining authentication and reducing manual management efforts.

Then there's workload identity federation, which allows you to configure identities from each cloud provider or any OAuth 2.0-compliant authorization service. The following are examples:

- **Azure**: Use Azure service principals and managed identities
- **Google Cloud**: Leverage Google service accounts
- **AWS**: Use AWS IAM roles

To set up identity federation in MongoDB Atlas, follow these steps in order using the Federation Management console:

1. Add and verify your domains.
2. Configure your identity provider with Atlas.
3. Connect your domains with your identity provider.
4. Activate your identity provider.

You can find detailed guides for each identity provider in the Atlas documentation.

Lastly, we have X.509 certificates, which enable mutual **Transport Layer Security** (**TLS**). By using X.509 certificates, we can take advantage of mutual TLS.

Mutual TLS builds upon the standard TLS handshake by requiring both the client and the server to authenticate each other's certificate. This mutual authentication ensures that both parties involved in a communication are trusted.

X.509 is ideal for authenticating applications that need to connect to your clusters.

Selecting the best authentication method for your database users depends on your specific security and operational needs. By evaluating these options, you can better protect your data and operations.

Authorization

Having discussed authentication in Atlas, it's natural to move on to authorization, which answers the question, "What are you allowed to do?" In Atlas, this is managed through RBAC.

Implementing authorization is closely related to the zero-trust security model and the principle of least privilege. Zero trust emphasizes that no one should be trusted by default, continuously validating access rights. Meanwhile, the principle of least privilege ensures users have only the permissions necessary for their roles. Together, these principles guide the configuration of RBAC in Atlas, enhancing security by strictly controlling and verifying access.

Role-based access control

RBAC defines a framework for managing and restricting database access based on predefined roles. Each role encompasses specific privileges, which determine what actions a user can perform. By assigning roles to users, you can control their access and actions within the database and Atlas efficiently. This approach enhances security by ensuring that users only have the permissions necessary for their work, adhering to the principle of least privilege.

It's important to understand that RBAC is applied to both Atlas users and database users. However, their roles and privileges are not shared. As we will explore shortly, Atlas users and database users each have their own distinct roles and privileges.

Let's visualize how RBAC can be applied in a real-world scenario for both Atlas users and database users:

For example, imagine a medium-sized software development company that leverages MongoDB Atlas to manage its project data. Within the company, there are different team members with distinct access needs:

- **Atlas users:**
    - **Platform administrators:** These users, responsible for managing the MongoDB Atlas account infrastructure, have roles that grant them permissions to deploy new clusters, manage settings, and oversee security protocols. With broad privileges, they ensure optimal performance and security of the company's cloud database infrastructure.

- **Database users:**

    - **Developers:** As database users, they require access to create, read, and update documents within specific collections. They are assigned a Developer database role, permitting them to perform **Create, Read, Update, Delete (CRUD)** operations relevant to their tasks.

    - **Data analysts:** Also database users, they depend on read access across several collections to derive insights and analyze data trends. Their Analyst role provides read privileges aligned with their analytical tasks, enabling them to run complex queries using MongoDB's powerful tools, such as the aggregation framework.

While these roles don't map directly to Atlas roles, you can get a basic picture of what RBAC can look like in a team setting.

Now that we know what RBAC is, let's start exploring the specifics of it in Atlas.

Atlas user roles

A good place to start is with the built-in roles for Atlas users. Built-in roles are predefined sets of permissions that you can assign to users to control their access and actions within Atlas. These roles help simplify user management by providing a quick way to grant appropriate levels of access without having to define custom roles manually.

For Atlas users, we have roles for both organizations and projects. Organizations manage things such as Atlas user access, billing, and various administrative tasks. Given this, organization roles are tied to these types of tasks. The following are examples:

- **Organization Owner:** As the pinnacle of management, the Organization Owner has the authority to govern every aspect of the organization. This includes overseeing settings, handling billing, and managing users and projects, providing comprehensive control over administrative functions.

- **Billing Admin:** Focused exclusively on financial operations, this role handles billing details and manages payment methods. While crucial for financial transparency, the Billing Admin doesn't possess rights to alter project settings or non-financial administrative tasks.

- **Organization Member:** These members have a limited view into the organization, with restricted administrative privileges. They can access organization details but lack rights to create, modify, or delete clusters, or to manage user access, ensuring secure organizational operations.

Within each organization, projects act as individual environments tailored for specific applications. Project roles are crafted to complement organizational roles and provide granular control within projects. Each project can have unique roles:

- **Project Owner**: Holding full access, the Project Owner can configure and manage every aspect of the project. From creating clusters to setting up monitoring tools and backups, this role allows comprehensive management, including handling user permissions and integrating observability tools such as the Query Profiler for data analysis.

- **Project Data Access Read Only**: Ideal for users needing visibility into databases without the ability to alter them, this role provides viewing privileges in Data Explorer and observability tools, ensuring data integrity and preventing unauthorized changes.

- **Project Cluster Admin**: Specializing in cluster operations, this role allows pausing, editing, and resuming clusters, but not creating new ones. It ensures precise control over existing cluster configurations while sidelining broader creation tasks reserved for higher roles.

> The Project Data Access roles are unique since they give control plane users access to the data plane. This should be considered when granting these roles to users.

It's important to note that these roles are hierarchical. Higher-level roles in the organization have overarching permissions that can affect multiple projects, while project-specific roles are more focused and restricted in scope.

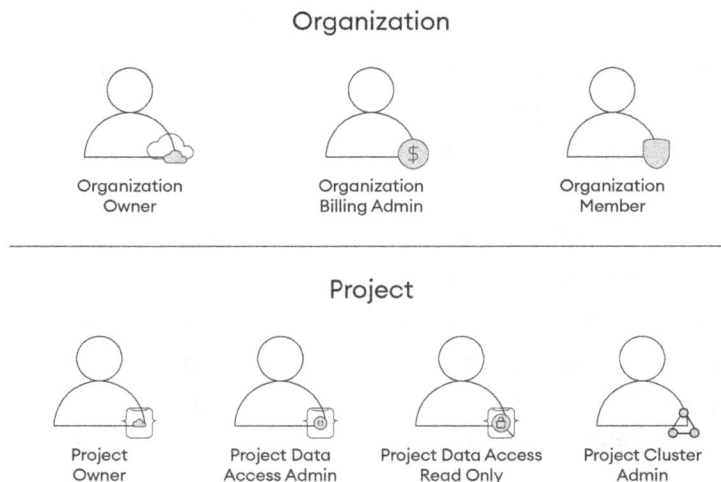

Figure 8.4: The hierarchical relationship and differences between organization and project roles

While this is not an exhaustive list, it gives you a sense of the kinds of built-in roles available. If you want a more comprehensive list of all the built-in roles, you can check out the Atlas documentation (https://www.mongodb.com/docs/atlas/reference/user-roles/).

So, how do we assign an Atlas user a role? Here's a way: We can assign roles when we invite someone to our organization, as follows:

```
atlas users invite --email user@example.com --username user@example.com
--orgRole <orgId>:ORG_MEMBER --projectRole <projectId>:GROUP_READ_ONLY
--firstName Example --lastName User --country US --output json
```

Database user roles

Let's shift our attention to the database user, which deals with managing the data directly. In MongoDB, a database user serves as a credential for authenticating to your cluster, acting as a unique entity with specific permissions that determine actions you can perform within the database. Similar to Atlas users, database users have their own set of built-in roles that we can take advantage of, such as the following:

- **atlasAdmin**: The atlasAdmin role can perform a wide range of administrative tasks. This includes managing shards, configuring database settings, and performing operations across all databases within the cluster. It's ideal for users who need comprehensive control and oversight.

- **readWriteAnyDatabase**: This role allows users to execute both read and write operations on any database within the cluster. It's a versatile choice for those who need broad access for data manipulation but don't require administrative permissions.

- **readAnyDatabase**: Tailored for users who only need to read data, the readAnyDatabase role grants permission to access and view data across all databases in the cluster. It restricts any data modifications, making it perfect for analysts or team members focused on data examination without altering it.

This is not an exhaustive list of database user roles, but it gives you a sense of the types of built-in roles available to us.

We'll need a database user for when we begin working with Atlas Search and Vector Search, so let's go ahead and create that user now so we can see how database roles are used.

To create a new database user, run the following command:

```
atlas dbusers create readWriteAnyDatabase --username searchDemoUser
--projectId <projectId>
```

- **`atlas dbusers create`**: This is the command to create a new database user in an Atlas project.
- **`readWriteAnyDatabase`**: This specifies the role to be assigned to the user.
- **`--username searchDemoUser`**: This flag sets the username for the new database user. In this example, the username given is `searchDemoUser`. This is the name the user will use to authenticate with the databases in the specified project.
- **`--projectId <projectId>`**: The `--projectId` flag specifies the unique identifier for the MongoDB Atlas project where this user will be created. `<projectId>` should be replaced with the actual project ID string. This ID ensures that the user is added to the correct project environment within your Atlas organization.

We now have a database user we can use for the rest of this chapter to connect to our cluster. In our case, the built-in roles worked great for us. But what if we need more granular control over the privileges for a certain role?

Custom roles

We have the ability to create custom roles for database users. Custom database user roles allow you to tailor access control to fit the specific needs of your application or organization. While MongoDB Atlas provides a set of built-in roles that cover common use cases, creating custom roles provides flexibility when you need more granular permissions.

With custom roles, we can do the following:

- **Define specific privileges**: Assign precise privileges to a role, such as read or write access to specific databases or collections, or even administrative operations such as index management
- **Enhance security**: Limit users to only the resources and actions they require, reducing potential exposure from overly permissive access
- **Improve management**: Streamline role management by grouping user permissions, making it easier to assign and update access controls as your team or application evolves

Creating a custom role in MongoDB Atlas involves identifying the actions and resources needed for a particular user or application, and then executing these definitions through the Atlas UI or API.

To create a custom database role, run the following command:

```
atlas customDbRoles create customRole --privilege FIND@
databaseName,UPDATE@databaseName.firstCollectionName,UPDATE@databaseName.
secondCollectionName
```

- **atlas customDbRoles create**: This is the command to create a custom database role.
- **customRole**: This is the name of the custom database role being created. You can choose any name that makes sense for the role's purpose and scope.
- **--privilege**: This flag is used to specify the privileges that the role will have. Each privilege is defined with an action and a target, formatted as ACTION@TARGET.
- **FIND@databaseName**: This specifies a privilege allowing the custom role to perform read operations (such as querying documents) within the entire databaseName. FIND is the action, and databaseName is the target database on which this action can be performed
- **UPDATE@databaseName.firstCollectionName**: This grants the privilege to perform update operations on firstCollectionName within databaseName. UPDATE is the action, and databaseName.firstCollectionName specifies the collection on which this privilege is applicable.
- **UPDATE@databaseName.secondCollectionName**: Similarly, this grants the privilege to perform update operations on secondCollectionName within databaseName. Again, UPDATE is the action, and databaseName.secondCollectionName is the target collection.

We can make roles even more granular by specifying specific actions, as in the following command:

```
atlas customDbRoles create customRole --privilege GET_CMD_LINE_OPTS
```

GET_CMD_LINE_OPTS is a specific privilege that allows the user to access the command-line options with which the MongoDB instance was started.

Or we can make it so custom database roles inherit privileges from other roles, as in the following command:

```
atlas customDbRoles create customRole --inheritedRole read@databaseName
```

- **--inheritedRole**: This flag is used to specify that the new custom role will inherit permissions from another predefined role. In MongoDB, predefined roles come with a set of specific built-in privileges that can be leveraged to create a custom role with similar permissions.
- **read@databaseName**: This indicates the inherited role from which the custom role will

derive its permissions. The read role is a predefined MongoDB role that grants privileges to read data from all collections within a specified database. @databaseName specifies the particular database where this read access applies.

As we can see, Atlas offers vast and robust solutions for authenticating and authorizing users. Hopefully, this gives you a sense of what's possible with Atlas, and you can apply it to your own Atlas deployments. But security doesn't begin and end with just authentication and authorization. In the next section, we'll take a look at more security features available in Atlas to keep your data protected.

Securing your Atlas deployments

Now that we have covered authentication and authorization, let's take a look at some other features that keep your Atlas deployments secure so you can rest easy. But first, have you ever wondered why so many organizations struggle with security breaches, even after investing heavily in security tools? The answer often lies in their approach. Security is bolted on as an afterthought rather than built into the foundation of their systems. When it comes to your data platform, this distinction makes all the difference.

MongoDB Atlas embraces a **security by design** philosophy, where robust security measures are integrated from the ground up rather than added as a layer after the fact. This proactive approach ensures that your data remains protected throughout its life cycle, from creation to deletion.

Why security from the beginning matters

Think of security like the foundation of a house. It's much easier (and more effective) to build it properly from the start than to try retrofitting it later. When security is an afterthought, the following could occur:

- Vulnerabilities may be deeply embedded in your architecture
- Remediation becomes exponentially more complex and costly
- Compliance requirements may force disruptive changes
- Your data remains at risk during the gap between deployment and security implementation

By incorporating security from day one, you create a defense-in-depth strategy that protects your data at multiple levels. This approach aligns with modern security best practices and reduces your overall risk exposure.

Atlas security tooling: Comprehensive protection

MongoDB Atlas provides an extensive security toolkit that covers every aspect of database security. Let's explore what this means for your deployments:

- **Network security**: Atlas provides multiple layers of network protection to secure your database infrastructure:

    - **Mandatory TLS encryption for all connections**

        All data transmitted between your application and Atlas is encrypted using TLS. This prevents the unauthorized interception of data during transmission and protects against man-in-the-middle attacks.

    - **IP access lists to control who can connect**

        You can specify which IP addresses or CIDR blocks are allowed to connect to your clusters. This creates a first line of defense by preventing connection attempts from unauthorized networks or locations.

    - **Private endpoints and Virtual Private Cloud (VPC) peering for isolation from the public internet**

        These features allow your applications to connect to Atlas without exposing traffic to the public internet. By establishing private network connections, you reduce the attack surface and minimize exposure to external threats.

- **Authentication and authorization**: We implement comprehensive identity and access management to ensure only authorized users can access our data:

    - **RBAC with granular permissions**

        RBAC allows you to assign specific permissions to users based on their responsibilities. This implements the principle of least privilege, ensuring users have access only to the resources they need to perform their job functions.

    - **Database user authentication with multiple mechanisms**

        Atlas supports various authentication methods, including username/password, X.509 certificates, **OpenID Connect (OIDC)**/OAuth 2.0, and LDAP. This flexibility enables you to implement the authentication strategy that best meets your security requirements.

- **Integration with identity providers through OIDC**

  OIDC integration allows you to use your existing identity provider (such as Entra ID, Okta, or Auth0) to manage Atlas access. This centralizes user management and enables SSO capabilities.

- **Organization and project-level access control**

  Atlas organizes resources hierarchically, allowing you to set permissions at different levels. This structure enables you to implement consistent access policies across teams while maintaining appropriate separation of duties.

- **Data protection**: Atlas safeguards your data with multiple encryption options and security features:

  - **Encryption in transit using TLS/SSL**

    All communications between clients and Atlas are encrypted using modern TLS protocols. This ensures data confidentiality during transmission and helps satisfy compliance requirements for data protection.

  - **Encryption at rest using AES-256 encryption**

    All data stored in Atlas is automatically encrypted using industry-standard AES-256 encryption. This protects your data from unauthorized access if storage media is compromised or stolen.

  - **Optional customer-managed encryption keys (BYOK)**

    For enhanced control, you can use your own encryption keys managed in a cloud key management service. This adds a layer of separation between your data and the database service provider.

  - **Client-Side Field Level Encryption and Queryable Encryption for sensitive data**

    These advanced features encrypt specific fields in your documents before they leave your application. This protects highly sensitive information such as **Personally Identifiable Information** (PII) from database operators.

- **Monitoring and auditing**: Our platform offers extensive visibility into database activity to help you maintain security compliance:

  - **Continuous monitoring for suspicious activities**

    Atlas actively monitors for unusual access patterns, authentication attempts, and other security events. This helps detect potential security incidents early so you can respond quickly.

  - **Comprehensive audit logs for tracking access and changes**

    Detailed logs record who accessed your database, what actions they performed, and when. These logs provide an audit trail that's essential for security investigations and compliance reporting.

  - **Integration with leading SIEM solutions**

    Security Information and Event Management (SIEM) integration allows you to incorporate Atlas security data into your broader security monitoring infrastructure. This creates a unified view of your security posture.

  - **Activity tracking at the organization and project levels**

    Atlas records administrative actions at both the organization and project levels. This multi-level tracking provides visibility into both strategic configuration changes and tactical operational activities.

The beauty of Atlas's approach is that many of these security features are enabled by default, requiring no additional configuration. This reduces the risk of misconfiguration while ensuring your deployments start with a strong security posture.

By building on this secure foundation, you can focus on creating value with your applications rather than worrying about security vulnerabilities in your data layer. As we progress through this section, we'll explore each of these security aspects in greater detail, providing you with a comprehensive understanding of how to maximize the security of your Atlas deployments.

Compliance and standards

MongoDB Atlas maintains rigorous compliance certifications to meet regulatory requirements across industries. These certifications ensure Atlas adheres to global security frameworks when handling your sensitive data:

- **SOC-2:** Verifies robust controls for security, availability, processing integrity, confidentiality, and privacy.
- **ISO/IEC 27001:** Confirms the implementation of a comprehensive information security management system.
- **PCI DSS:** Meets PCI DSS requirements for applications processing payment information.
- **HIPAA:** Supports compliance with safeguards for **Protected Health Information (PHI)** for healthcare organizations.
- **GDPR:** Provides tools and controls to help meet GDPR requirements for handling the personal data of EU citizens.
- **FedRAMP Moderate:** Meets security standards for cloud services used by US federal government agencies and contractors.

> If you're interested in learning more about the regulations and standards Atlas meets, visit the **MongoDB Trust Center** (https://www.mongodb.com/products/platform/trust).

MongoDB continuously maintains these certifications through regular third-party audits, allowing you to build compliant applications without duplicating security controls.

Shared responsibility model

Have you wondered where your security responsibilities end and MongoDB's begin? The shared responsibility model clarifies this boundary, ensuring you understand exactly who handles which aspects of security in your Atlas deployment.

Understanding the division of security duties

The shared responsibility model is a security framework that divides protection responsibilities between MongoDB (the cloud service provider) and you (the customer). This clear delineation helps prevent security gaps while avoiding redundant efforts.

MongoDB Atlas takes responsibility for the following:

- Physical infrastructure security
- Network infrastructure
- Database software security and patching
- Encryption of data in transit
- Default encryption of data at rest
- Authentication mechanisms
- High availability and disaster recovery infrastructure
- Compliance certifications and audits

As an Atlas customer, you're responsible for the following:

- Proper configuration of network access (IP access lists, private endpoints)
- User access management and identity controls
- Selection of appropriate authentication methods
- Data classification and protection policies
- Application-level security controls
- Client-side encryption implementation (if needed)
- Monitoring and responding to security events
- Backup management and testing

This division allows you to focus on securing your application and data while MongoDB handles the underlying infrastructure security. Think of it as MongoDB securing the house, while you control who gets the keys and what they can access inside.

Understanding where these responsibilities fall is key to maintaining a secure deployment. When security incidents occur, they often exploit gaps in this understanding, for example, when customers assume MongoDB handles certain access controls that are actually their responsibility.

By recognizing your security obligations within this model, you can implement appropriate controls and processes to ensure comprehensive protection across your entire database environment.

Encryption in MongoDB Atlas

Data security doesn't end with compliance and shared responsibilities. How your data is actually protected as it moves through your systems is equally important. MongoDB Atlas employs a comprehensive encryption strategy that protects your data throughout its life cycle: in transit, at rest, and in use.

Encryption in transit

Have you ever worried about your sensitive data being intercepted as it travels across networks? Encryption in transit addresses this concern by securing data as it moves between your application and the database.

What is encryption in transit?

Encryption in transit protects your data while it's moving across networks: between your application servers and MongoDB Atlas clusters or between nodes within a cluster. It ensures that even if someone intercepts your network traffic, they can't read or modify your data.

In MongoDB Atlas, encryption in transit is implemented using TLS, the successor to SSL. TLS creates a secure encrypted channel for data transmission by doing the following:

1. Authenticating the identity of the server
2. Establishing a secure encrypted connection
3. Ensuring data integrity during transmission

Always-on protection

Unlike many database systems where encryption in transit is optional, Atlas takes a security-first approach by making TLS encryption mandatory. This means the following:

*   All connections to your Atlas clusters are always encrypted
*   TLS is enabled by default and cannot be disabled
*   No sensitive data ever travels "in the clear" across networks

This mandatory encryption protects against various network attacks, including the following:

*   Man-in-the-middle attacks, where attackers attempt to intercept communications
*   Packet sniffing, which could expose sensitive queries or results
*   Session hijacking attempts

Atlas uses TLS 1.2+ by default, which represents the current security standard for encrypted communications. This implementation ensures your data remains protected according to modern security practices, without requiring any additional configuration on your part.

By making encryption in transit non-optional, Atlas eliminates a common security gap and ensures your data is always protected as it moves between systems, giving you one less security concern to worry about.

Encryption at rest

What happens to your data when it's stored on disk? Is it still protected against unauthorized access? With Atlas's encryption at rest, you can be confident that your data remains secure even when it's not actively being processed.

What is encryption at rest?

Encryption at rest protects your data while it's stored on physical media: hard drives, SSDs, or backup storage. It ensures that if someone gains physical access to the storage devices or extracts raw data files, they can't access the actual contents without proper authorization and decryption keys.

In MongoDB Atlas, the following applies to encryption at rest:

- Enabled by default on all clusters
- Implemented using industry-standard AES-256 encryption
- Applied to all data files, indexes, and logs

This ensures complete protection of your stored data without requiring any additional configuration or management on your part.

How Atlas implements encryption at rest

Atlas uses a two-tier encryption architecture:

- **Volume-level encryption:** Your cloud provider's disk encryption secures the entire storage volume
- **Database-level encryption:** MongoDB encrypts individual data files before they're written to disk

This layered approach provides defense in depth, ensuring your data remains protected even if one security layer is compromised.

Bring Your Own Key (BYOK)

For organizations with stringent security or compliance requirements, Atlas offers **Bring Your Own Key (BYOK)** encryption. This feature gives you complete control over your encryption keys by allowing you to do the following:

- Use your own encryption keys stored in your cloud provider's key management service (AWS KMS, Azure Key Vault, or Google Cloud KMS)
- Manage key rotation according to your security policies
- Revoke access to data by revoking the key, providing an emergency "kill switch" if needed

Here's how BYOK enhances your security posture:

Customer Key Management Service → **Master Key Encryption** → **Data Encryption Keys** → **Encrypted Data**

With BYOK, you maintain control of the master key that encrypts all data encryption keys. If you revoke access to this key, the data becomes inaccessible: even to MongoDB.

By implementing encryption at rest with optional BYOK, Atlas ensures your data remains secure throughout its life cycle, protecting against unauthorized access even if physical storage media is compromised. Remember, losing your key means losing your data.

Encryption in use

With Atlas, you are able to take advantage of MongoDB's CSFLE and Queryable Encryption, which we covered earlier.

Network security enhancement

Beyond encryption, securing the network pathways to your database is important for a comprehensive security strategy. MongoDB Atlas offers multiple approaches to network security, each providing different levels of isolation and protection. Let's explore how you can enhance the security of your database network connections.

Network peering

Have you ever needed to securely connect your application infrastructure to your database without exposing it to the public internet? Network peering creates a direct, private connection between your **Virtual Private Cloud (VPC)** and the Atlas VPC.

With network peering, traffic flows directly between the two networks, bypassing the public internet entirely. This approach does the following:

- Reduces network latency by creating a more direct path
- Improves security by keeping traffic off the public internet
- Allows private IP communication between your resources and Atlas
- Maintains network isolation from other Atlas customers

Setting up network peering is straightforward through the Atlas UI or API. The process involves creating a peering connection in your cloud provider and accepting it in Atlas, with automatic routing table updates to enable communication.

Consider network peering in the following instances:

- You need maximum performance for high-throughput applications
- You want to use private IP addressing for your database connections
- You have compliance requirements necessitating private network communication
- You operate in the same cloud provider and region as your Atlas deployment

Private endpoints

What if you need the security benefits of private networking but can't set up network peering? Private endpoints provide a simpler alternative, creating a private connection to your Atlas clusters without requiring complete VPC peering.

Private endpoints work by establishing a private link between your VPC and Atlas using your cloud provider's private connectivity service:

- **AWS:** AWS PrivateLink
- **Azure:** Azure Private Link
- **Google Cloud:** Private Service Connect

The key advantages of private endpoints include the following:

- Simpler setup than full VPC peering
- Support for cross-cloud connectivity
- More granular access control
- No need for overlapping IP addresses or route table modifications

Private endpoints are ideal in the following instances:

- You need private connectivity with minimal configuration
- Your applications span multiple cloud providers
- You require multiple private connections to the same Atlas deployment
- You have limited permissions to modify VPC configurations

IP access list

Atlas provides IP access lists as a basic but effective security measure. This feature restricts database access to specific IP addresses or CIDR blocks that you explicitly allow.

IP access lists control which connections can access the database:

- Only listed IP addresses can establish connections to your clusters
- You can add temporary access entries that expire automatically
- Both individual IP addresses and CIDR ranges are supported
- Changes take effect immediately for robust access control

While less secure than private networking options, IP access lists provide protection by doing the following:

- Preventing connection attempts from unknown sources
- Limiting the attack surface for brute-force attempts
- Creating an additional layer of defense beyond authentication
- Providing temporary access for maintenance or development needs

IP access lists are particularly useful in the following cases:

- Development environments with changing access needs
- Remote work scenarios requiring temporary access
- Adding a security layer to public-facing applications
- Quick implementation of basic network security

> IP access lists can now be locked, which helps prevent any accidental changes to who can access your Atlas clusters.

By combining these network security approaches, or selecting the one that best fits your needs, you can significantly enhance your Atlas deployment's security posture, ensuring that only authorized systems can even attempt to connect to your database.

Auditing capabilities

Auditing is a vital feature in MongoDB Atlas that helps ensure the security, compliance, and transparency of your database operations. With multiple tools available to monitor user activities and system events, Atlas empowers administrators to maintain tight control over their environments.

Audit log

The audit log in MongoDB Atlas is designed to capture and record key events to help you monitor and analyze operational and administrative actions. Available for clusters sized M10 and larger, audit logs track activities such as CRUD operations, authentication attempts, and configuration changes such as updates to encryption keys or user roles. You can apply audit filters to focus on specific events, ensuring you capture only the information most relevant to your compliance or security needs. These logs are securely stored within Atlas, preserving their integrity and accessibility for later analysis.

Activity feeds

MongoDB Atlas also provides activity feeds that offer visual, real-time insights into system-level and project-specific events:

- **Organization activity feed**: Tracks high-level activities at the organizational level, such as billing updates, team management, or administrative changes
- **Project activity feed**: Focuses on events within individual Atlas projects, covering tasks such as database configurations, cluster operations, and user authentication attempts

These feeds let administrators quickly review and monitor actions within their deployments without needing to dive into detailed logs. The ability to distinguish between organization-wide and project-focused activities ensures that relevant information is accessible with minimal effort.

Using audit logs and activity feeds together

By leveraging audit logs and activity feeds together, administrators gain both granular and high-level perspectives on database activity. Audit logs provide in-depth information about specific events, while activity feeds help identify broader trends or patterns in system behavior. Together, these tools enable organizations to meet regulatory requirements, detect potential security risks, and maintain operational clarity across their cloud database environments.

Configuring auditing in Atlas

Atlas makes auditing straightforward to implement. Available on M10+ clusters, auditing features can be tailored to your specific needs:

- **Default authentication auditing**: Automatically enabled for all M10+ clusters, tracking authentication attempts without any additional configuration
- **Custom audit filters**: Create JSON-formatted filters to specify exactly which events you want to track, focusing your audit logs on the most security-critical operations
- **Audit log access**: Retrieve and analyze logs through the Atlas UI, API, or CLI with 30 days of retention

The compliance connection

For regulated industries, auditing isn't just useful; it's mandatory. Atlas's auditing capabilities help satisfy requirements from multiple compliance frameworks:

- SOC-2 requirements for monitoring system access
- HIPAA mandates for tracking who accessed PHI
- PCI DSS requirements for user activity monitoring
- GDPR provisions for demonstrating data protection measures

By implementing comprehensive auditing in Atlas, you create a verifiable record of database activity that both protects your data and demonstrates compliance to auditors and regulators.

Remember that auditing does introduce some performance overhead, so configure your filters to capture what's necessary for security and compliance without excessive detail that could impact performance. With thoughtfully implemented auditing, you gain visibility into database operations while maintaining the performance your applications require.

Securing your Atlas deployment: Best practices

Now that we've explored the comprehensive security features of MongoDB Atlas, how do we bring it all together to create a holistic security strategy? Let's examine some best practices and actionable recommendations to maximize your Atlas security posture.

The most effective security strategies implement multiple layers of protection: no single security measure is sufficient on its own. For MongoDB Atlas, consider implementing the following:

- **Defense in depth:** Combine network security, encryption, and access controls to create overlapping layers of protection
- **Principle of least privilege:** Grant users and applications only the permissions they absolutely need
- **Zero-trust architecture:** Verify every access request regardless of source, with no implicit trust granted

Security implementation checklist

Start with this practical checklist to enhance your Atlas deployment security:

1. **Network security foundation:**
   - Use private endpoints or VPC peering whenever possible
   - Restrict IP access lists to specific addresses rather than wide CIDR ranges

2. **Authentication and access control:**
   - Implement strong password policies for database users
   - Use OIDC federation with your identity provider for centralized user management
   - Create role-based access controls with custom roles for fine-grained permissions

3. **Data protection:**
   - Consider BYOK for sensitive production environments
   - Identify fields containing sensitive data and implement CSFLE or Queryable Encryption as appropriate
   - Rotate encryption keys regularly according to your security policies

4. **Monitoring and detection:**
   - Configure alerts for suspicious authentication or access patterns
   - Implement custom audit filters for collections and operations
   - Regularly review audit logs for unexpected activity

By methodically implementing these security measures, you'll create a robust security posture that protects your data while enabling your applications to function efficiently and securely. Remember that security is a journey, not a destination; continuous improvement and vigilance are key to maintaining your security posture in the face of evolving threats.

Deprecating services in Atlas

As MongoDB Atlas continues to grow and adapt to changing customer needs, we sometimes face the difficult decision to deprecate certain services. These decisions aren't made lightly; they involve careful consideration of usage patterns, customer feedback, and strategic direction.

By September 30, 2025, several MongoDB Atlas features will reach their end of life and be removed from the platform. If you're using any of these services, it's important to understand what's changing and plan your migration strategy well in advance.

The affected features include the following:

- Atlas Data API and custom HTTPS endpoints
- Atlas Device Sync
- Atlas Device SDKs (Realm)
- Atlas Data Lake (preview)

Additionally, Atlas Edge Server (preview) was discontinued in September 2024.

Serverless clusters

Serverless clusters were designed to provide an on-demand database experience with automatic scaling based on workload. However, these clusters will be transitioning to the Flex cluster tier, which offers the following:

- Similar automatic scaling capabilities
- More predictable pricing model
- Greater control over resource allocation
- Improved performance for varied workloads

If you're currently using serverless clusters, your instances will be automatically migrated to the Flex tier before the end-of-life date. This transition should be seamless, with minimal impact on your applications and workloads.

Before these deprecations take effect, here are some key considerations to keep in mind:

- **Assess your current usage:** Take inventory of which deprecated services you're actively using
- **Evaluate alternatives early:** Start testing potential replacement solutions well before the end-of-life date

- **Plan for migration costs**: Budget for development time and possible infrastructure changes

- **Consider architectural impacts**: Some alternatives may require adjustments to your application architecture

- **Test thoroughly**: Ensure your chosen alternatives meet your performance and reliability requirements

- **Communicate with stakeholders**: Keep your team informed about upcoming changes and migration plans

Next steps

Remember that MongoDB's support team is available to help guide you through these transitions. Don't hesitate to reach out through the MongoDB Support Hub for assistance with your migration strategy.

When planning your migration away from deprecated Atlas services, consider these key factors:

- **Timeline assessment**: Create a realistic schedule that completes migration well before the September 30, 2025, deadline

- **Resource planning**: Allocate appropriate development resources for each affected component

- **Dependency mapping**: Identify all integration points with deprecated services throughout your application stack

- **Testing strategy**: Develop a comprehensive testing plan covering all migration phases

- **Fallback options**: Prepare contingency plans in case you encounter unexpected challenges

By starting your migration planning early, leveraging available resources, and working closely with MongoDB's support team, you can ensure a smooth transition to alternative solutions. Remember that MongoDB and its partner ecosystem are actively developing resources to make these migrations as seamless as possible.

Whether you choose to build custom solutions using MongoDB drivers, leverage serverless architectures, or adopt partner offerings, the key is to begin your evaluation process now to allow ample time for implementation and testing before the deprecation deadlines arrive.

For the most up-to-date information and guidance, don't hesitate to contact MongoDB Support. They can provide recommendations based on your specific use cases and requirements.

Summary

In this chapter, we've explored MongoDB Atlas and its role as a comprehensive data management solution for modern developers. We began by setting up an organization and examining the various tools available for interacting with Atlas deployments. These tools provide the foundation for efficiently managing your data environment.

We then walked through the important considerations for sizing an Atlas cluster, ensuring you can make informed decisions based on your application's specific needs. Building on this, we explored how Atlas handles scaling, both automatically and on demand, allowing your database to grow alongside your application without service interruptions.

Security formed a significant portion of our discussion, covering both authentication and authorization mechanisms. We examined how to implement proper access controls and the methods available to secure your Atlas deployment against unauthorized access and potential threats.

Finally, we reviewed the deprecated services in Atlas, helping you plan for future changes and updates to the platform.

MongoDB Atlas stands out as more than just a database service; it's an integrated platform that supports diverse workloads while addressing the needs of development teams in organizations of all sizes. From start-ups to large enterprises, Atlas provides the tools needed to build, scale, and maintain modern applications efficiently.

As you continue your journey with MongoDB, we encourage you to experiment with the features we've discussed. Start small, test in non-production environments, and gradually incorporate these powerful capabilities into your production systems. The more you explore Atlas, the better you'll understand how it can help solve your unique data challenges.

What will you build with MongoDB Atlas?

9

Atlas Search

This chapter dives into some of the standout features of MongoDB Atlas: **Atlas Search** and **Vector Search**. One of the great advantages of these features is their seamless integration into Atlas, enabling you to start using your data right away without the need for additional software in your tech stack.

While both Atlas Search and Vector Search are designed to help you perform searches, they operate in distinct ways. Atlas Search is a full-text search feature. It allows you to create search indexes on your collections, enabling efficient and powerful lexical searches across your data.

On the other hand, Vector Search harnesses embedding models to conduct semantic searches. This capability brings the power of AI to your fingertips, allowing you to perform more nuanced searches based on meaning rather than just keywords. When combined, these features enable hybrid searches, supercharging your search results with both keyword precision and contextual understanding.

In this chapter, we'll explore these features in detail and provide you with plenty of hands-on opportunities to engage with them.

This chapter will cover the following topics:

- Getting started with Atlas Search
- The mongot
- Search Nodes
- Atlas Search indexes
- Atlas Search queries
- Atlas Vector Search
- Generating vector embeddings with Voyage AI

- Vector Search indexes
- Performing vector searches with $vectorSearch
- Bringing your data to life with hybrid search, RAG, and AI agents

By the end of this chapter, you'll understand how to implement both keyword-based and semantic searches in MongoDB Atlas. These search capabilities can transform how you interact with your data, moving beyond simple queries to finding information based on context and meaning.

Whether you're building a recommendation system, enhancing user search experiences, or creating AI-powered applications, the combination of Atlas Search and Vector Search provides the tools you need.

We're excited to guide you through these techniques step by step. Get ready to apply these concepts in practical scenarios that will help you build more intelligent and responsive applications with MongoDB Atlas!

Technical requirements

To follow along, you'll need to have the following:

- MongoDB Atlas account
- Python 3.7+
- The MongoDB Shell

You can find the coding examples used on GitHub at: `https://github.com/PacktPublishing/The-Official-MongoDB-Guide`.

Getting started with Atlas Search

Let's begin with Atlas Search because understanding its capabilities will lay a solid foundation when we move on to Vector Search. Before diving in, let's clarify a common misconception: you might initially think Vector Search is superior due to its ability to comprehend meaning. However, this isn't always the case. Full-text search can often be more than sufficient for certain use cases, and it requires significantly fewer resources to execute.

As we explore each feature, consider the diverse scenarios where they shine and how you might leverage them in your own applications.

Tools to get started with Atlas Search

Getting started with Atlas Search is now easier than ever, thanks to the release of new onboarding tools and resources.

One of these tools is the **Atlas Search Playground**, a sandbox environment designed to help you explore the capabilities of Atlas Search without the need for a full Atlas setup. This tool offers a straightforward way to experiment with creating search indexes and queries on your data, all within a simple, user-friendly interface. Suitable for both beginners and experienced users, it provides an opportunity to understand and work with the features of Atlas Search effortlessly.

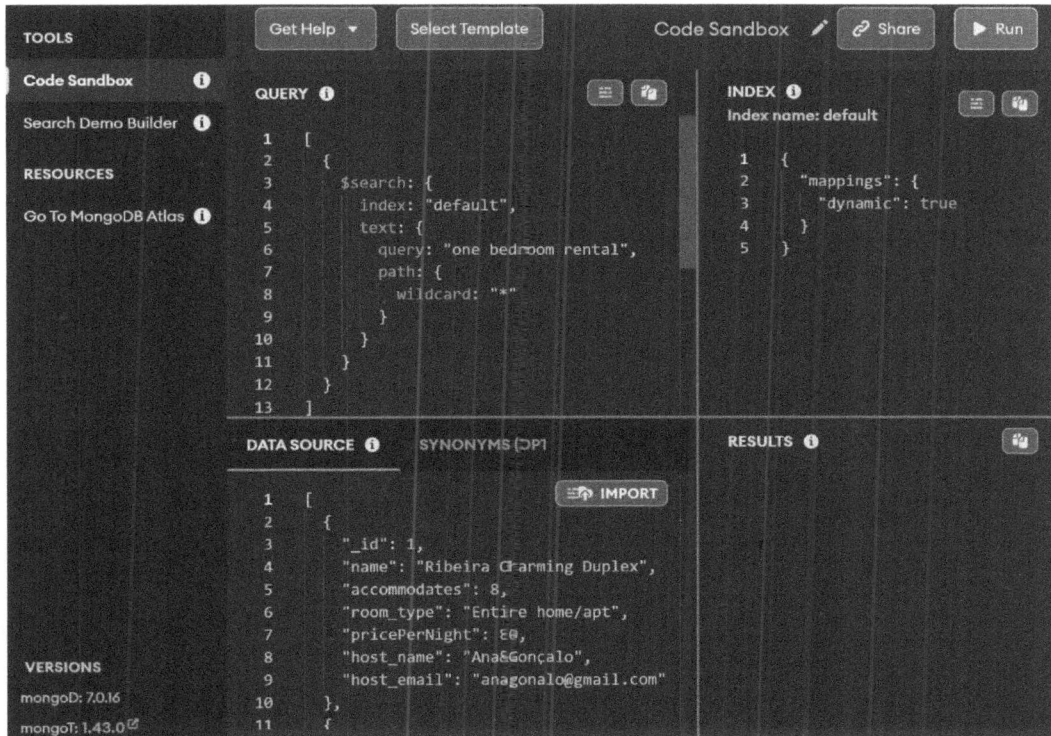

Figure 9.1: Atlas Search query through Code Sandbox in the Atlas Search Playground

Key features include the following:

- **Instant access**: There's no need for sign-ups or logins. You can head straight to the **Playground Environment** page and start experimenting with the search features immediately.

- **Playground workspace**: In this workspace, you can easily add and modify data, create and test search indexes, and run queries in real-time. It's a practical setting for trying out new ideas and understanding how search functions.

- **Preconfigured templates:** Use a range of sample templates to simulate real-world scenarios and test your search skills across various use cases in a straightforward way.

- **Shareable snapshots:** You can generate unique URLs for each session to share your experiments and findings with colleagues or collaborators, facilitating easy communication and collaboration.

One of the ways to use Atlas Search Playground is to copy and paste a small sample of documents in your collection that aren't being returned, and troubleshoot your query with everything right in front of you. It's easier to deal with a couple of hundred documents versus thousands or even millions.

Playgrounds make it easy by allowing existing Atlas Search users to align their configurations with the Atlas Search Playground by copying and pasting documents, search index definitions, and queries into the respective editor panels.

Another option we have is with the recently launched **Search Demo Builder**, which is a dynamic tool designed to simplify your experience with MongoDB Atlas Search. Nestled within the Atlas Search Playground, it provides a user-friendly interface for exploring and configuring key search features such as searchable fields, autocomplete, and facets, without the need for extensive technical expertise or manual query writing. Search Demo Builder empowers you to experiment and visualize these functionalities directly, enhancing your understanding and capabilities.

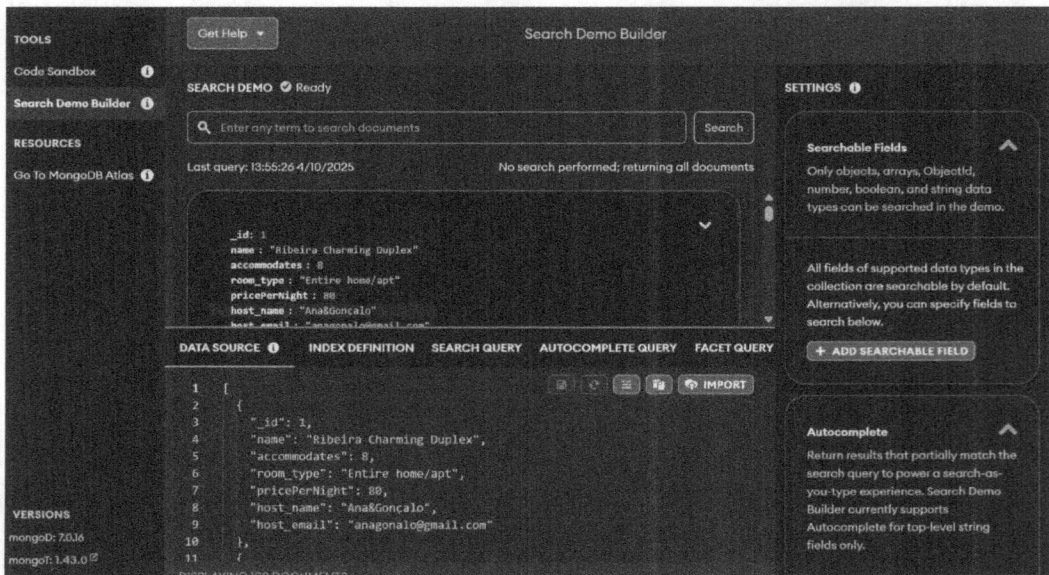

Figure 9.2: Atlas Search query using Search Demo Builder in the Atlas Search Playground

Key features include the following:

- **Searchable fields**: By default, the tool leverages dynamic fields, but you also have the flexibility to specify particular fields for your searches
- **Autocomplete**: Configure autocomplete on string fields to enable a search-as-you-type experience, complete with an index definition and an autocomplete query
- **Filters and facets**: These interactive elements can be set up using arrays of strings and numbers, providing a robust filtering experience
- **Experience preview**: Observe how your configurations affect search results in real time through the interactive preview screen
- **Auto-generated definitions**: The tool generates index and query definitions based on your configured search features, streamlining the setup process

This has many benefits, such as the following:

- **Instant setup**: Start exploring Atlas Search immediately using preloaded datasets or by uploading your own collection, with no complex setup or sign-up required
- **Guided exploration**: Benefit from step-by-step tours and tooltips that make the tool accessible for users of all skill levels, ensuring a smooth learning curve
- **Interactive workspace**: Experiment with features such as autocomplete and facets in a visual, hands-on environment that encourages creativity and immediate insight into your configurations
- **Shareable outputs**: Easily copy and use auto-generated indexes and query definitions outside the tool, supporting broader project use and collaboration

To begin using either one of these tools, visit the following link and get started exploring Atlas Search on your own: `https://search-playground.mongodb.com/tools/code-sandbox/snapshots/new`.

So, what will we be using in this section? We'll be using the MongoDB Shell, and we'll also need an M0+ cluster that has the `sample_mflix` sample data. With this, you should be able to follow along with no problems.

The mongot

Before we begin using Atlas Search, let's familiarize ourselves with the underlying technology so we can understand what is happening when we perform a search. This will provide insights into the Atlas Search process known as mongot, explaining how it serves as the backbone for creating and managing search indexes and queries within MongoDB Atlas.

By now, you're likely familiar with how indexes and queries function in MongoDB. However, Atlas Search introduces a unique approach, using its own indexing technology based on Apache Lucene. Like the index in the back of a book, a search index is a mapping between terms and the documents that contain those terms. Search indexes also contain other relevant metadata, such as the positions of terms in documents.

Enter mongot, a specialized process within Atlas Search that functions as an abstraction layer, integrating the Apache Lucene engine seamlessly with MongoDB. Through this integration, mongot enables you to manage search indexes efficiently, catering to rules specified in your index definitions.

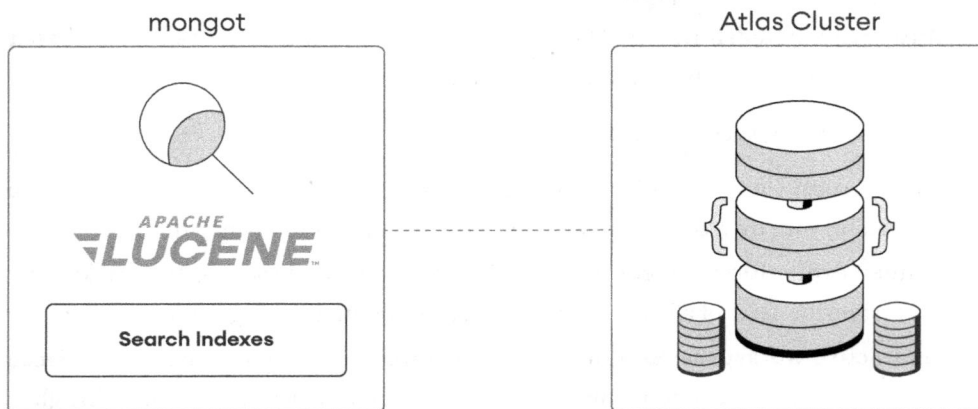

Figure 9.3: Atlas Search architecture showing mongot and Lucene

It's important to know that mongot is separate from the mongod process, which performs the core database functions. In a coupled architecture, these two processes share and compete for the same resources. We can improve this with something new called Search Nodes.

Search Nodes

So, what are Search Nodes? **Search Nodes** provide dedicated infrastructure specifically optimized for Atlas Search and Vector Search workloads. Rather than running the mongot process on the same nodes as your database (mongod) processes, Search Nodes allow you to deploy mongot on separate, purpose-built infrastructure.

Think of this as giving your search engine its own apartment rather than having it share space with your database operations; each has room to breathe, grow, and operate without disturbing the other.

Why move to dedicated Search Nodes?

When the mongot and mongod processes share the same infrastructure (as in the coupled architecture we discussed earlier), several challenges emerge:

- **Resource contention**: Both processes compete for the same CPU, memory, and disk resources
- **Performance limitations**: Heavy search workloads can impact database performance, and vice versa
- **Scaling constraints**: You can't independently scale your search infrastructure based on specific search workload needs
- **Availability risks**: Resource exhaustion from one process could impact the other

Let's look at how Search Nodes address these challenges.

Benefits of dedicated Search Nodes

- **Workload isolation**: With Search Nodes, your search operations run independently from your database operations. This separation ensures the following:
    - Heavy search indexing won't slow down your core database operations
    - Database load spikes won't impact search query performance
    - Each workload gets dedicated resources optimized for its specific needs

    You might ask, *How much difference does this really make?*. In many cases, we've observed 40–60% decreases in query time for complex search operations after migrating to dedicated Search Nodes.

- **Independent scaling**: One of the most powerful advantages of Search Nodes is the ability to scale your search infrastructure independently of your database tier, as follows:
    - Add more Search Nodes to handle higher query volumes
    - Upgrade to memory-optimized Search Nodes tiers for larger indexes
    - Configure search resources specifically for vector search workloads
    - Scale back search resources during low usage periods without affecting database performance

- **Enhanced availability**: Search Nodes improve overall system reliability in several ways:

  - A minimum of two Search Nodes ensures redundancy for your search workloads
  - Maintenance operations on your database cluster won't affect search availability
  - Scaling operations are less disruptive to search functionality

- **Optimized performance**: Search Nodes are designed specifically for search workloads, offering the following:

  - Hardware configurations optimized for search operations
  - Support for concurrent segment search (parallelizing query execution across index segments)
  - Memory-optimized options specifically designed for Vector Search

When should you use Search Nodes?

While the coupled architecture (where mongot runs on the same nodes as mongod) works well for development and testing, Search Nodes are strongly recommended for production environments, especially in the following cases:

- Your workload includes more than 2 million documents to index
- Your indexed data exceeds 10 GB
- You perform more than 10,000 queries in a 7-day period
- Search performance is important to your application
- You're implementing vector search at scale

Let's consider a practical example. Imagine you're building an e-commerce application with the following:

- 5 million product documents
- Full-text search on product descriptions and features
- Vector search for visual similarity and recommendation features

With the coupled architecture, you might need to provision much larger database instances than necessary just to accommodate the search workload. With Search Nodes, you can do the following:

- Configure your database tier (M30, for example) based purely on your database requirements
- Deploy S30 Search Nodes optimized specifically for your search and vector workloads
- Scale each independently as your application grows

Getting started with Search Nodes

Ready to migrate to Search Nodes? Here's how to get started:

1. Ensure that your cluster is running on a dedicated tier (M10 or higher).

2. Verify that your deployment is in a region that supports Search Nodes.

3. Enable Search Nodes through the Atlas UI or API.

4. Configure the appropriate search tier and node count for your workload.

When you enable Search Nodes, Atlas seamlessly builds indexes on your new Search Nodes while continuing to serve queries from your existing setup, ensuring zero downtime during the transition.

Now that we have a basic understanding of how Atlas facilitates search, let's shift our attention to seeing it in action by creating a search index. Once we have created a search index, we'll then explore how to use it to perform a search.

Atlas Search indexes

Before we begin, let's take a moment to review one of the movie documents in the sample_mflix database. This will give you a sense of what we're working with:

```
{
  "_id": ObjectId('573a13b2f29313caabd3a6e5'),
  "title": "V for Vendetta",
  "plot": "In a future British tyranny ...",
  "directors": ["James McTeigue"],
  "cast": ["Natalie Portman", "Hugo Weaving"],
  "genres": ["Action", "Drama", "Thriller"],
  "imdb": { rating: 8.2, votes: 709175, id: 434409 },
  "rated": "R",
  "metacritic": 62,
  "released": ISODate("2006-03-17T00:00:00.000Z"),
  "languages": ["English"],
  "fullplot": "Tells the story of Evey Hammond and her ...",
  "year": 2005,
  "writers": [],
  "type": "movie",
  // ...
}
```

We'll be using the plot, directors, and released fields for most of our examples in this section.

Let's start with a simple example and then dive into the components of a search index to understand what is happening.

Suppose we want to index the plot field, enabling easy searchability of movie plot descriptions. Here's how you can achieve this using the createSearchIndex method in the MongoDB Shell:

```
db.movies.createSearchIndex(
  "plotIndex",
  {
    "mappings": {
      "fields": {
        "plot": {
          "type": "string"
        }
      }
    }
  }
)
```

Here's what each part of the command does:

- **Name the index**: Begin by naming your index. In our case, we'll call it plotIndex.
- **Define fields**: You can choose to index specific fields or the entire document. In this example, we're focusing on the plot field for text searches.
- **Specify data type**: Specify the expected data type. For the plot field, this is a string. We'll explore data types further in a bit.

Similar to other indexes, search indexes take up space on disk and are continuously updated when documents are inserted, updated, or deleted. The mongot process uses MongoDB change streams to keep search indexes up to date.

Now, it's time to go over each of these components together.

Creating a search index starts with a key process known as **tokenization**. This involves transforming your data into searchable pieces, known as **tokens** or **terms**. An analyzer facilitates this process by handling tokenization, normalization, and stemming, making data consistently represented and easier to search.

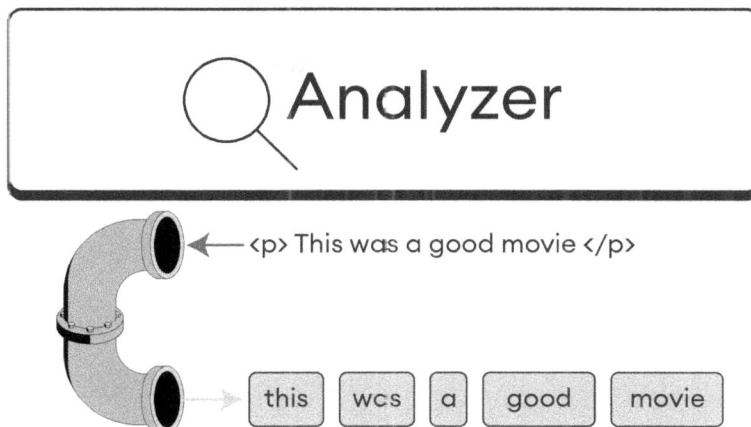

Figure 9.4: Analyzer breaking input into tokens in Atlas Search

While analyzers are an important piece of the indexing puzzle, they are beyond the scope of this chapter. It's worth noting that they play a vital role in dictating how data is parsed and indexed. Further exploration into analyzers can enhance your understanding of Atlas Search capabilities and can be explored in greater depth in the MongoDB documentation.

Field mapping: dynamic versus static

Effective indexing requires thoughtful field mapping, which impacts both the size and performance of your search indexes. Here's how different approaches can be leveraged:

- **Dynamic mapping**: Best for dynamic data where field structures are unpredictable or frequently changing. Every field of a supported data type within a document gets indexed. For example, in a movie catalog app, dynamic mapping would index all fields (title, plot, genre, etc.) without predefined specifics. This flexibility, however, leads to larger index sizes and potential performance overhead. We can create a search index with dynamic mapping by running the following command:

  ```
  db.movies.createSearchIndex(
      { "mappings": { "dynamic": true } }
  )
  ```

  To index every field in the movie collection, we use the mappings field in the index definition and set the dynamic option to true. Since we didn't provide a name for this index, it will be saved as default. Now, each field in the movies collection document will be indexed. This means that we can create a search query for any of the fields.

- **Static mapping**: Ideal when your document structure is static and well defined. Only specified fields are indexed, such as `plot` and `released` in the `movies` collection, allowing for a more efficient use of resources. This focused indexing reduces computational load and keeps the index lean. We can see what this looks like in the following:

```
db.movies.createSearchIndex(
    "plotReleasedIndex",
    {
        "mappings": {
            "dynamic": false,
            "fields": {
                "plot": {
                    "type": "string"
                },
                "released": {
                    "type": "date"
                }
            }
        }
    }
)
```

When using static mapping, we must specify the data type for each field, as in the preceding example, where the `plot` field is defined as `string` and the `released` field is defined as `date`.

Keep in mind that MongoDB accommodates polymorphic data. If an attempt is made to insert a document with a field value data type differing from the one specified in the search index, that particular document won't be included in the index.

In scenarios where a mixed approach is needed, fields can be selectively assigned `dynamic` or `static` properties, targeting specific document areas only. Consider situations such as indexing the `plot` field statically while allowing the `released` field, which might contain subdocuments, to remain dynamic to accommodate variations. We can see what this looks like in the following:

```
db.movies.createSearchIndex(
    "plotReleasedIndex",
    {
        "mappings": {
            "dynamic": false,
```

```
        "fields": {
          "plot": {
             "type": "string"
          },
          "released": {
             "type": "embeddedDocument",
             "dynamic": true
          }
        }
      }
    }
  )
```

Now, both the plot field and all the released subdocuments are indexed.

Choosing the right data types

By now, you have probably already figured out that specifying the correct data type is important in an Atlas Search index, and you would be correct in that assumption. Atlas Search supports a variety of data types, each catering to different aspects of your data. Here's a small sample of the data types available to us:

- **Basic types**: string, number, boolean, and date
- **Complex types**: array, objectId, document, and EmbeddedDocument

These types map closely to MongoDB's BSON structure, ensuring seamless integration. For example, the number data type maps to the BSON double, 32-bit, and 64-bit integer types.

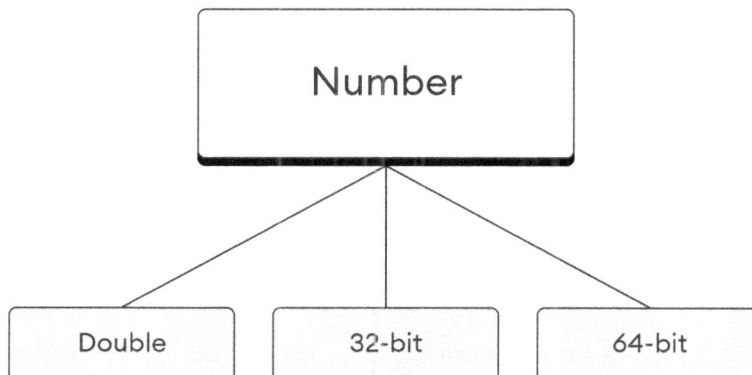

Figure 9.5: Number data type mapped to BSON types in Atlas Search

For nuanced data needs, fields can be assigned multiple data types, allowing complex queries that enhance how you interact with your database. For example, let's say we want to assign multiple data types when we index the `directors` field in the `movies` collection, so that it can be either a name or an `objectId` type. We can do this with the following index:

```
db.movies.createSearchIndex(
  "directorsIndex",
  {
    "mappings": {
      "dynamic": false,
      "fields": {
        "directors": [
          {
            "type": "string"
          },
          {
            "type": "objectId"
          }
        ]
      }
    }
  }
)
```

Here, we assign the `directors` field to an array of objects, with each object defined either as an `objectId` or `string` type in a search index. This will enable us to create a search query using a director's `name` or `objectId` value.

This was just a taste of what we can do with Atlas Search indexes, but by understanding and leveraging these components (index types, analyzers, field mappings, and data types), you're equipped to create finely-tuned search indexes that cater to specific application needs.

Explore the MongoDB documentation and experiment with different configurations to further your understanding and abilities with Atlas Search indexes (`https://www.mongodb.com/docs/atlas/atlas-search/index-definitions/`).

Now that the search index is set, the mongot process can query documents we want to search.

So now, how do we execute a search query? This is where the MongoDB aggregation comes into the picture.

Atlas Search queries

To execute an Atlas Search query, the $search or $searchMeta stage is used within an aggregation pipeline. It is important to note that the search stages must be the first stage in the aggregation pipeline for a query to execute correctly.

The $search stage performs a full-text search on a specified field or fields that are defined in the search index, whereas the $searchMeta stage is used to return a summary of your results.

For instance, if you wanted to obtain the number of documents from a search query, it would be more performant to use the $searchMeta stage instead of adding a count stage to the end of your search pipeline.

Let's see them both in action to get a better understanding, starting with the $search stage. We'll expand on our earlier example by constructing an aggregation pipeline that integrates the $search stage with the plotIndex we previously configured, in the following code:

```
db.movies.aggregate([
    {
      "$search": {
        "index": "plotIndex",
        "text": {
          "query": "space",
          "path": "plot"
        }
      }
    }
  ])
```

Let's break the preceding code down:

- **db.movies.aggregate()**: This is the MongoDB method used to run an aggregation pipeline on the movies collection.
- **$search**: This initiates a full-text search operation within the aggregation pipeline.
- **"index": "plotIndex"**: This specifies which search index to use. In this case, it's using plotIndex, which is an index we created previously that targets the plot field in the documents.

- **"text"**: This keyword indicates that the following operation is a text search, meaning it will search through text-based data within the specified fields. We're not limited to just the text operator (we'll learn more about this shortly):

  - **"query"**: **"space"**: This is the search term you're querying for within the plot field. The text search will look for documents containing the word "space".

  - **"path"**: **"plot"**: This determines the field within each document to search. Here, it's set to the plot field, which contains textual descriptions or summaries of movies.

After running the command, we should receive documents similar to the following:

```
{
  _id: ObjectId("573a1398f29313caabcea2cc"),
  plot: 'The young attendees of a space camp find themselves in space for
real when their shuttle is accidentally launched into orbit.',
  genres: [
    'Adventure',
    'Family',
    'Sci-Fi'
  ],
  runtime: 107,
  rated: 'PG',
  cast: [
    'Kate Capshaw',
    'Lea Thompson',
    'Kelly Preston',
    'Larry B. Scott'
  ],
  title: 'SpaceCamp',
  released: 1986-06-06T00:00:00.000Z,
  directors: [
    'Harry Winer'
  ]
  // ...
}
// ...
```

We can confirm that the documents returned indeed include the word space, aligning with our search objective. However, we can enhance the readability of the results by adding the limit and project stages to display only the title and plot fields. Additionally, by incorporating the meta aggregation operator in the projection stage, we can gain insights into how each result was scored. Here's how you can achieve this:

```
db.movies.aggregate([
  {
    "$search": {
      "index": "plotIndex",
      "text": {
        "query": "space",
        "path": "plot"
      }
    }
  },
  { "$limit": 3 },
  {
    "$project": {
      "_id": 0,
      "title": 1,
      "plot": 1,
      "score": { "$meta": "searchScore" }
    }
  }
])
```

After running the command, you should see something similar to the following:

```
{
  plot: 'The young attendees of a space camp find themselves in space for
real when their shuttle is accidentally launched into orbit.',
  title: 'SpaceCamp',
  score: 3.5627431869506836
}
```

Now, we can easily see the `title` and `plot` fields in our results. We also see how each document was scored. Atlas Search has a relevance-based scoring system. The document with the highest score is the most relevant and is returned first. Atlas Search gives documents a higher score if the query term appears frequently in a document, and a lower score if the query term appears across many documents in the collection.

Earlier, we mentioned that we can also use the `$searchMeta` stage. Let's update our previous search query to use the `$searchMeta` stage and add the `count` field to it:

```
db.movies.aggregate([
    {
      "$searchMeta": {
        "index": "plotIndex",
        "text": {
          "query": "space",
          "path": "plot"
        },
        "count": {
          "type": "total"
        }
      }
    }
  ])
```

We should see that it counts the total number of documents returned from the query. In this case, there are 97 documents returned:

```
{
  count: {
    total: 97
  }
}
```

Atlas Search operators and collectors

Operators specify the type of search operation you want to perform in the `$search` aggregation pipeline stage, whether you're combining multiple search conditions with `compound` or implementing specific `text` searches. Meanwhile, collectors help organize the returned search results by aggregating them according to certain criteria, such as grouping by values or ranges. By thoughtfully applying both operators and collectors, you can create precise, insightful search queries that ultimately enhance data retrieval and analysis.

So far, we have only used the text operator in our search queries, but we have quite a few other operators at our disposal. I can't go over all of them here, but to give you an idea, here's a small list of some of my favorites:

- **Text operator (text)**: The text operator enables full-text search capabilities. It allows you to search for terms within string fields. For instance, it can be used to look for documents containing specific words or phrases. This is useful when you need precise or broad matching.

- **Compound operator (compound)**: By combining multiple search criteria into a single query, the compound operator enhances query complexity and flexibility. It facilitates logical operations such as must, mustNot, should, and filter to build composite queries. For example, you can search for documents that must have certain fields and must not include others.

- **Range operator (range)**: This operator helps specify numeric or date ranges for filtering. It is ideal when you want to find documents within a specific numerical threshold or date range.

- **Embedded document operator (embeddedDocument)**: Use this when you need to perform searches within nested structures. It allows querying specific fields within embedded documents, which is good for dealing with complex data models.

- **Near operator (near)**: The near operator is for geospatial queries. It allows you to search for documents containing geo-coordinates within a specific proximity. Whether it's finding the closest locations or sorting results by distance, the near operator integrates geographic considerations seamlessly into your search.

Compound operator

One of the most powerful operators at our disposal is the compound operator. The compound operator in Atlas Search is designed to combine various other operators using rules called **clauses**. Think of these clauses as conditions, or arrays of search operators that together can help formulate sophisticated queries. The following shows an example of how a compound operator query is formed:

```
{
  "$search": {
    "index": <index name>, // "default" when omitted
    "compound": { <must|mustNot|should|filter>:[ {<operator>} ],
        "score": <options>
    },
  },
}
```

Here's a breakdown of how each clause functions, including the `should` clause:

- **The `must` clause:**

  - **Purpose:** Requires all conditions to be met for document inclusion in results

  - **Example use case:** Find movies containing both `poet` and `Elizabeth` in the plot, ensuring exact matches, sorted by score

- **The `filter` clause:**

  - **Purpose:** Ensures all conditions are met for inclusion, without influencing document score

  - **Efficiency benefit:** Efficiently eliminates documents without computationally expensive scoring

  - **Example use case:** Filter documents with `poet`, returning only those that meet the condition with a score of zero

- **The `mustNot` clause:**

  - **Purpose:** Excludes documents meeting specified conditions

  - **Scoring impact:** Assigns a score of zero to matching documents

  - **Example use case:** Exclude movies with `poet` or `Elizabeth`

- **The `should` clause:**

  - **Purpose:** Requires any condition to be met, allowing partial matches

  - **Scoring impact:** Scoring affected by each matching condition; more matches yield a higher score

  - **Example use case:** Search documents with `poet` or `Elizabeth`, returning those where either term is present, with higher scores for more matches

  - **The `minimumShouldMatch` option:** Fine-tunes the number of required matching conditions

  - **Example:** With a `minimumShouldMatch` value of 2, only documents containing both `poet` and `Elizabeth` are returned, similar to using the `must` clause

Each clause plays a unique role in configuring your search queries, giving you control over document inclusion, scoring, and performance. Understanding these elements allows you to tailor your strategy to specific data retrieval needs. Let's look at an example of the compound operator in action:

```
db.movies.aggregate([
  {
    "$search": {
      "index": "plotIndex",
      "compound": {
        "must": [{
          "text": {
            "query": "space",
            "path": "plot"
          }
        }],
        "mustNot": [{
          "text": {
            "query": "aliens",
            "path": "plot"
          }
        }]
      }
    }
  }
])
```

Let's break the preceding code down:

- Inside the $search stage, a compound operator is used to combine multiple search criteria, allowing for flexible query building with logical operators such as must and mustNot
- The must clause specifies conditions that must be met:
  - It includes a text search where the query is "space"
  - The search is conducted on the plot field of the documents
- The mustNot clause defines conditions that must not be met:
  - It includes a text search where the query is "aliens"
  - This, too, is applied to the plot field

This is just a simple example of what the compound operator can achieve, but here's a challenge: build upon it by adding another clause. Instead of using the text operator, consider trying one of the many other available operators. Explore the possibilities and enjoy experimenting!

> Remember to update your Search index if you decide to perform a search query on a different field from the plot field.

Search facets

Let's move on to facets, but what exactly are facets? **Facets** enable you to group search results by a category or range and return the count for each specified group. These groups are commonly referred to as **buckets**. Have you ever searched for a product on a website, and in the sidebar, you see a list of brands with an associated number next to them? That's a faceted search in action, making it easier for users to narrow down results.

We can see how facets work by creating one for the movies collection. Let's create a search query to figure out how many movies within a release date range are in each genre. To do this, we need to use the range operator with facets.

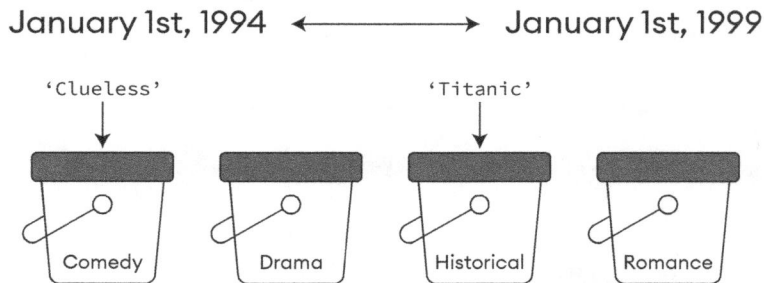

Figure 9.6: How facets operate in Atlas Search

Before we can create our search query, we need to define a new search index that can be used for facets. For facets to work on a particular field, it needs to have one of the following field mappings:

- token
- date
- number

Let's run the following command to create a new search index named genresFacetedIndex:

```
db.movies.createSearchIndex(
    "genresFacetedIndex",
    {
      "mappings": {
        "dynamic": false,
        "fields": {
          "genres": {
            "type": "token"
          },
          "released": {
            "type": "date"
          }
        }
      }
    }
)
```

Let's look at the preceding code in detail:

- The index is named genresFacetedIndex.

- Faceted indexes require specific field types, so we set the dynamic option to false. This means that fields are not indexed automatically; only specified fields are indexed.

- For the genres field, the type is specified as token. The genre field is a string, but we must use the Atlas Search token type in order to enable faceting on these fields. With the token type, Atlas Search indexes the terms in the string as a single token for efficient filtering or sort operations. This configuration allows faceting based on string values, categorizing search results into different genre buckets.

- For the released field, the type is specified as date. This setup enables storing and querying date-type data, which is useful for filtering movies by their release date range.

With our new search index successfully created, we can now create our search query that finds movies based on their release date and buckets them by genres. To do this, run the following command:

```
db.movies.aggregate([
   {
     "$searchMeta": {
       "index": "genresFacetedIndex",
       "facet": {
         "operator": {
           "range": {
              "path": "released",
              "gte": ISODate("2000-01-01T00:00:00.000Z"),
              "lte": ISODate("2000-01-31T00:00:00.000Z")
            },
          },
          "facets": {
            "genresFacet": {
              "type": "string",
              "path": "genres"
            }
          }
        }
      }
    }
  }
])
```

Here's a breakdown of the preceding code:

- Use the $searchMeta stage to retrieve the count of each genre.

- Define the search index as genresFacetedIndex.

- Specify a facet operator; you can choose any operator available in Atlas Search.

- Use the range operator to search for movies with a release date between January 1st, 2000, and January 31st, 2000.

- Define the buckets for each genre to see movie counts for each genre within the specified date range.

- Within the facet operator, create a subdocument field named facets, where you can specify multiple facets or groupings, each with its own data type, path, and optional fields.

- Define the name of the facet, which is how the facet counts will be referenced in the results. Name it genresFacet.

- Provide parameters, including the field being queried and its data type. Query the genres field, which is a token type.

When we run our search query, we get a document with the name of our facet and each genre in its own bucket:

```
{
  count: {
    lowerBound: 57
  },
  facet: {
    genresFacet: {
      buckets: [
        {
          _id: 'Drama',
          count: 39
        },
        {
          _id: 'Comedy',
          count: 13
        },
        {
          _id: 'Romance',
          count: 13
        },
        {
          _id: 'Biography',
          count: 11
        }
      ]
    }
  }
}
```

Remember that the count includes only movies from January 1, 2000, to January 31, 2000, since we defined the range operator.

This is just scratching the surface of what Atlas Search can accomplish. Beyond these examples, features such as fuzzy search, autocomplete, synonym mapping, pagination, and more can be implemented. These more advanced capabilities are worth exploring further, and the concepts covered here can serve as a solid starting point.

Atlas Vector Search

Have you ever tried searching for something when you only had a vague description rather than exact keywords? If you've been working with Atlas full-text search, you're already familiar with its powerful capability to match and rank documents based on words and phrases. But what about searching for the **meaning** behind those words?

From keywords to meaning

While Atlas full-text search excels at matching keywords and phrases (**lexical search**), Atlas Vector Search takes your search capabilities to the next level by understanding the meaning of your query (**semantic search**).

Think of the difference this way:

- **Full-text search**: Finds documents containing specific keywords, such as database, scalable, and cloud
- **Vector search**: Understands the meaning and context of a search query, such as I need a reliable database solution that grows with my business, and can find relevant documents even without matching exact keywords

This unlocks the ability to do some really interesting stuff with our data, such as the following:

- Find conceptually related documents even without keyword matches
- Improve recommendation systems by focusing on meaning rather than exact matches
- Enable natural language queries that understand user intent
- Power multimodal search across text, images, and other data types

This is not an exhaustive list, but it gives you a general idea of what you can do with Vector Search.

What are vectors, and why do they matter?

Vector embeddings are numerical representations of your data (whether that's text, images, or audio) stored as arrays of floating-point values. Each number in this array represents a dimension in a high-dimensional space, collectively capturing the semantic meaning of your data. Let's look at an example:

```
// Example of a dense vector embedding (simplified)
const vectorExample = [0.023, -0.112, 0.438, 0.067, -0.291, ...]; //
typically hundreds or thousands of dimensions
```

You've already been working with vectors in Atlas full-text search, though you might not have realized it. Those were **sparse vectors**, where most dimensions are zeros, primarily indicating the presence or absence of specific words (similar to TF-IDF calculations).

Dense versus sparse

Traditional text search relies on statistical measures of word frequency and uniqueness. This works well for finding documents containing specific terms, but it misses the contextual understanding that humans naturally bring to language.

Atlas Vector Search uses **dense vectors** instead, where the following apply:

- Virtually no dimensions are zero
- Each dimension contributes to the semantic meaning
- The vector captures complex relationships between concepts
- Similar concepts cluster together in the vector space

How Atlas Vector Search works

At a high level, Atlas Vector Search follows these steps:

1. **Embedding generation**: AI models convert your data into dense vector embeddings.
2. **Vector indexing**: Atlas stores these vectors in an efficient, searchable format.
3. **Similarity matching**: When you search, your query gets converted to a vector and compared with stored vectors.
4. **Result ranking**: Documents are returned based on vector similarity, not keyword matching.

Let's explore each of these steps by building a vector search query that helps us find movies based on a user's query.

Setting up the environment

In order for us to get started, we'll first need to set up our environment. For this, we'll be using a Python virtual environment, which can be created by running the following command in the directory you want to work in:

```
python -m venv vs-demo
```

Once that is finished, we can activate the virtual environment by running the following command:

- **On macOS/Linux:**

```
source vs-demo/bin/activate
```

- **On Windows:**

```
.\vs-demo\Scripts\activate
```

When the virtual environment is activated, you'll see the environment's name in the command prompt. Once activated, we can install packages using `pip` that will only be available in this virtual environment.

Let's go ahead and install pymongo since we'll be using it to interact with our MongoDB database:

```
pip install pymongo
```

The last thing to do is create two files: `data.py`, `index.py` and `search.py`. We'll use these two files throughout this section. Let's get started with generating some vector embeddings for our data.

Generating vector embeddings with Voyage AI

Now that we understand how Atlas Vector Search works at a high level, let's dive deeper into the first step: **embedding generation**. This is where we convert our movie plots into vector embeddings that can be searched and compared.

> Generating embeddings requires an API key for your chosen model. This usually requires a credit card, and it does have a cost. Low-cost and free models are available on `huggingface.com`.

Understanding embedding models

For our movie search to work, we need to convert the text descriptions in our `plot` fields into numerical vectors. However, not all AI models are created equal for this task.

Large language models (LLMs) such as GPT or Claude excel at generating text and conversation, but they're not specifically optimized for creating the consistent numerical representations we need for vector search.

Embedding models, however, are purpose-built to transform content into dense vector representations that capture semantic meaning. These specialized models ensure that similar concepts are positioned close together in the vector space, regardless of the specific words used.

> While LLMs can generate embeddings, dedicated embedding models produce higher-quality vectors for search applications, with better performance and more consistent results.

Leveraging Voyage AI for embeddings

We'll be using Voyage AI to generate the embeddings for our data, which has recently become part of the MongoDB family! MongoDB's acquisition of Voyage AI brings state-of-the-art embedding technology directly into our database ecosystem.

Voyage AI offers several advantages for our movie search application:

- **Industry-leading accuracy**: Voyage AI models are the highest-rated zero-shot embedding models on Hugging Face
- **Optimized for search**: These models are specifically designed for retrieval tasks
- **Seamless integration**: It is soon to be natively integrated within MongoDB Atlas

Keep in mind that you are not limited to only using Voyage AI with Atlas Vector Search. You have the ability to use any embedding model that you want with Atlas Vector Search.

Implementing embedding generation for the movies collection

Let's create the embedding vectors for our movies collection. We'll focus specifically on generating embeddings for each document's plot field. There are more than a few ways of generating embeddings. A lot of vector embeddings have packages that we can install, which makes generating embeddings for our data easy. This is the approach we'll be taking, which means we have to install the package for Voyage AI.

To do this, run the following command in your virtual environment:

```
pip install voyageai
```

With that complete, we can add the following code to the data.py file:

```
import os
import requests
import key_param
from pymongo import MongoClient
import voyageai

vo = voyageai.Client(api_key=key_param.voyage_api_key)

mongodb_client = MongoClient(key_param.mdb_uri)
```

```
#  Database name
DB_NAME = "sample_mflix"
# Name of the collection with full documents- used for summarization
FULL_COLLECTION_NAME = "movies"
db = mongodb_client[DB_NAME]
full_collection = db[FULL_COLLECTION_NAME]

chunked_docs = full_collection.find({}, {"plot": 1})

for doc in chunked_docs:
    embedding = vo.embed(doc["plot"], model="voyage-3-lite", input_
type="document").embeddings[0]
    print(doc["plot"])
    print(embedding)
    full_collection.update_one({"_id": doc["_id"]}, {"$set": {"plot_
embedding": embedding}})
```

Let's see what happens in the preceding code:

- **Library imports**: The code imports libraries, including pymongo for MongoDB connectivity and voyageai for generating embeddings

- **API client initialization:**

  - It creates a Voyage AI client instance using an API key stored in key_param.voyage_api_key

  - It initializes a MongoDB client connection with the connection string from key_param.mdb_uri

- **Database configuration:**

  - It targets the sample_mflix database, and specifically, the movies collection

  - It sets up references to both the database and collection for easy access

- **Document processing**: It queries the collection to retrieve all documents, but selects only the plot field for each document

- **Loop through documents:** For each movie document retrieved, the code does the following:

  - It uses Voyage AI's embed() method to generate vector embeddings from the movie plot text

  - It specifically uses the voyage-3-lite model, optimized for document embedding

  - It extracts the first (and only) embedding from the returned results

- **Data persistence:**

  - It updates each document in MongoDB by adding a new field called plot_ embedding containing the vector representation

  - It uses MongoDB's update_one() method with the document's _id value as the identifier

Now that we've generated embeddings for our movie plots, we've completed the first step in our Atlas Vector Search implementation. Our database now contains the vector representations needed for semantic search. In the next section, we'll explore how to index these vectors for efficient searching and build our first vector search queries.

Vector Search indexes

Now that you've successfully generated vector embeddings for your movie plots, you need a way to efficiently compare these vectors to find similar content. But how do you efficiently search through vectors with hundreds or thousands of dimensions? This is where Atlas Vector Search indexes come into play.

Understanding the technology behind Vector Search

When we work with high-dimensional vector data, traditional search methods aren't efficient. MongoDB Atlas uses **hierarchical navigable small world (HNSW)** graphs to power Vector Search. But what exactly is HNSW, and why is it so effective?

The evolution to HNSW

HNSW evolved from two important data structures:

- **Skip lists**: These are sorted linked lists with multiple layers, each containing list points. This structure increases search efficiency.

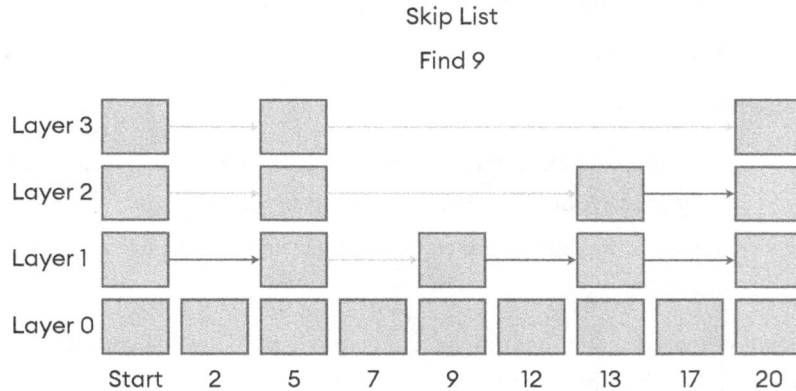

Figure 9.7: Skip list layers for navigating to value 9

- **Navigable small world (NSW) graphs**: Points (vertices) in these graphs are connected by links (edges) that represent similarity. They enable efficient similarity searches but may return suboptimal results.

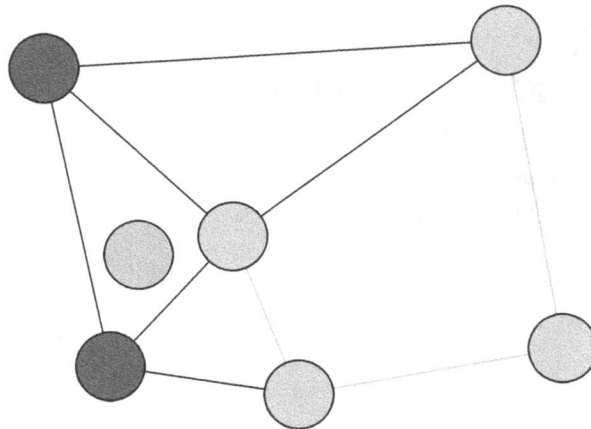

Figure 9.8: NSW graph showing nearest neighbor traversal

HNSW combines the best of both approaches. Like a skip list, it has multiple layers, and like NSW, it uses proximity graphs. The bottom layer contains all points with shorter connections, while the upper layers have fewer points with longer connections, similar to zooming in and out on a map.

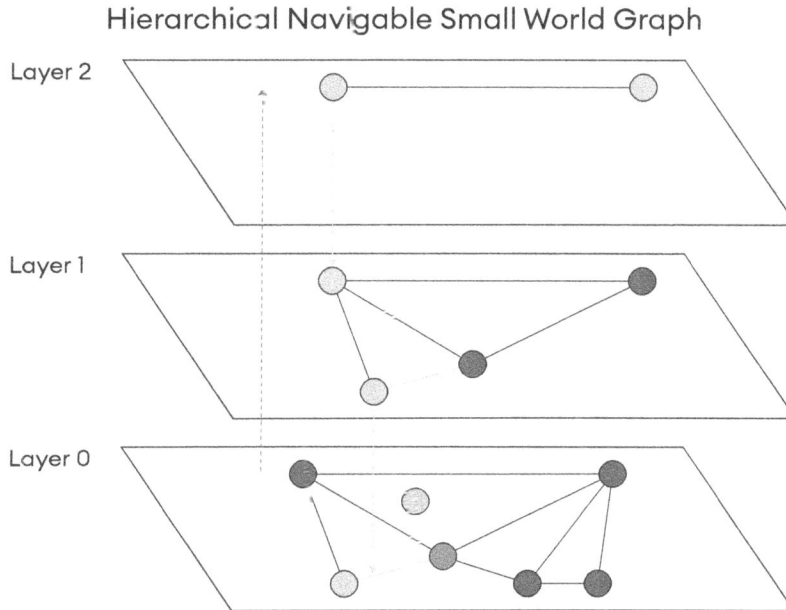

Figure 9.9: HNSW traversal from top layer to target point

Creating a Vector Search index

There are a couple of ways we can create a vector search index, but in our case, we'll use the Python driver to create the index.

Inside the index.py file, run the following command to create a vector search index:

```
import key_param
import pymongo
from pymongo.mongo_client import MongoClient
from pymongo.operations import SearchIndexModel

mongodb_client = MongoClient(key_param.mdb_uri)

#  Database name
DB_NAME = "sample_mflix"
# Name of the collection with full documents- used for summarization
```

```python
FULL_COLLECTION_NAME = "movies"

db = mongodb_client[DB_NAME]
full_collection = db[FULL_COLLECTION_NAME]
search_index_model = SearchIndexModel(
  definition={
    "fields": [
      {
        "type": "vector",
        "numDimensions": 512,
        "path": "plot_embedding",
        "similarity": "cosine"
      },
      {
        "type": "filter",
        "path": "year"
      }
    ]
  },
  name="vector_plot_index",
  type="vectorSearch"
)

full_collection.create_search_index(search_index_model)
print("Index created successfully")
```

Let's break down the code to understand what is happening better:

- SearchIndexModel creates a blueprint for the search index and includes the following:

  - A vector field that does the following:

    - Points to plot_embedding in your documents
    - Uses 512 dimensions (matching your embedding model's output size)
    - Implements cosine similarity for measuring vector closeness

  - A filter field on year that does the following:

- Allows you to narrow search results by movie release year
- Combines traditional filtering with vector similarity

- `full_collection.create_search_index(search_index_model)` applies the index definition to your collection. Once created, MongoDB Atlas builds and optimizes the index.
- A simple `print` statement confirms that the index was created successfully.

Understanding similarity functions

When configuring your vector search index, you'll need to choose a similarity function, which greatly impacts your search results:

- **Euclidean similarity:** This measures the straight-line distance between vectors in multi-dimensional space. This works well when the absolute magnitudes of your vectors matter.
- **Cosine similarity:** This measures the angle between vectors, ignoring magnitude. This is useful when you care about directional similarity but not size. Note that cosine doesn't work with zero-magnitude vectors.
- **Dot product:** Similar to cosine, it measures the angle but also considers magnitude. For optimal results with the dot product, your vectors should be normalized to unit length.

Which one should you choose? First, check your embedding model's documentation; use what the model was trained with. If that information isn't available, experiment with each function to see which gives the best results for your specific use case.

Pre-filtering your vector searches

One of the powerful features of Atlas Vector Search is the ability to pre-filter your data before running similarity comparisons. This has the following benefits:

- Makes your searches more efficient by reducing the search space
- Improves result relevance by excluding irrelevant data
- Enhances performance for multi-tenant applications by restricting searches to specific data subsets

In the preceding example, we added a filter on the year field, which will allow us to focus searches on movies from specific years.

Important considerations and limitations

Here are some key points to remember when working with Vector Search indexes:

- **Memory requirements**: HNSW requires a lot of memory. For production workloads, use dedicated search nodes to separate Vector Search from your main cluster operations.

- **Field limitations**: You can only use the vector field type on fields that contain vector embeddings.

- **Array limitations**: You can't index fields in subdocuments within an array field. Don't store embeddings in documents that are part of an array.

- **Vector dimensions**: The number of dimensions must be less than or equal to 8,192.

- **Vector types**: Your vector field must contain an array of numbers (BSON double) or BSON BinData vectors with specific subtypes.

- **Index status**: Monitor your index's status through the Atlas UI. Indexes are only fully operational when they show the "Active" status.

Another thing to consider is how much space each vector takes in the database. Recently, MongoDB released vector quantization to address this particular problem. **Vector quantization** is a technique that compresses high-dimensional vectors into more compact representations by reducing the number of bits used to store each dimension. It works by mapping continuous float values to a smaller set of discrete values, effectively trading a small amount of precision for significant storage savings. Think of it as similar to how JPEG compression works for images: you sacrifice a bit of quality to dramatically reduce file size.

When working with MongoDB Atlas, you have two quantization options at your disposal: **scalar quantization** and **binary quantization**. Scalar quantization divides each dimension's range into equal bins, converting float values to discrete integers, reducing memory usage to approximately 1/4 of the original. Binary quantization is even more aggressive, converting each dimension to a simple 0 or 1 based on whether it's above or below a midpoint (typically 0), shrinking memory requirements to about 1/24 of the original size. This is particularly effective for normalized embeddings such as text-embedding-3-large from OpenAI.

The benefits of vector quantization are substantial, especially as your vector collections grow. For applications with over 10 million vectors, quantization can dramatically reduce resource consumption while maintaining search quality through techniques such as candidate rescoring. You'll experience faster queries, lower memory usage, and reduced costs, all while scaling your vector search capabilities to handle larger datasets. This makes previously impractical applications feasible by bringing down the resource requirements to manageable levels.

Performing vector searches with $vectorSearch

Now that you've created your vector embeddings and successfully indexed them, it's time to unleash the true power of Atlas Vector Search! Are you ready to see how we can query data based on semantic meaning rather than exact text matches?

In this section, we'll walk through performing vector searches using the $vectorSearch aggregation stage. This powerful feature allows you to find documents based on the semantic similarity between your query and the vector embeddings in your database.

Let's look at a complete example of how to perform a vector search:

```python
import key_param
from pymongo import MongoClient
import voyageai

vo = voyageai.Client(api_key=key_param.voyage_api_key)

mongodb_client = MongoClient(key_param.mdb_uri)

#  Database name
DB_NAME = "sample_mflix"
# Name of the collection with full documents- used for summarization
FULL_COLLECTION_NAME = "movies"

db = mongodb_client[DB_NAME]
full_collection = db[FULL_COLLECTION_NAME]

query = "A movie about a life altering event that changes the
protagonist's life forever."
query_embedding = vo.embed(query, model="voyage-3-lite", input_
type="query").embeddings[0]

pipeline = [
    {
        '$vectorSearch': {
            'index': 'vector_plot_index',
            'path': 'plot_embedding',
            'queryVector': query_embedding,
```

```
                'numCandidates': 200,
                'limit': 10,
                'filter': {
                    'year': {
                        '$lt': 1960
                    }
                },
            }
        },
        {
            '$project': {
                'title': 1,
                'plot': 1,
                'year': 1,
                'score': {
                    '$meta': 'vectorSearchScore'
                }
            }
        }
    ]


results = full_collection.aggregate(pipeline)
for result in results:
    print(f"Title: {result['title']}, Year: {result['year']}, Score:
{result['score']}")
    print(f"Plot: {result['plot']}")
```

Let's break down what's happening in this code:

- **Importing libraries:** We start by importing the necessary libraries, including PyMongo for MongoDB interactions and Voyage AI for generating embeddings

- **Setting up connections:** We create clients for both MongoDB and Voyage AI, using connection parameters stored in a separate file for security

- **Defining the query:** We create a natural language query describing the kind of movie we're looking for, which is one about a life-altering event

- **Generating query embeddings:** We convert our text query into a vector embedding using the same model we used to index our data (voyage-3-lite)

- **Creating the pipeline**: We define an aggregation pipeline with two stages:
  - The $vectorSearch stage, which performs the semantic search
  - A $project stage that shapes our output
- **Vector Search parameters**:
  - index: The name of our vector search index
  - path: The field containing our vector embeddings
  - queryVector: Our query converted to an embedding
  - numCandidates: How many candidates to consider (200 in this case)
  - limit: How many results to return (10)
  - filter: A pre-filter to limit results to movies before 1960
- **Retrieving the score**: We use the special $meta: vectorSearchScore operator to include the similarity score in our results
- **Executing and displaying**: We run the aggregation pipeline and print out the results, showing each movie's title, year, similarity score, and plot

Understanding the results

When we run this code, we get these fascinating results:

```
Title: White Shadows, Year: 1924, Score: 0.7545456886291504
Plot: In Paris a wild girl becomes possessed by the soul of her twin who
died to save her life.

Title: For Heaven's Sake, Year: 1926, Score: 0.7396184802055359
Plot: An irresponsible young millionaire changes his tune when he falls
for the daughter of a downtown minister.

[...additional results omitted for brevity...]
```

Notice something about these results? Our query was about a life-altering event that changes the protagonist's life forever, and the system returned movies with plots that match this concept semantically. The first result features a character whose life is dramatically changed by supernatural possession, while the second shows a character whose life is transformed by falling in love.

None of these matches would have been found with a traditional keyword search, as they don't share the exact words from our query. This demonstrates the power of semantic search: finding results based on meaning rather than just matching text!

ANN versus ENN: understanding search approaches

Atlas Vector Search supports two distinct search approaches, as we will discuss in the following subsections.

Approximate nearest neighbor (ANN) search

ANN search uses the HNSW algorithm to efficiently find vector embeddings that are closest to your query vector without scanning every single vector in your dataset. Here's what you should know about ANN:

- Optimized for speed and efficiency, especially with large datasets
- Doesn't scan every vector, making it faster but potentially less accurate
- Tuned using the numCandidates parameter to balance speed versus accuracy
- Recommended for most production use cases, especially with large collections

Exact nearest neighbor (ENN) search

Recently added to Atlas (available in MongoDB v6.0.16, v7.0.10, v7.3.2, or later), ENN search exhaustively compares your query vector with every indexed vector to find the absolute closest matches. Here's what you should know about ENN:

- Provides 100% accuracy by calculating the distance between all embeddings
- More computationally intensive and may impact query latency
- Ideal for benchmarking ANN accuracy or for smaller datasets
- Perfect for queries with highly selective pre-filters (affecting <5% of data)

To enable ENN search in our example, we would modify our $vectorSearch stage to include the exact: true parameter:

```
'$vectorSearch': {
    'index': 'vector_plot_index',
    'path': 'plot_embedding',
    'queryVector': query_embedding,
    'exact': true,  # Enable Exact Nearest Neighbor search
    'limit': 10,
    'filter': {
        'year': {
            '$lt': 1960
        }
    }
}
```

When using ENN search, you don't need to specify numCandidates since the algorithm examines all vectors.

Optimizing Vector Search performance

To get the best results from your vector searches, consider these best practices:

- **Tune numCandidates for ANN searches:** Start by setting numCandidates to at least 10–20 times your limit value
- **Use pre-filters wisely:** Pre-filtering with the filter option improves performance by reducing the search space
- **Choose between ANN and ENN based on your needs:**
  - Use ANN for most production scenarios
  - Use ENN for small datasets or when validating ANN accuracy
- **Ensure embedding model consistency:** Use the same embedding model for indexing and querying

Vector Search opens up exciting possibilities for building semantically aware applications. You can find similar documents, implement recommendation systems, or create natural language interfaces to your data, all powered by the semantic understanding of your content.

Bringing your data to life with hybrid search, RAG, and AI agents

Now that you've explored the depths of Atlas Search and Atlas Vector Search, let's dive into the exciting possibilities these powerful tools unlock. What happens when you combine traditional search capabilities with vector embeddings? A world of intelligent applications awaits!

Hybrid search: the best of both worlds

By leveraging both Atlas Search and Atlas Vector Search together, you can do the following:

- Capture both semantic meaning and exact keyword matches
- Deliver more relevant results by considering multiple search dimensions
- Balance precision and recall based on your specific use case
- Fine-tune search experiences that truly understand user intent

Hybrid search empowers you to create search experiences that understand not just what users are looking for, but what they truly mean.

Retrieval-augmented generation (RAG)

RAG represents one of the most practical applications of vector search technology. By connecting your MongoDB data to LLMs, you can do the following:

- Ground AI responses in your own authoritative data
- Reduce hallucinations and increase accuracy
- Create domain-specific AI assistants that truly understand your business
- Maintain control over information sources while leveraging AI capabilities

With Atlas Vector Search as your retrieval engine, building RAG applications becomes straightforward and scalable, ensuring your AI solutions have access to the most relevant information from your databases.

AI agents: taking action with your data

AI agents represent the next evolution: systems that not only retrieve and generate but actually take action based on your data. Atlas Vector Search enables agents to do the following:

- Understand complex user requests through semantic understanding
- Retrieve relevant context before executing tasks
- Learn from previous interactions stored in your database
- Orchestrate multiple tools and systems with intelligence

Integration ecosystem: build faster with leading AI tools

One of Atlas Vector Search's greatest strengths is its extensive integration ecosystem. You don't need to build everything from scratch! MongoDB has partnered with leading AI platforms to make implementation seamless:

- **AWS Bedrock**: Connect your vector data directly to Amazon's foundation models
- **LangChain and LangGraph**: Build sophisticated RAG pipelines with minimal code
- **LlamaIndex**: Create structured data access patterns over your MongoDB collections
- **Microsoft Semantic Kernel**: Integrate with Microsoft's AI orchestration framework
- **Haystack**: Build production-ready search and RAG applications
- **Spring AI**: Integrate vector search capabilities in your Java Spring applications
- **Google Vertex AI**: Connect seamlessly with Google's AI/**machine learning (ML)** ecosystem

With Atlas Search and Vector Search at your fingertips, the possibilities are nearly endless. From intelligent document retrieval to conversational shopping assistants to knowledge management systems that truly understand context, your data can now power experiences that were previously impossible.

Summary

In this chapter, we explored two standout features of MongoDB Atlas: Atlas Search and Atlas Vector Search. Both features are seamlessly integrated into Atlas, allowing users to tap into their data without requiring additional software. These tools enable advanced search capabilities that go beyond basic queries, helping developers unlock deeper insights and build smarter applications.

Atlas Search provides full-text search functionality that empowers efficient keyword-based searching across collections. By implementing search indexes and crafting queries, it allows for features such as fuzzy matching, autocomplete, and synonym mapping, ensuring highly responsive search experiences tailored to your application's needs.

Atlas Vector Search brings AI-powered semantic search to MongoDB Atlas by leveraging vector embeddings generated by ML models. This feature enables searches based on contextual meaning rather than just keywords, making it ideal for use cases such as recommendation systems, image similarity searches, or natural language processing. When combined with Atlas Search, these capabilities enable hybrid searches that merge keyword precision with semantic understanding, delivering richer and more nuanced search results.

We demonstrated how to implement both Atlas Search and Atlas Vector Search, walking through hands-on examples of index creation, query design, and hybrid search strategies. Additionally, we explored practical applications, showcasing how these tools can transform search experiences and elevate AI-powered solutions. So, whether you're building a recommendation system or enhancing user interactions, MongoDB Atlas has the tools to bring your data to life!

10

Unlock Your Exclusive Benefits

Your copy of this book includes the following exclusive benefits:

- ⌁ Next-gen Packt Reader
- 📄 DRM-free PDF/ePub downloads

Follow the guide below to unlock them. The process takes only a few minutes and needs to be completed once.

Unlock this Book's Free Benefits in 3 Easy Steps

Step 1

Keep your purchase invoice ready for *Step 3*. If you have a physical copy, scan it using your phone and save it as a PDF, JPG, or PNG.

For more help on finding your invoice, visit https://www.packtpub.com/unlock-benefits/help.

Note: If you bought this book directly from Packt, no invoice is required. After *Step 2*, you can access your exclusive content right away.

Step 2

Scan the QR code or go to `packtpub.com/unlock`.

On the page that opens (similar to *Figure 10.1* on desktop), search for this book by name and select the correct edition.

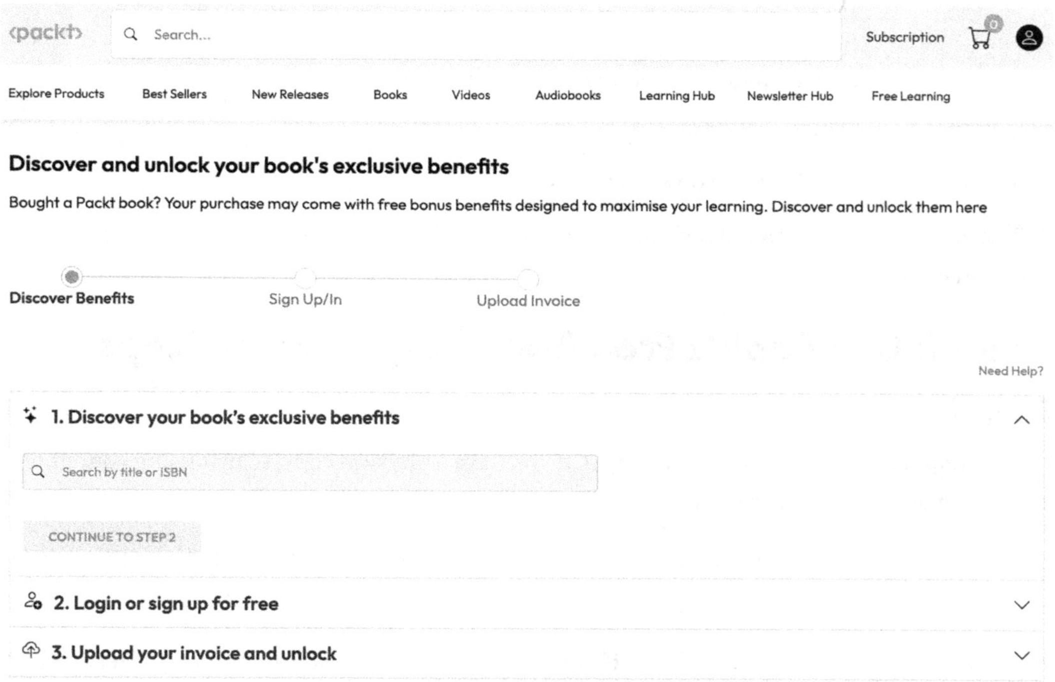

Figure 10.1: Packt unlock landing page on desktop

Step 3

After selecting your book, sign in to your Packt account or create one for free. Then upload your invoice (PDF, PNG, or JPG, up to 10 MB). Follow the on-screen instructions to finish the process.

Need help?

If you get stuck and need help, visit `https://www.packtpub.com/unlock-benefits/help` for a detailed FAQ on how to find your invoices and more. This QR code will take you to the help page.

Note: If you are still facing issues, reach out to `customercare@packt.com`.

Index

‹packt›

packtpub.com

Subscribe to our online digital library for full access to over 7,000 books and videos, as well as industry leading tools to help you plan your personal development and advance your career. For more information, please visit our website.

Why subscribe?

- Spend less time learning and more time coding with practical eBooks and Videos from over 4,000 industry professionals
- Improve your learning with Skill Plans built especially for you
- Get a free eBook or video every month
- Fully searchable for easy access to vital information
- Copy and paste, print, and bookmark content

At www.packtpub.com, you can also read a collection of free technical articles, sign up for a range of free newsletters, and receive exclusive discounts and offers on Packt books and eBooks.

Other Books You May Enjoy

If you enjoyed this book, you may be interested in these other books by Packt:

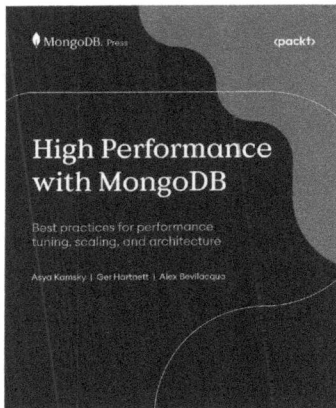

High Performance with MongoDB

Asya Kamsky, Ger Hartnett, Alex Bevilacqua

ISBN: 978-1-83702-263-2

- Diagnose and resolve common performance bottlenecks in deployments
- Design schemas and indexes that maximize throughput and efficiency
- Tune the WiredTiger storage engine and manage system resources for peak performance
- Leverage sharding and replication to scale and ensure uptime
- Monitor, debug, and maintain deployments proactively to prevent issues
- Improve application responsiveness through client driver configuration

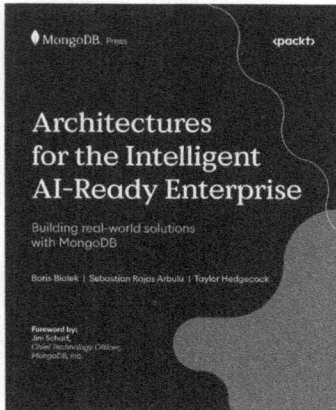

Architectures for the Intelligent AI-Ready Enterprise

Boris Bialek, Sebastian Rojas Arbulu, Taylor Hedgecock

ISBN: 978-1-80611-715-4

- Design AI-ready data architectures that scale in production
- Define systems of action and explain why they matter for enterprises
- Modernize legacy systems for AI-ready, unified architectures
- Implement governance, privacy, and compliance frameworks for AI
- Explore real-world AI implementations for over six industries
- Deploy production RAG and agentic systems with MongoDB
- Apply semantic data protection in regulated industries
- Build domain-specific AI agents and intelligent copilots
- Apply MCP, causal AI, and multi-agent systems for future-ready architectures

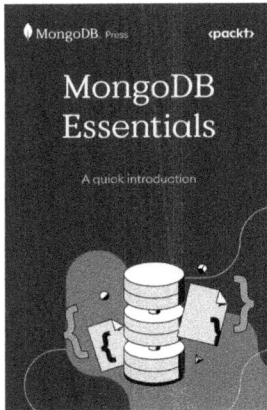

MongoDB Essentials

ISBN: 978-1-80670-609-9

- Understand MongoDB's document model and architecture
- Set up MongoDB local deployments quickly
- Design schemas tailored to application access patterns
- Perform CRUD and aggregation operations efficiently
- Use tools to optimize query performance and scalability
- Explore AI-powered features such as Atlas Search and Atlas Vector Search

Packt is searching for authors like you

If you're interested in becoming an author for Packt, please visit authors.packt.com and apply today. We have worked with thousands of developers and tech professionals, just like you, to help them share their insight with the global tech community. You can make a general application, apply for a specific hot topic that we are recruiting an author for, or submit your own idea.

Share your thoughts

Now that you've finished *The Official MongoDB Guide*, we'd love to hear your thoughts! Scan the QR code below to go straight to the Amazon review page for this book and share your feedback or leave a review on the site that you purchased it from.

https://packt.link/r/183702197X

Your review is important to us and the tech community, and will help us make sure we're delivering excellent quality content.

www.ingramcontent.com/pod-product-compliance
Lightning Source LLC
Chambersburg PA
CBHW081045220326
41598CB00038B/6992

* 9 7 8 1 8 3 7 0 2 1 9 7 0 *